EUROPE:
CHAINED BY
HISTORY

Bob —
thanks for your
interest in this book.
Enjoy!

EUROPE:
CHAINED BY
HISTORY

What Force Can Break The Chain?

L A R R Y   J .   H I L T O N

For information about this title or to order other books and/or electronic media, contact the publisher:
Newport Publishing
P.O. Box 6532
Chandler, AZ 85246
newportbookpublishing@gmail.com

ISBNs:
Hardcover 978-0-9967861-0-2
Softcover 978-0-9967861-1-9
eBook 978-0-9967861-2-6

Printed in the United States of America
Cover and Interior design: 1106 Design

To my granddaughters, Ava and Elle:
Cultivate your garden.

CONTENTS

PREFACE

When the World Trade Center was struck in 2001 by extremists attacking the heart of Western Civilization, I was motivated to learn more about our civilization and where it came from. Since I own the full set of *The Story of Civilization,* by Will and Ariel Durant, I thought that was a good place to start. Through reading these books, I discovered Voltaire and his lifelong fight against intolerance and superstition: He said that if a country has only one religion, it is autocratic; if it has two religions, they will kill each other, and if it has a hundred religions, they will live peacefully. Western Civilization is facing intolerance and violence from religious extremists, and it is time to become reacquainted with Voltaire and the Age of Enlightenment.

The roots of Western Civilization are, of course, in Europe. As a financial advisor for more than four decades and an avid reader of European history, I have become increasingly concerned about its future. European nations have experienced fear and distrust of each other for almost 2,000 years. How can they now collaborate to define, approve, and implement a unified fiscal policy that provides each country with enough revenue to effectively operate while allowing business to grow and prosper? How can they build a common political perspective that supports European security? I decided to discuss my concerns against the backdrop of a brief history of Austria and its capital, Vienna. Looking at Europe through the window of Austrian history illustrates how Europe got to where it is today, and it may point the way to a brighter future.

I selected Austria and Vienna as a focus for this book for two reasons: First, I have had the good fortune to spend significant time in the city of Vienna. As a college student in 1962, I was selected to study Austrian history at the University of Vienna for a semester, and it was a fascinating time for a naive young American from the Midwest to experience central Europe. Vienna was only seventeen years removed from World War II and only seven years from unification after the Communists had departed. Its historic buildings were gloomy and dark with grime accumulated for more than three hundred years, and few funds were available to clean them. But the city was alive with politics of various sorts, and this twenty-year-old ravenously took it all in. After all, John F. Kennedy was our president, and our generation felt we could change the world.

In 2012, I went to Vienna again, this time to spend a month just living there. I was pleasantly surprised to find that funds received when Austria joined the European Union had been used to restore the beautiful buildings in the central city to their original glory. Vienna was again a vibrant city of cafes, music, museums, and parks. It is a remarkably easy city to get around in, with an efficient subway system and street cars that allow visitors to view the city as they travel. Austria exports lumber and chemicals from its forests and mountains, and it has the lowest unemployment rate in Europe. But I found myself asking, "What will happen if their neighbors are all financially broke and can't buy their goods?"

My second reason for choosing Vienna is its location as the geographic center of Europe. Vienna was first founded as an outpost to oppose barbaric Germanic tribes who lived across the Danube River. After the Dark Ages, it was again inhabited to serve as a sentry to watch for Turks from the "Mysterious East" and protect Christian Europe from the Muslims. Situated at the center of Europe, Austria found itself continuously fighting various enemies while aligning itself with ever-changing "friends." Because of their central location and pivotal role in history, Austria and Vienna have much to teach us about modern Europe and its chances of succeeding with a unified fiscal policy or common defense.

As a college student in Vienna, one of the courses I studied was the European Common Market. How could Europe possibly compete against the unified economic force of America in the new world created at the end of the war? Winston Churchill thought the only way Europe could avoid World War III was for France and Germany to join together in a United States of Europe. In 1990, the proposal for a monetary and political union was largely the work of Helmut Kohl, the German Chancellor, and Francois Mitterrand, the French President. They claimed at the time that a monetary union of Europe would eliminate currency risk. Their vision became reality with the launching of a common currency in the late 1990s—the *euro.*

The great mistake of their reasoning is that monetary union simply converts monetary risk into credit risk—the risk that a government might be unable to pay its creditors. In sum, never in history has there been an economic and financial disaster on the scale of the current monetary union in Europe.[1] What can be done?

In talking with friends and clients, I am discovering that few Americans know much about the history of Austria or Vienna, or even where they are located on a map of Europe. Unless they are on a Danube River cruise with one day to see the city, Americans rarely seem to visit this beautiful city. My story will provide a glimpse of the fascinating history of the area, including the trials its people have endured for 2,000 years with recurring wars, plagues, and poor harvests caused by floods or drought, and their experiences under extraordinary rulers such as Marcus Aurelius and Josef II, and interesting ones such as Maria Theresa and Franz Josef.

History, including the history of religion, politics, and economics, is really nothing more than the story of people: how they worked, what they ate, how they played, what they wore, how they thought, how they lived, and how they died. Whether they lived in an ancient Roman fort in old Vienna or in Austria before World War II, they laughed, cried, made love, and worried about their finances—just like us. Looking at their lives will show us much about the multiple challenges facing Europe today.

ACKNOWLEDGMENTS

Many people encouraged me as I deeply immersed myself in this book for many months. First among them is my editor, Anne Edwards, whose work consistently helped me to better express what I wanted to say. I have been very fortunate in having several friends who are writers, such as Larry Schweikart, Richard Parry, and Fern Welch, who not only provided encouragement but also served as models for me to follow. Tom Schildgen at Arizona State University was a tremendous help in getting books I needed through the Inter-Loan Library System; and Chris Johnsten, with the College of Liberal Arts at ASU, patiently read the manuscript to provide both proofing and constructive comments.

I want to thank writers whom I have never met who provided great inspiration as I worked on the book. Reading Will and Ariel Durant's eleven volumes of *The Story of Civilization* opened my eyes to how history could be written as an unfolding story that leads us from the past to the present. Too often I encounter people who tell me they hated history in school, or it bored them, and they saw no point in reading about kings, presidents, treaties, and wars of long ago. If their history classes could have been taught like the Durants write, their experience might have been very different.

One of my most important sources was the diary of Anna Eisenmenger, a record revealing the hardships faced by one middle-class family during the hyper-inflation in Vienna after the First World War. When I mentioned to a colleague in finance that I intended to write a chapter on hyper-inflation without using any numbers, he asked how. I told him I would describe the way one family lived in 1923, when a single egg cost the same as a million eggs had cost a decade earlier.

George Clare's book, *Last Waltz in Vienna,* should be required reading in schools. His firsthand account of the horrors of anti-Semitism gave me a genuine sense of what it must have meant to be Jewish as the Nazis assumed power. Versions of his story were played out in millions of lives throughout much of Europe during the Holocaust, but Clare's heart-breaking tale of just one family—his own—will bring the tragedy to life for every reader.

I deeply appreciate the support of my family, friends, co-workers, and clients who showed a surprising interest in the progress of this book—a project that, for me, has been truly a labor of love.

INTRODUCTION

American Nobel Prize laureate William Faulkner said, "history is not *was,* it *is.*" I take this to mean that, while history is constantly evolving, a better understanding of it will help us survive the political and economic winds now swirling around the globe. After majoring in history, I have never lost my passionate interest in the subject. I am writing this book not as an academic historian but as a storyteller, believing that a fast walk through Vienna's 2000-year history will highlight political, economic, and social mistakes of the past and suggest a better direction for the future.

Before going all the way back to ancient Vienna, then known as Vindobona, I will begin the city's story with a glimpse of the German occupation and the takeover of Austria, known as the *Anschluss,* on March 12, 1938. Jewish Austrians were dragged from their homes to face insult, injury, or worse, often by ordinary Austrian citizens who had for years been increasingly influenced by anti-Semitic writers and speakers. What happened in Vienna was similar to events in other countries taken over by Germany.

Early images of atrocities in Vienna will be seen through the eyes of seventeen-year-old Georg Klaar, whose family's long and distinguished history in the city meant nothing to their persecutors in 1938. Jews had long been restricted to occupations within medicine, law, banking, or retail, and Georg's father, Ernst, was a banker. The Klaars were among many upstanding residents of Vienna who were victimized simply because they were Jewish.

Georg Klaar's firsthand account will show us the horrors, the hatreds, and the loss of human dignity that occurred in 1930s Vienna as though we were standing beside him. A million deaths is a statistic, but one family's tragedy is a personal story to which we can all relate.[2] It is not easy to fathom the idea that countless numbers were killed because of anti-Semitism, but one family's experience brings it home. The Klaars' story is an integral part of the story of Vienna.

As it has for centuries, the Danube River continues to provide a major means of transport and a fertile landscape throughout Austria. This bustling highway for modern commerce was a decisive factor for the earliest settlements in and around Vienna, and ruins at the city's Hoher Market reveal the remnants of Vindobona, a city once occupied by 30,000 inhabitants of the Roman Empire. We will taste the flavors of Vienna's beginnings by visiting this ancient city. In doing so, we will find that while the Romans were stern masters of the lands they occupied, their enlightened policies allowed conquered peoples to participate in Roman citizenship. We will learn how the city provided, even during its earliest days, strategic defense against external threats to a mighty empire.

In a later era, Vienna provided defense for another enormous kingdom, the Habsburg Empire, arguably the most powerful since Rome.

It once encompassed today's countries of Austria, Hungary, the Czech Republic, Slovakia, Poland, Slovenia, Croatia, Bosnia, Serbia, Romania, and parts of Italy. Of the Habsburg Empire's sixty million inhabitants, only eight million were Austrian, but Vienna was situated strategically at the easternmost edge of Western Europe, so it became the empire's capital city for 640 years. For centuries, the city stood as the bastion of defense against external threats—especially from the Turkish warriors who threatened Christian Europe throughout the Middle Ages.

Eighteenth-century Austria was dominated by two Habsburg Emperors who tried to usher their medieval empire into the Age of Enlightenment, personified by Voltaire and Rousseau in France: Maria Theresa worked to unify her empire by instituting far-reaching reforms, and her son, Josef II, wielded his sovereign power to abolish serfdom, foster religious and social tolerance, and create a more just system of taxation. We will see how the reforms of Maria Theresa and Josef II were consistently resisted by powerful individuals and groups who benefitted from the status quo.

Decades later, the vast Habsburg Empire fell apart after the reign of Emperor Franz Josef I. The empire effectively ended with the assassination in 1914 of his nephew and heir, Archduke Franz Ferdinand, during a parade in his honor in the city of Sarajevo, Bosnia. The Archduke's death signaled that strategic alliances created by European countries to protect themselves from their neighbors were becoming fatally compromised by continual rivalry among the allies. Europe was experiencing the "unintended consequences of well meaning but flawed decisions," and it had become ripe for the horrors of World War I.

After World War I, Austria experienced severe hyper-inflation, and the Austrian krone collapsed. Food shortages turned to widespread famine, and money became worthless. The diary of war widow Anna Eisenmenger will provide a vivid picture of daily life, where money was falling in value by the minute, and people were forced to turn to illegal practices to keep their families alive.

Ten years of deepening worldwide depression and a lack of European leadership moved the world toward a second brutal world war, and as anti-Semitism and Adolf Hitler gained political steam, Nazi Germany annexed Austria in 1938. Religious hatred of the Jews evolved into deadly racial hatred, ultimately leading to the Holocaust. From 1938 until 1945, there was no Austria, and only in 1955 did this country regain complete independence on the condition that it would be forever neutral. To this day, Austria is not a member of NATO.

After relating the depressing events of World War I, worldwide economic collapse, and World War II, I wanted to introduce a reason for optimism about the future of Europe, and I found such a reason in the philosophy, writings, and actions of one man: Voltaire—an eighteenth-century icon of the French Enlightenment. One might ask, "Why Voltaire? What's he even doing in this book about Austria and Vienna?" The question is worth asking because Voltaire never even visited Austria, let alone Vienna. But an examination of his life and works provides a light in the darkness for people facing the crises within today's Europe, the U.S., and other countries around the world.

In 2012, during my second trip to Vienna, I made a four-day pilgrimage to Voltaire's two homes in Geneva, Switzerland, and learned more about this brilliant and versatile figure. I realized then that it would be challenging to demonstrate how and why an understanding of Voltaire's life is instrumental to an understanding of modern Vienna, Europe, and

Western Civilization. Because his presence in our civilization is so strong, I decided that a full chapter would be needed to explain his enduring influence. I consider Voltaire to be one of the greatest human beings our world has produced—not because he was a perfect man, but because his ideas point the way to political and religious freedom for all of us.

We believe that our world should function rationally, based on commonsense values and the ability to compromise, yet we continue to experience rigid polarization, conflict, violence, and war brought on by self-interest, greed, intolerance, and ignorance. We live in a world where too many care too little for reason, a world where radical extremists engage in warfare without respect to borders, especially against those who respect plurality, diversity, and freedom. For them, there is only one proper way to think, feel, or act. While moderate members of such groups may share many of their views, only extremists among them act on a belief that all who don't agree with them must submit or be killed, including members of different sects within their own faith.

Winston Churchill was right: Europe must form a United States of Europe among member states who band together in a true economic and political union. From an economic standpoint, this is the only way European nations can compete commercially with the United States and China. And, beyond economic concerns, the very survival of the European Union and even of its member nations may depend upon the unity of Europe in the face of political and military storms now on the horizon.

How can we hope for such an outcome when the story of Vienna, from its earliest beginnings to 1938, underscores *disunity* among the European states? The long history of factional disputes within the City of Vienna, the Austrian Empire, and Europe itself, led to competition, suspicion, hatred, economic collapse, two world wars, the rise of anti-Semitism, and—ultimately—the Holocaust. Vienna's history is, in many ways, a microcosm of the history of Europe, and the same divisions that undermined the city's unity have long undermined political relationships within the European continent.

Once again, we can turn to Voltaire for the antidote to the fragmentation of Europe and even of the world. Human freedom, with respect for differences, was the underlying theme of almost everything Voltaire wrote or talked about. In a later decade, perhaps influenced by his ideas, the Founding Fathers were more passionate about their common cause of freedom than they were about their different views of how to achieve it. Freedom was the unifying motive for the allied powers during World War II, and it remains the key to unity of purpose and practice among European and Western nations today.

As difficult as it was for the leaders of the American Revolution to unify a nation, it will be even more difficult for European leaders, first to agree with each other, and then to nudge the European states, with their diverse interests, languages, and cultures, toward a unified political, economic, and military structure. But the prosperity and survival of each and all of them may depend on their ability to put differences aside, and for the sake of freedom, to form what may become a more perfect union.

CHAPTER I

Vindobona

In 1938 Vienna, Saturday, March 12 was cold, with a bit of snow still on the ground, but it was a bright, sunny day, and a slight smell of spring was in the air. When seventeen-year-old Georg Klaar went into his father's study and opened the window overlooking Nussdorferstrasse, a major street north of the central city, he could see flags flying from rooftops and windows. Many of them were the new Nazi Party flag, boasting a large black swastika in a white center circle on a red background, and some were the familiar red and white Austrian flag. Most of the Nazi flags looked homemade, as though they were hastily painted or sewn by eager hands during the night.[3]

The housekeeper, Helene, entered the room to put breakfast on the table. When Georg turned to greet her, he saw at once that she was crying.

"Oh, Herr Georg," she sobbed, "What are they going to do to our lovely little country? What is going to happen to our Austria?"[4]

It would have been more appropriate to ask what was going happen to the Klaar family. They were Jews who could trace their history in Vienna back to 1780 and the days of Habsburg Emperor Josef II. Georg's father was an accountant for the Länderbank, a successful and carefully managed bank that had survived the hyper-inflation of the twenties and the Great Depression of the thirties. But Austria was facing a crisis greater and more threatening than any of the past, even the Turkish Siege of 1683, and the future was nothing if not uncertain.

Georg heard the roar of men shouting at the top of their lungs, so he stepped back to the open window, only to see that Nussdorferstrasse was still quite empty—until the first lorry came into sight, a huge swastika flag fluttering overhead. Then there were more vehicles, all packed with screaming men wearing swastika armbands. Georg later learned that they were members of the *Sturmabteilung,* or *SA,* an Austrian Nazi paramilitary organization that was illegal in Austria but still a powerful force that intensified the danger for Austrian Jews.

When he heard a sharp cry directly below the window, Georg looked down to see a policeman with a swastika brassard newly on his sleeve and his truncheon held tightly in his fist. With berserk fury, he was striking a man who was cowering at his feet. Georg had seen this same police officer on traffic duty; they had chatted when they met in the shops around the corner, and the officer had given his father a polite salute in the street. Now, with the full strength of his powerful body, he was clubbing some poor soul who had called out his opposition to the ecstatic Nazis. Within seconds, a friendly neighborhood police officer and polite protector of the public was transformed into a brutal persecutor and tormentor. More clearly than anything else could have done, this single incident drove home to Georg the change taking place in his city.[5]

The *Anschluss,* or incorporation of Austria as part of Germany, was all but official. The Austrian Jewish community had heard about the anti-Semitic policies of their neighboring country, but the excesses were minimized with talk such as, "Hitler won't last long," or "Perhaps it won't be so bad after all." Besides, during recent days, Georg's father, Ernst, had gone to the bank every morning, had his midmorning snack at Würstel-Biel, and come home to lunch as usual; his mother, Stella, had done her shopping and checked Helene's dusting like she always had, and Georg had gone to school each day without incident.[6]

But nothing is more impermanent than permanence or as insecure as security. There is a saying that Jews are just like everyone else in this regard, only *more* so. Their permanence is impermanent, like everyone's, only more so, and their security is insecure, like everyone's, only more so.[7]

One of the first high-ranking Germans to arrive in Vienna on the wave of the *Anschluss* was Heinrich Himmler, chief of the German police. Himmler had landed with his aides at the Aspern Airport that very morning at 4:30 a.m. The surrender of the Austrian government had made his task only too easy, as the complete Austrian police files were already in his hands by the time Georg saw the first lorry.[8]

From his window, Georg saw the white snow turning into dirty slush under the exhaust fumes of innumerable vehicles and the stomping jackboots of Austrian SA members. By now, he could clearly make out what the SA men were shouting: "Ju-da verr-rrecke! Ju-da verr-rrecke! Ju-da verr-rrecke!" (Perish Judah!) As he listened to the sound of a thousand voices screaming out in the full fury of hate, he knew it was a sound he would never forget.[9] Only a few moments later, units of the German Wehrmacht began to roll by, and Georg stared in fascination at the steel-helmeted soldiers sitting stiffly upright in their vehicles, motionless, with their hands clasping the barrels of their rifles.[10]

The phone rang, startling Georg and causing him to turn away from the mesmerizing scene outside. It was a neighbor calling to relay a message from good friends of the Klaars, the Mautners: "Love to you all, we have gone on a journey. Will be in touch." Richard and Kathe Mautner were among the relatively few who had left just in time. Richard was a pessimist in the best of times, but he was also a realist who had accurately seen doomsday coming for Austrian Jews. Unlike most, even if they recognized the danger, he had acted early and decisively. Richard had been secretly moving money to Switzerland since mid-1936, and only a few days before the Nazis arrived in Vienna, he had told his wife, Kathe, to start packing. In the early morning hours of March 11, their driver, already wearing a swastika brassard on his arm, had driven the two to the Austrian-Swiss border. The Austrian border guards did not yet have a clear idea of what was going on in Vienna, and they were impressed by the driver's swastika armband and his smart "Heil Hitler" salute. The Mautners had crossed the border without any trouble.[11]

As Georg walked outdoors to get a closer look at the activity in the street, fear was in the air. He was only a few blocks from home when the first squadron of German bombers appeared over Vienna. Flying very low, in exact formation, they looked big and black against the blue sky, their engines throbbing menacingly. Squadron after squadron of Luftwaffe planes appeared until there were hundreds of them circling over the city, and Georg described what he saw as a "plane-blacken'd sky." It was literally true.[12]

Georg thought back to New Year's Day, a little more than two months earlier, when a lead newspaper article had called for government action to stop further immigration of Jews into Austria and recommended a review of all naturalizations granted to Jews after 1918. After reading it, his father had said nothing but was quiet the rest of the morning and had left to visit his mother, Julie, in a pensive mood. His thoughts became clear over lunch with his wife and son when he asked if either of them had read that day's news. When they said they had, his father's next words hit Georg like a bombshell:

> I would expect the Neueste Nachrichten, that Nazi rag, to write in this vein. But for the Reichspost; practically a government newspaper, to write virtually the same does go too far. You know, Stella, I think I should ask the bank to pay me off. Let's take the money, something like forty thousand schillings I'd get, not much, but enough for a new start and go to Switzerland.

Georg and his mother had looked at each other in stunned surprise, hesitating to respond; quickly, perhaps too quickly, Georg thought, his father seemed to be merely toying with the idea of leaving, as he said, "What would happen to my mother and Sally if I did that? Who'd look after them? I'd like to go, but how can I?"[13] At forty-eight, Ernst was reluctant to give up the comfortable existence he had worked for all his life: his lovely home, successful career, and a city that had been the Klaar hometown for generations. But even his attachment to work and home might not have stopped him had his feelings of responsibility and love toward his mother, Julie, and sister, Sally, been less strong. It was at that moment that Ernst Klaar had decided to stay in Austria, even though he recognized the danger sooner than many.[14]

Late on the night of March 12, there was a loud knock on the door at the home of Emil and Selma Ornstein, long-time neighbors across the street from the Klaars. Emil was a prominent businessman and a leading Freemason who was proud of his role as a community leader and his title, "Commercial Councillor." He was also proud of Selma, his elegant platinum-blond wife, and of Ilse, their fifteen-year-old daughter. When Emil opened the door that night, the caretaker of his house was standing there with two Austrian policemen and two German S.S. men in black uniforms. They stormed into the Ornstein home, searched every nook and cranny, emptied drawers on the floor, and finally handcuffed Emil's arms behind his back and led him away. His so-called crimes were being a prominent businessman, a Freemason, and a Jew.

A week later, the Klaar family saw in the newspaper a photograph of Emil Ornstein taken with other Jews who had fallen into the hands of the Gestapo. They all looked sickly and ill groomed, partly because the Germans wanted the Jews to look unkempt, and they were not allowed to shave. Emil was never seen or heard from again. After this incident, Georg's father changed his mind about leaving Vienna, as there was no doubt left in Ernst Klaar's mind that he had to get his family out of Austria before the same thing happened to them.[15]

Ernst, Stella, and their son Georg found that leaving Austria was difficult now, as the fox was already guarding the henhouse. To emigrate, they needed to prepare many documents and pay all taxes, and doing this was more easily said than done. The Austrian government had transformed its proverbial inefficiency into all-but-official state policy intended to offend and harass Jewish petitioners. Negative surprises waited for Jews at every office, and there was an ever-present risk of being hijacked from a queue by a passing German patrol. After a few hours of waiting, they might learn they had done their paperwork wrong and had to return to the starting point. After queuing for more hours, they would be told to get a chit from another official before they could talk to the person they had just spoken to, the stamp they had received was not correct, or they had the wrong paper.[16]

Georg writes of his father's frustrating experience with a government official when he tried to get a certificate that he owed no taxes, one of the requirements for emigration:

The official, a youngish man with a little Hitler mustache, welcomed us with an almost friendly sounding "Heil Hitler" but after looking at us added "Oh well, as you aren't allowed to say that, good morning, and what can I do for you?" Father explained that he needed his tax clearance. "Have you paid everything?" the man asked. Father said he had and the man started to rummage through his files. "Well, well, well," he said and you could see that whatever he had found fairly pleased him no end. "I can't give you a certificate." "Why not? I've paid my taxes," Father replied. "Now have you really?" the man said, clicking his tongue against his teeth with glee. "What about your brother then?" he asked. "Which of my brothers are you talking about?" Father replied. "I'm talking about that nut job half-brother of yours. The one the

Christian taxpayers of this city have been maintaining in the loony bin for the last twenty years. Aryans don't pay for insane Jews any more you know. You Jews have the money anyway. It is up to you. You either pay for his keep or you don't get your certificate. Please yourself."

Under Austrian law, Ernst Klaar had no financial responsibility for a half brother, but the Nazis were in charge now, and what they said went.[17]

Obtaining the proper documentation was not the only problem the Klaar family faced. Even if they received permission to leave, what country would take them in? Within hours of the German absorption of Austria, Czechoslovakia, long hailed as the only true democracy and the most liberal state in Central Europe, closed its border to all Austrian Jewish refugees. The Belgian Parliament announced there would be no wholesale admission of foreigners into their country; and the United States made it clear that German and Austrian immigration quotas would not be increased. To prevent Polish Jews from fleeing to Poland, a Polish law passed on March 25, 1938, decreed that Polish citizens who had not visited Poland for five consecutive years would be deprived of citizenship. By June of the same year, if a Polish Jew affected by this regulation returned to Poland anyway, he was placed in a concentration camp for political prisoners. Worldwide unemployment and trade union opposition to immigrants were the most frequent reasons given for keeping Jews out, and many countries jumped on that bandwagon.[18]

After paying their taxes and buying tickets, there was often little money left, so Jews trying to emigrate found that entry permits were difficult to obtain. Only small amounts of Austrian schillings could be exchanged for foreign currency, and the exchange rates were exorbitant. Because the procedures and policies were all but designed to deplete an applicant's funds, it became difficult to prove he had sufficient funds to sustain himself in his new country.[19]

Early in the afternoon on the day Ernst Klaar saw the newspaper photograph of his friend Emil Ornstein, he sat in his bedroom armchair doing his best to hold back tears. When he could finally speak, he said to his son, "It is the end for us. If only, oh, if *only* I had done what I said a few weeks ago, got my money from the bank and taken mother and you to Switzerland."[20]

Georg describes his father's anguish:

I had never seen my father cry before, had never heard that racking sound of pain and despair of a crying man, had never witnessed that choking struggle with which a man, overcome with grief, tries to regain control over himself. Father had broken down because he had finally realized the total collapse of his world, the end of his career and that he was also afraid they might come for him as they had done for Emil Ornstein.[21]

Georg heard his father ask, "What is going to happen to my mother?" A final parting with Ernst's mother, Julie, was now inevitable, and the knowledge that he would probably never see his mother alive again brought a deeper grief to Ernst than the loss of his home and career. Georg wondered if his father's despairing cry was another way of expressing a longing to be a child again—to be under his mother's protection from a world he could no longer face. How could his father, this giant of his childhood, be so vulnerable that he would cry out for his mother?[22]

The night of March 11, 1938, marked the dramatic end to one thousand years of the peaceful residence of Jews in Austria. Within a matter of days or, at most, a few months, nearly all of Austria's Jews had lost their means of livelihood as well as their homes.[23] Who *were* the people who surged through the streets breaking into Jewish homes and shops to loot and steal? Unfortunately, Austrians themselves had willingly bought into Nazi propaganda proclaiming that the Jews had exploited and injured their society, and they were all too ready to exact revenge.

Jewish men, women, and children were repeatedly forced to don their finest clothes and wash the streets, sidewalks, and buildings of Vienna, frequently with small brushes and water mixed with acid. They were met by the cheers and jeers of crowds of Austrian onlookers. In Währing, one of Vienna's wealthiest sections, Jewish women were ordered to scrub streets in their fur coats, and some of the Austrian Nazis then urinated on their heads.[24] Laughing with glee, they taunted the women, saying, "Work for the Jews, at last the Jews are working! We thank the Führer he has created work for the Jews."[25]

Anti-Semitism in Austria of 1938 is only one reflection of the human tendency to place blame on others for our own failings or insecurities. When things go wrong in society, hate and fear of "the other" can grow to the point that violent acts of persecution are committed against neighbors who have an appearance, religion, or conviction different from our own. Sometimes hatred and fear are actively encouraged by our leaders; and sometimes, we are led to war.

How did Vienna become a hotbed of European anti-Semitism? After all, as one of the leading cultural centers of Europe, the city had given rise to greatness in music, the arts, and the sciences for hundreds of years. Austria was the country of Mozart, Beethoven, Schubert, and Strauss; artists such as Klimt; architects such as Fischer von Erlach, and pioneers in psychology such as Freud. Her long history included the rule of relatively enlightened and benevolent leaders such as Roman emperor Marcus Aurelius, Habsburg emperors Maria Theresa and Josef II, and master politician Prince Metternich.

But the story of Vienna and Austria reveals the repeated failure of peoples and nations to forgive slights, capitalize on strengths, and solve problems through collaboration. If we are to better understand our world today, it behooves us to understand the history of a city and country of contradictions: heartbreaking beauty, fading glory, and, at times, hatred and violence. So let us go back in time to the founding of Vienna, a desolate outpost of the Roman Empire, built along the Danube to protect the empire from invasion by Germanic tribes in the north. Let us go back to the very beginning.

Imagine that you are nineteen-year-old Lucius, a legionnaire from the small village of Patavium, or Padua, in northern Italy. In AD 178, you are part of Caesar's Legio XIII or Thirteenth Legion, consisting of five thousand men divided into ten divisions. Your legion is quartered in Vienna, then known as *Vindobona*, a remote settlement at the far reaches of the Roman Empire. Like most of your comrades, you are a career soldier who has enlisted at an annual pay rate of 1,200 sesterces

($180) plus a cash bonus at retirement that will be equal to thirteen years of salary. You plan to retire happily someday in the province where you serve most of your career, but that day is far away, so you do not think of it often. What you may not realize is that the empire's twenty-five-year service requirement is an effective cost-cutting measure. Many troops die during their last nine years of service.[26]

At the age of only sixteen, Lucius had donned the toga, the white robe of manhood, as a symbol of his right to vote and his duty to serve in the Roman army. He is now more impressive than he is handsome, as rigorous training and three years of military duty have already hardened his expression. He is coarse, tough, and prepared to kill without compunction or to be killed without complaint. Like a typical Roman, he is orderly, conservative, loyal, sober, reverent, tenacious, severe, and practical. He enjoys discipline and will have no nonsense about liberty. With some effort, he can love beauty, but he can seldom create it. He faithfully follows his code but cannot understand philosophy, pure science, or Christ. He can only rule the world.[27]

The name *Vindobona* is of Celtic origin, referring to the Celtic leader, *Vindos*, and his personal estates (from the Latin: *bona*).[28] The Romans subdued the Celts in 15 BC and selected the flat, elevated area between two mountain chains, the Alps and the Carpathians, as an ideal site for a fortress. The Celtic fishing village of Vindobona became part of the north-south trade route between the Scandinavian countries and Italy, a route that crossed the Danube, a critically important river for transportation of food and goods. By the time Lucius arrived, Vindobona had reached a population of 30,000, comprised mostly of Roman soldiers, their families, and merchants who supplied their needs.

The construction of a Roman fortress in AD 97 attracted many people who occupied and further developed Vindobona and the surrounding lands.[29] The fortress itself was built on a standard model used throughout the empire. Its drab but monumental stone buildings, watchtower, and walled-in square made it look something like a small urban center of today. Central buildings in provincial fortresses were examples of some of the greatest architectural structures of their time, and they undoubtedly made an intimidating impression on local residents.[30]

The religious and economic center of Vindobona was the forum, where council members met to govern the town and nearby areas. Baths, theaters, and temples were located within the settlement as well as trade workshops, shops, and taverns. One large building within the fortress was reserved for the camp commander, usually situated near the heavily guarded treasury, and there were long lines of wooden barracks for the troops. But the grim uniformity of the military camp was interrupted by granaries, a kitchen, ovens, latrines, a hospital, armories, leather-works, and a veterinary building. On the outskirts of most towns was an oval amphitheater where public games, gladiator fights, and animal baiting took place and legionnaires practiced daily weapons training. But the location of the amphitheater in Vindobona is not known.

Apart from the forum itself, the most important public building housed the baths. They were the center of life in the Roman world, and entrance fees were subsidized to make this pastime affordable for all. The baths provided for good hygiene, physical training, and relaxation. Except for changing rooms and toilets, each room was furnished with cold and warm water, and there was an outdoor area for exercise. A library was often available, as well as reading rooms, surrounding gardens, a courtyard, shops, restaurants, art galleries, and debating halls. Sometimes there were popular gambling rooms, as well as clusters of rooms set aside for prostitutes.

Lucius spent his leisure time visiting the baths, inns, and taverns, where he could hear the latest gossip. In the back rooms of these establishments, he frequently indulged himself in gambling or enjoyed female companionship. At the baths, he would first go into the apodytarium to undress and then into the unctarium, where his body was rubbed with oil made from the olive tree. Like most Romans, he loved the common practice of having fragrant ointments and oils massaged into his skin. In a warm bath called the calidarium, he would wash himself with a novelty item that the Romans had obtained from the Gauls—soap—made from tallow and the ashes of the elm or beech tree. Next, he relaxed in the steam room before cooling off in the tepidarium and taking a final plunge into the frigidarium.[31]

Romans placed great emphasis on hygiene, and they were aware that waste and sewage water could cause disease. In large towns and fortresses, they built public latrines and sewage systems with running water to flush the latrines and clean the special sponges that were used as an early version of toilet paper. Each visitor purchased this item upon entering a room that contained forty to fifty seats. Because toilets were arranged next to each other, visits to the latrines were also social occasions.

In addition to practicing good hygiene, people in Vindobona were able to follow a healthy diet, as food was available in apparent abundance. Their horticultural skills made it possible for Roman farmers to grow vegetables that varied in taste and size. Fruit was also an important part of every meal, and the cultivation of cherries, plums, pears, apples, and grapes has been confirmed.[32] Sheep and goat meat were as cheap and plentiful as beef, though chicken was rather pricey. Meats such as other kinds of poultry or venison were seldom consumed, but people prized imported mussels such as oysters.

People used their animals not only for food but also for labor, transportation, and clothes. Cattle pulled carts and served as draft animals for working the field, and animal dung was spread over the fields to fertilize their crops. Sheep wool and the fur and skin of other animals were used to make garments, and goat hair was used for weatherproofing material.

There were no weekends as we know them, and the majority of the population worked in the same houses they lived in. Smaller dwellings had no kitchens, so their occupants bought food from shops along the main roads. How people lived, including what they ate, was strongly affected by their social status, as determined by the professional guild to which they belonged.[33]

Because it was considered substandard, barley was fed to horses or used for beer brewing. Seminola, coarsely ground flour made from durum wheat, was used for making pasta and pearl barley, and spelt, another species of wheat, was ground with water to make porridge, a staple of the less privileged. The poor also valued onions and garlic, eaten fresh or cooked as a separate dish.

Affluent Romans dined on courses of roast beef, testicles, kidneys, sow bellies, cheesecake, lobster, goose, and mullets, but only after whetting their appetites with olives, sausage, pomegranate, bread made with finely ground flour, and dormice dipped in a mixture of honey and poppy seeds. Reclining on couches, they watched as entertainers performed in an open space and smoky light glimmered from oil lamps.[34] Murals and mosaics graced most of their houses, and their furnishings, though few, were elegant.

The troops were well supplied, so Lucius had access to plenty of healthy food. His diet consisted of meat from cattle and pigs, animal products such as eggs, milk, and cheese, and foodstuffs from plants, like vegetables and legumes. Costs for his supply of grain, bacon, cheese, salt, and vinegar were deducted from his pay. In the barracks, he lived with seven other soldiers in two rooms equipped with fireplaces and flour mills. He and his comrades prepared their own meals.

In domestic life, the heads of Roman households had exclusive power over their family members, servants, and slaves. Those who could afford to do so sent their children to private teachers. Women could neither vote nor hold public functions, though in rare cases, they were known to have managed companies. There are numerous indications that women engaged in trade, social professions, and the service sector. That they were sometimes entrepreneurs is demonstrated by the example of Atilia, a female brick-factory owner in Vindobona.[35]

The army played a significant role in spreading Roman customs and ideals wherever they went. Inscriptions discovered on various objects indicate that most legionnaires and a large number of civilians were literate, so it was quite likely that Lucius could read and write.[36] To regulate daily life in Rome's vast empire, a large administrative organization was needed, so each town had an army garrison to keep the peace. Lucius and his well-disciplined comrades participated in regular military drills, watched over municipal offices, and ensured that people obeyed Roman laws.

With each conquest, Rome gave people a degree of independence while incorporating them into the Roman system. This carefully graduated scheme of submission allowed for limited freedom while providing rewards for civic participation. It also minimized rebellion and attached great numbers of people to Rome. The Romans wanted peace, and they were prepared to grant the gift of Roman citizenship to those they conquered as the supreme reward for good behavior. Provincials who served in the army received automatic citizenship when they were discharged.

Roman citizenship was not lightly regarded, as citizens had the full protection of Roman law. An accused person could claim the right to be tried by the emperor or a judge responsible to the emperor, and his person was inviolable until a trial took place. This system of granting citizenship was remarkably successful, even though the empire included savage Berbers, cultivated Greeks, resourceful Syrians, and stubbornly clannish Gauls. They all seemed content to live as Romans. The commonwealth was bonded together by law, an undisputed military supremacy, the lure of citizenship, and economic prosperity generated by the lucrative trade that flowed under the shelter of an almost universal Roman Peace.

Before the army's arrival, supplying remote outposts such as Vindobona was difficult. Local production of food and goods was insufficient, and supplies had to be brought in from other areas. But roads were poor, bridges unsafe, oxcarts slow, inns rare, and robbers plentiful, so traffic often moved along canals and rivers, and coastal towns imported goods by sea rather than across the hinterland.

To solve this problem, Romans built a vast network of solidly constructed roads, making possible the fastest mail delivery the world would know until the advent of the railroad. Roman roads were usually straight, three feet in depth, and built on a foundation of rubble that supported tiers of stone and concrete topped by pavement, making them strong enough to support heavy-wheeled traffic. By the time Lucius reached Vindobona, Roman roads extended more than 180,000 miles from Spain to Asia.

The roads defended, unified, and vitalized the Roman Empire by quickening the movement of troops, goods, intelligence, customs, and values. At every ten miles, there was a stopping place where fresh horses could be hired, and at every thirty miles, an inn that served as a store, saloon, and brothel. The roads were channels of commerce that played a major role in populating and enriching Italy and much of Western Europe. They were like tentacles stretched across vast lands that Rome could use to make its laws the will of the people.

Roads of medieval and eighteenth-century Europe would not improve on the roads of Rome. In 54 BC, well before the road system had reached its zenith, Caesar wrote a letter in Britain that reached Cicero in Rome in twenty-nine days, while Sir Robert Peel, hurrying from Rome to London in 1834, needed thirty days to complete the journey.[37]

Lucius and other Romans enjoyed a standard of living that was not to be seen again until the second half of the nineteenth century. They enjoyed plenty of goods, food, exercise, and recreation. They had healthy hygienic practices such as the nearly universal use of baths, fresh running water, clean public latrines, and sophisticated sewer systems. They had impressive civic buildings, an extensive road system, and a sophisticated infrastructure. The presence of police and fire brigades, as well as the Roman military, ensured strict law enforcement and a measure of public safety. These attributes made Roman towns and cities among the most livable in the world.[38]

Religion was a well-integrated part of Roman culture throughout the empire. During the time of Augustus, Roman poet Ovid said, "It is convenient that there should be gods, and that we should think they exist."[39] Daily life was punctuated with religious activities, including sacrifices offered on domestic or community altars. There were sacrifices designed for every occasion, usually consisting of wine, fragrant essences, incense, herbs, fruits, or honey. For more important occasions, an animal such as a bull was led to the altar accompanied by a flute player and a priest who recited prescribed prayers. The animal was stunned with a hammer and killed with a knife or axe before the priest wet the altar with as much blood as possible.

Each year was adorned with more than a hundred holy days, and religious festivals were occasions for feasting and celebration.[40] Romans believed in many deities, though the primary gods within the state religion were Jupiter, Juno, and Minerva. Foreign deities were tolerated, and the only obligatory element in religious life was participation in the cult of the emperor. Among the national gods, Jupiter (or Jove) was the favorite. He was revealed in the expanse of the sky, the light of the sun and moon, a bolt of lightning, a shower of fertilizing rain, and in the trembling of leaves that announced a storm.

Juno was the god of the home, and his two-faced image reflected not that he was deceitful but that he watched over all who entered and exited at every door. The spirit of Juno resided in the woman of the house, giving her the capacity to bear a child, and the month of June was named for him. The important goddess Minerva was the personification of wisdom and memory.

Greek gods invaded the Roman pantheon and found new names: The Roman god Mercury was the Greek god Hermes, the god of travels and commerce; Venus was the Greek Aphrodite, the goddess of love and beauty; Neptune was the Greek Poseidon, the god of the sea, and Baccus was the Greek Dionysus, the god of wine and theatre. The earth itself was a deity, Terra Mater, or Mother Earth, and a Roman's deepest piety turned toward the earth as the source and mother of his life.

The gods were neglected in the autumn as attention turned to harvesting the crops, but December was again rich in religious feasts. The Saturnalia took place from December 17 to 23, when gifts were exchanged, and the distinction between slave and free men was abolished for a time, so that slaves might sit down with their owners and give them orders.

Roman religion served a great purpose for the empire by leading participants to be pious and obedient to the demands of the state. But some have said that it was a lesser belief because it stressed rituals over substance, and its gods rewarded gifts rather than goodness. Surviving Roman prayers were nearly always for material goods, martial victory, and other external benefits. Roman religion may have failed to satisfy the needs of the people because it left too many questions unanswered: It said little about death and the afterlife; it was sternly masculine and failed to speak to women, and it derived its sanctions from ancient legend, with little to say about the present.[41]

Even with the ultimate triumph of Christianity in the ancient world, the religion of Rome was to have lasting influence. The robes of Christian priests, the shape of Christian churches, the order of services, the offerings at the altar, the title of the supreme pontiff, and the very language of Christian ceremonies were all derived from religious practices of ancient Rome. This can be seen in traditions surrounding Christian marriage: Roman betrothals were legal bonds, and relatives gathered to feast and witness the contract. Weddings were celebrated with ritual and song. The groom placed an iron ring on the fourth finger of the bride's left hand because it was believed that a nerve ran from this finger to her heart. Marriage required the consent of the bride and groom, and the ceremony was concluded by *confarreatio*—literally, eating cake together. The two families feasted at the home of the bride and followed the couple to the garlanded door of their new home, where the bridegroom lifted his bride over the threshold and presented her with the keys to the house.[42]

In his outpost of Vindobona, Lucius almost certainly practiced his religion by sacrificing to the gods and asking them for military success. He was miserably cold during the winter, unbearably hot during the summer, and the sole reason he was there was to prevent the crossing of the Danube by the Germanic barbarians on the other side. He needed to believe that the gods would bring him success in his mission. The young soldier had heard that the barbarians on the other side of the river were wretchedly destitute and unable to read or write. Could these stories be true? If they were as ignorant as people said they were, how could they be a threat?

Centuries later, Edward Gibbon, the famous eighteenth-century historian and author of *The Decline and Fall of the Roman Empire*, would describe the barbarians as follows:

The Germans, in this time, had no cities, and that they affected to despise the works of Roman industry, as places of confinement rather than security. Each barbarian fixed his independent dwelling on the spot to which a plain, a wood, or a stream of fresh water, had induced him to give preference. Neither stone, nor brick, nor tiles, were employed in these slight inhabitations. They were indeed

no more than low huts, of circular figure, built of rough timber,
thatched with straw, and pierced at the tip to leave a free passage
for the smoke.[43]

The little clothing worn by the Germans was made from the skins of animals with which their forests were plentifully stocked, and their wealth was measured almost solely by their enormous herds of cattle. During times of peace, they were addicted to gambling that inflamed their passions and excessive drinking that extinguished their reason, but both pastimes brought them relief from the discomfort of their harsh lives. As Gibbon said:

These barbarians are by turns the most indolent and the most
restless of mankind. They delight in sloth, they detest tranquility,
the languid soul, oppressed with its own weight, anxiously required
some new and powerful sensation; and war and danger were the
only amusements adequate to his fierce temper. The sound that
summoned the German to arms was grateful to his ears.[44]

The dark, gloomy German forests put fear into the Romans, as they believed they were havens for evil.[45] And the cold winters that chilled Lucius were scarcely felt by the hardy Germans, who could not endure the Italian summer heat. In the summer, the Danube was a barricade for the Romans, but severe winters tended to freeze the great river, which then became a bridge the barbarians could cross. When the Danube and its sister river, the Rhine, froze solid, they could easily pull their heavy carts across rivers that were impediments to their movements in warmer seasons.[46]

What the Roman soldiers had, that the barbarians lacked, was *discipline.* Lucius and his comrades had been trained for war since early childhood, and they studied military arts above all else. Their military strength was matched by a desire for peace and security for themselves and all who dwelled in the empire. As Gibbon wrote:

> *If a man were called upon to fix the period in history of the world which the condition of the human race was most happy and prosperous, he would without hesitation name that which elapsed from the accession of Nerva (AD 96) to the death of Marcus Aurelius (AD 180). Their united reigns are possibly the only period of history in which the happiness of a great people was the sole object of government.*[47]

After the reign of Nerva came four more great emperors: Trajan, Hadrian, Antonius Pius, and Marcus Aurelius. Even though they were different from each other in temperament, they all possessed qualities of dignity, authority, and calm impartiality associated with enlightened leadership; and they all cared deeply about the welfare of the people they ruled.

The last of them, Marcus Aurelius, embraced the teachings of *Stoicism* before he reached full manhood, putting on the cloak of the philosopher at the age of twelve. He slept on a little straw on the floor, resisting the pleadings of his mother to use a couch. All Italy and all the provinces acclaimed him as the fulfillment of Plato's dream—that mankind will prosper when philosophers are rulers and rulers are philosophers. But the long peace under his predecessors, Hadrian and Pius, had emboldened rebels within the empire and barbarians outside of it, and the challenges he was to face would be severe, indeed.[48]

For about two hundred years following the accession of Augustus in BC 27, the Mediterranean world had been almost completely at peace. War, when waged, was confined to frontier areas. Never in human history was there so long a span of general tranquility. Rome virtually ruled the world, with only the savage tribes of northern Europe and central Africa living outside the great Pax Romana, or Roman Peace.

Safe from raids by marauding combatants, people lived out their lives in quiet contentment, going about their business in the knowledge that they were sheltered by Rome, a stern but generous master that demanded only unyielding obedience to its laws. Rome even granted to communities the right to adapt those laws to local circumstances. Under Roman protection, trade flourished, cultivation expanded, and prosperity came to regions that had never before progressed beyond a subsistence level.

A severe crisis occurred when the army returned to Italy from the wars in Syria in AD 161, just as Marcus Aurelius became emperor. Soldiers brought back with them the worst enemy of all—the plague. Black pestles covered its victims, and sufferers with stinking breath were racked with a hoarse cough. Wagons clattered through streets carrying heaps of bodies out of cities. By 166, the disease had spread throughout Italy, and in Rome alone, two thousand people died each day. The plague ultimately claimed the lives of five million throughout the empire, and many localities were so stricken that they reverted to a primitive existence. Famine followed, and people yielded to a bewildered pessimism. They flocked to soothsayers and altars clouded with smoky incense or sought consolation in a new religion, Christianity, that spoke of personal immortality and peace in a life after death.[49]

Amid these difficulties, in AD 167, came the news that the German tribes along the Danube had crossed the river, overwhelming the Roman garrison of twenty thousand and pouring unhindered into the empire, advancing as far as Venice and Verona. Never before had the Germans moved with such unity and force. Despite years of being defeated, the fertile barbarians had grown in numbers and strength, while the barren Romans were becoming fewer and weaker.

Marcus Aurelius realized that there must be a war to the death and that one side must destroy the other or go under. Only a man schooled in the Roman and Stoic sense of duty could have transformed himself so completely from the mystical philosopher that he preferred to be into an imposing and successful general. Aurelius rallied his forces and began to fight back in 168 AD. Between 171 and 174, he was on the Danube frontier directing a desperate war that he knew could mean the end of the empire. He acted with surprising decisiveness, energy, and courage, all the more admirable in a man who hated war. Inspiring his army to move as a force of disciplined strength, he drove the barbarians all the way back to the Danube.[50]

Marcus Aurelius had a Stoic temperament to the point that it was said of him that neither grief nor joy changed his countenance. Such consistency in an emperor would be almost beyond belief if we did not have the testimony of his *Meditations*, a work that celebrates Stoic virtues and documents the emperor's heroic search for self-knowledge. In his writing, we find the man who ruled the greatest empire on earth recording this liberating thought:

> *Don't look down on death, but welcome it. It too is one of the things required by nature. Like a new set of teeth, a beard, the first grey hair … So this is how a thoughtful person should await death: not with indifference, not with impatience, not with disdain, but simply viewing it as one of the things that happen to us. Remember how you anticipated the child's emergence from its mother's womb? That's how you should await the hour when your soul will emerge from its compartment.*[51]

This glimpse of a philosopher pondering the problems of mortality and destiny while leading his great army in a conflict on which the fate of the empire turned is one of the most intimate portraits that time has presented of its great men. *Meditations* is a private journal of a man who senses he has not long to live, contemplating human life and the mysterious ways of the gods. We can imagine him scratching out his thoughts by a flickering oil lamp in the cold and inhospitable environment of Vindobona. It is the record of his ambivalence, one moment filled with wonder at the grandeur and order of the universe and the next, railing with disgust at the folly of mankind and the arbitrariness of fate.[52]

In AD 180, sickness struck Marcus Aurelius while he was in Vindobona. After refusing all food and drink for six days, he covered his head with a sheet and died at the age of fifty-nine. When his body reached Rome, people had already begun to worship him as a god who had consented, for a while, to live on earth. Although he did not use these exact words, his legacy includes two well-known axioms: "Vanity of vanities, all is vanity," and "This, too, will pass away."[53]

During the final illness of Marcus Aurelius, did Lucius and other young soldiers keep vigil for their great emperor-general? Whatever the case, at the death of Aurelius, a great dream faded. He had set the highest possible standard for integrity and responsibility. Perhaps no man in history ever had a more elevated sense of duty. But as a Stoic emperor, he had a problem: on the one hand, he had to love mankind, but on the other, he despised what they wanted and hated what they loved. He had discovered that not all men wished to be saints, and he sadly reconciled himself to a world of corruption and wickedness. The obvious sign of his greatness was that he was a standing refutation of the famous words of Lord Acton, "Power tends to corrupt and absolute power corrupts absolutely." Aurelius had absolute power but had never used it for selfish, despotic, or corrupt purposes.

The son of Marcus Aurelius, Commodus, inherited his father's throne, but not his character, courage, or administrative skill. With the death of Aurelius, the great Pax Romana was virtually over.[54] And Rome's inability to civilize the Germanic provinces north of the Danube ultimately led to its fall. The task was too great for an empire suffering from old age. With its citizens living in sterile comfort, Rome was losing its vitality just as the northern barbarian tribes were advancing in robust health and reckless strength. As the Germans multiplied, Roman families were dying out. During this process, the Romanization movement was reversed, and the barbarians began to barbarize Rome. People who inhabited the region around Vindobona reverted to living by herding, hunting, tillage, and war, and they did not retain the complex abilities needed to administer a thriving city.

Like many remote provinces, Vindobona lost its connection to Roman civilization, and the municipal character of the Roman Empire simply ceased for 700 years. Europe moved inevitably into the Dark Ages. And yet, the way was being prepared for a promising new beginning. The great Roman Empire was dying, but the states of modern Europe were waiting to be born.[55]

CHAPTER 2

The Greatest Test

An examination of Austria's experience during what has been called the "Dark Ages" reveals that humanity has not progressed as far as we would like to believe since medieval times. The insecurity that excites greed, the hate that fosters cruelty, the poverty that causes fear, the filth that generates disease, and the ignorance that begets superstition still survive in modern civilization. Dogmatism continues to move many toward intolerance, and inquisitors still look for circumstances that permit them to oppress, kill, ravage, and destroy.

Man occupies territory with the permission of physical geography, divided from his fellows by mountains, rivers, and seas; he is therefore destined to live in a semi-isolation that gives rise to diverging languages, cultures, and creeds. People fear what seems alien, and instead of fostering unity, the panorama of delights among diverse peoples causes nations to focus on their differences, self-imprisoned by suspicion of their neighbors. This is true in today's Western civilization and throughout the world.

At no time was the legacy of human conflict more apparent than in Vienna after the death of Marcus Aurelius in AD 180, when all of Europe fell into a chaotic mix of conquest, barbarization, and disintegration in an endless duel between East and West. Plague swept the Roman Empire in 542 and again in 566, and famine struck in 569. Poverty and war disrupted communications, discouraged commerce, and stifled literature and art.[56]

The impacts of the barbarian conquest on the Roman Empire were profound: Avars, equestrian nomads from central Asia, and Slavs crossed the Danube and took possession of imperial lands and towns. The barbarian conquerors lived by tillage, herding, hunting, and war, so they did not know how to manage the commercial complexities of cities. Occupied lands simply reverted to a rural state, and the municipal character of the Roman Empire literally ceased for 700 years. Much of the classical pagan culture survived, hidden within monasteries or practiced by a few families; but the physical and psychological foundation of social order had been so disturbed that it would take centuries to rebuild. As Will Durant wrote in *The Story of Civilization*:

Order is the mother of civilization and liberty; chaos is the midwife of dictatorship; therefore, history may now and then say a good word for kings. Their Medieval function was to free the individual from local domination, and to centralize in one authority the power to legislate, judge, punish, mint and make war. The feudal baron mourned the loss of local autonomy, but the simple citizen thought it good that there should be, in his country, one master, one coinage, one law.[57]

The name "Austria" was first written in 996 as "Ostarrichi," referring to the inhabitants who lived in the central Danube basin intending to shield Christendom and the empire from the heathen East.[58] Situated at the crossroads of Europe, Austria has always been forced to keep her eyes turned watchfully on all points of the compass, but mainly toward the plains which mark the beginning of the Asian steppes and beyond. It was from this direction that the white dust cloud rising in the summer heat gave the first warning of approaching armies. Austrians built their churches as outposts for protection as well as for praying; they were perched on crags or hills chosen for security rather than for comfort, and their stubby square towers were pierced with arrow slits.

Austrians were less concerned about the welfare of other states than about saving their own skins, but their fate was vitally linked to those of the larger lands surrounding them. Their territory both joined and divided the races and religions of all of Europe, for across Austrian lands, the Alps rose and the Danube flowed—Europe's greatest mountain range and her longest river. Winding through the Austrian valley from north to south was the ancient route that connected the Baltic and the Mediterranean. Here could be found all the main avenues of European trade and migration.[59]

Austrians were never to know the security provided by the English Channel that made it possible for England to grow strong or the shelter of the Pyrenees Mountains that allowed the Spaniards to slumber safely. Spain and France were traditional enemies of England, with historical axes to grind, but the impersonal enemies of Austria had ever-changing names and faces: The Avars, Magyars, Huns, Mongols, and Turks had differing weapons, faces, and helmets; but they all came from the East, and it was their common path that made them "the enemy."

While Austria fought successfully against almost everyone, she was driven to seek greater security by building various alliances with other European countries. Over time, this had the unintended effect of encouraging the development of her uniquely cosmopolitan culture. Her musicians and artists have come from the Germanic north, the Roman south, and the Slavic East.[60]

Most citizens of twenty-first century Europe were born into a nationalism that they accepted unquestioningly, like the air they breathed. But Austrians never developed a similar level of state patriotism. The Habsburg Empire arose as a feudal estate, and it was ruled like one. Austria's centrality to the empire may have caused it to remain what the emperors of the Dark Ages intended her to be when they drew their lines of defense across her territory: the reef to protect the culture of Christendom from the turbulent seas of the Turkish Empire. Austria was homeless, the property not of a nation but of a single family.

The usual method of empire building was to push out beyond an existing frontier and colonize, with more or less violence, weaker peoples on the path. But the Habsburgs were without equal in augmenting their private territorial possessions through treaty, marriage, and succession rather than conquest. The Austrian people were in every sense the personal servants of the Habsburg family who resided in their palace in

Vienna. In that sense, there was no true Austrian nation. The British ruled whatever they discovered while sailing in their ships and whatever they won through wars, but the Austrians simply administered what the Habsburg dynasty acquired through the use of a personal and bloodless weapon—the wedding ring.[61]

Early Austrians had to be greedy enough to seek food eagerly and gorge on it zealously, for they could never be sure when it would be available again. European forests were fearfully immense, harboring wild animals and impeding communications and unity until man felled the trees and the soil yielded to his will. People had to strike a balance between their jungle instincts and the inhibitions of a moral code. Instincts without inhibitions would have ended civilization, and inhibitions without instincts would have ended life. The problem of morality is to adjust inhibitions to protect civilization without enfeebling life, and the Austrians gradually succeeded in doing just this. Through five centuries, from 566 until 1106, Austrians developed greater sophistication in tilling the soil and rearing children, until they at last conquered their country for civilization.[62]

Generations of hardy peasants pushed back the beasts and the wilderness by taming the land with hoe and plow, planting fruit trees, herding flocks, and tending vines; and their miners dug salt, iron, copper, lead, and silver from the mountains. They combated their rural isolation with love, prayer, flowers, music, and beer.[63]

Roads were difficult to travel, so rivers played a leading role in the transport of goods, and trade began to flow more freely across the Danube. A major impediment to the river trade, however, was the imposition of toll stations where the river passed through a feudal baron's domain. There were seventy-seven toll stations on the Danube alone, and merchants could not avoid them, even at night, as a large chain was placed across the river at each stop. Barons felt justified in exacting these tolls on goods passing through their domains, as most gave protection and service to merchants by providing armed escorts and convenient hospitality. A boat could transport as much as five hundred animals could carry over land, and far more cheaply; so rivers became superhighways. They ultimately determined the spread of populations and the growth of towns.[64]

In the Middle Ages, daily life for a typical family was much different and far less comfortable than that of our Roman soldier in the previous chapter. The few windows in a medieval home had only wooden shutters to shelter its occupants against glare or cold. Heat came from one or more fireplaces, but drafts blew in through a hundred cracks in the walls, making high-backed chairs very popular.

Food was abundant, varied, and well prepared, but the lack of refrigeration put a premium on spices that could preserve or disguise meat. Some spices were imported from the Orient, but these were costly; so spices grown in domestic gardens, such as parsley, mustard, sage, savory, anise, garlic, and dill were widely used. Sugar was an expensive import that had not replaced honey. Desserts were usually made of fruit, nuts, and many varieties of pastry. Peasants flourished by eating coarse, whole-grain bread made of barley, oats, or rye baked in the home, but city dwellers preferred white bread bought from bakers. The most common meat was pork: pigs ate the refuse in the streets, and people ate the pigs. There were no potatoes, coffee, or tea.

In the thirteenth century, napkins were not used during the meal, so people wiped their hands on the tablecloth. Couples sat together, usually eating from the same plate and drinking from one cup. And though forks were known, they were seldom provided. Instead, each person received a spoon and used his own knife. Cups, saucers, and plates were usually made of wood.[65]

Cleanliness was not considered to be next to godliness in medieval times. Early Christians denounced Roman baths as places of perversion and promiscuity, and their general disapproval of the human body caused them to place no premium on hygiene. Cleanliness was next to *money*, and it varied with one's income. The rich had latrines, but most people managed with outhouses that might serve up to a dozen households.[66]

Unless it was boiled, water was seldom safe to drink, so all classes substituted beer and wine. Cider was made from apples or pears, providing a cheap intoxication for the peasantry, and drunkenness was a favorite vice of men and women, whether rich or poor. Beer was the regular drink of the poor, even for breakfast, and monasteries and hospitals normally allowed a gallon of beer per person per day.[67] Since there was no practice of after-dinner smoking, both sexes drank instead.

Medieval manners were usually coarse, though they were tempered by certain graces associated with feudal courtesy. Men shook hands when they met as a pledge of peace that showed their lack of readiness to draw their swords. Christianity was teaching a new respect for human life and work; and it was providing peace of mind by solving the baffling riddle of the universe, though this came at the cost of discouraging science and philosophy.[68]

To priests and theologians of the Middle Ages, a woman was still what she had been to the earliest Christians: a necessary evil, a natural temptation, a desirable calamity, a domestic peril, a deadly fascination, or a painted ill. She was the reincarnation of Eve, who had lost Eden for mankind, and she was still the favored instrument of Satan in leading men to hell. Civil law was even more hostile to her than canon law, and both codes permitted wife beating. It was a giant step forward when, in the thirteenth century, new laws and customs "bade a man beat his wife only in reason."[69]

A woman was raised to learn the arts of the home: to bake bread, puddings, and pies, cure meats, make soap and candles, make cream and cheese, brew beer, and make medicines from herbs. She also learned to spin and weave wool, make linen from flax, make clothing for her family, decorate the home, and keep it as clean as the male inmates would allow. She was, of course, expected to take responsibility for rearing the children.[70]

By AD 1256, most feudal lords were convinced that an emperor was necessary to keep central Europe from drifting into chaos. The pope supported the idea, as disorder in central Europe hindered recruitment for the next crusade to free the holy land from the Muslims. In 1273, Rudolph, Count of Habsburg, was chosen to lead the empire. As emperor, he was merely a figurehead, but as founder of a royal house, he was very effective. At Rudolph's accession, the Habsburg family controlled lands extending from modern Switzerland into Alsace in modern France, a substantial holding. But Rudolph used his position to acquire other territories for his family, setting an example that would be followed by most of his successors. Between 1273 and 1308, the Habsburgs rose from obscurity to become the most feared house in central Europe.[71]

After 1477, the history of the Habsburgs was the history of Europe. Maximilian I was the first Habsburg to use marriage-bed diplomacy to consolidate various provinces which made up the Austrian legacy.[72]

By 1580, even Portugal fell to the Habsburgs through marriage, along with their possessions in Africa and Brazil. Other dynasties achieved their greatness by wars and conquest, but the Habsburgs consistently acquired their vast properties through marriages and treaties. There seemed to be no conscious plan to dominate Europe, and many of the Habsburg marriages and successions were fortuitous rather than being part of a long-term scheme.[73]

We are fortunate to have a description of Vienna in the 1480 writings of an Italian visitor, Silvo Piccolomini, the future Pope Pius II. Piccolomini complained bitterly of bad food and bad wine—something almost unbearable for an Italian—and he condemned what he saw as irresponsibility and disorder among the people of Vienna:

Day and night there are brawls in the streets of the city, craftsmen against students, court employees against craftsmen, a guild against another. Seldom does festivity end except in a brawl, often with death as a result. Neither the city authorities nor the princes intervene to put an end to this wretched state of affairs. The common people think only of their stomachs and clothing. Whatever earned during the week with his hand spends all on his earnings on Sunday's merrymaking.[74]

On the eve of Martin Luther's revolution, the Germanic land was a scene of social and political chaos, with the Habsburgs and other great families failing to behave like responsible sovereigns. By nailing his *95 Theses* to the door of the church in Wittenberg in 1517, Luther merely struck the match that spread the fire of church reform across northern and central Europe. A report in 1561 also called for reform by saying that the church at Klosterneuberg, near Vienna, was a place where "priests and monks were living a life of pleasure with their concubines and indulging in feasting and dancing."[75]

Protestantism appealed not only to the nobility but to the exploited lower classes and all who were disgusted by the greed, hypocrisy, and increasingly secular lifestyle of Catholic prelates and clergy. Once the most desired of all careers in Vienna, the priesthood had no recruits in the twenty years preceding the Reformation begun in 1517. By the 1560s it was estimated that four-fifths of the population of Vienna were Protestant, and ten of the thirteen parishes lacked priests. Fiery Lutheran preachers castigated the pope as being the anti-Christ. Noblemen cantered on their horses down the aisles of St. Stephen's Cathedral, slashing religious images with their swords. By 1576, even the mayor of Vienna was Protestant.

While this was a high point of Protestantism in the city, a counterattack had already begun in 1551, when Emperor Ferdinand summoned the Jesuits to the University of Vienna. And by 1598, the Catholic Church was once again dominant. The Jesuit order acquired a complete monopoly on higher education in Austria because their philosophy was more attractive to the masses than Protestantism, with its discouraging doctrines of predestination and the total depravity of man. Emperor Maximilian II claimed he was "neither Papist nor Protestant; I am a Christian." But this was enough for the Cardinal of Trento, from present-day Italy, to allegedly lace the emperor's food with a lethal dose of poison when he visited Vienna. After the emperor's death, a Catholic doctor hastened to discover in his dissected heart a black substance which he said was the precise spot where the devil had made his lodging.[76]

Austria had long been the bulwark of Western civilization against the ambitious Turks, but it would also become become the bastion of the Counter Reformation and the seat of Catholic power during the Thirty Years War, from 1618 to 1648. Ferdinand II became emperor of the Catholic Habsburg Empire in 1619, and he began what was to be a brutal war between Protestants and Catholics for the minds of all Eastern Europe. On November 8 in 1620, just outside of Prague, the Battle of White Mountain resulted in a resounding defeat of the Protestant army by the Catholic League and the consolidation of Habsburg power.

Ferdinand II forced all Viennese citizens to profess themselves Catholics or emigrate. The results of this order were disastrous, as it caused those with strong principles to leave and those with weak ones to stay.[77] The departure of Vienna's entrepreneurial Protestant burgers was Germany's gain and Vienna's loss. The absence of the Protestant craftsmen, technicians, and businessmen would put a drag on Vienna's development for years to come.

Under Ferdinand III, until 1648, the war dragged on against not two armies but six: German, Danish, Swedish, Bohemian, Spanish, and French. To augment their armies, most governments relied heavily on foreign mercenaries led by adventurers—hirelings who fought not for faith, but for a fee, with no attachment to the people or causes for whom they fought.[78] The Habsburgs were blessed in that they could recruit fighters from loyal residents of their vast empire.[79]

Monarchs and morals alike collapsed during the holocaust that was the Thirty Years War.[80] And the fatalism of despair sparked the cynicism of brutality. The elevating ideas of religion and patriotism receded into the darkness of a generation of violence, and simple men fought over food, drink, or just plain hatred of one another.[81] Thousands of "witches" were put to death, and men began to doubt the creeds of those who preached Christ and practiced wholesale slaughter. They suspected their rulers of having no real faith and only a lust for power. Soldiers saw civilians as legitimate prey, forcing them to become servants, kidnapping their children for ransom, firing their haystacks, and burning their churches for fun.

The population of Germany and Austria declined from twenty-one million to a little more than thirteen million during the Thirty Years War. Thousands of fertile acres were left untilled for lack of men and draft animals. Peasants no longer bothered to plant their fields, as they had no assurance they could reap what they had sown. Both sides destroyed any crops remaining in the fields when they departed an area to prevent them from being used to feed the enemy. Once-wealthy merchants begged in the streets or robbed for bread.[82]

The spiraling costs of war exposed the real weakness of the Habsburg system. General inflation caused food prices to rise five times and industrial prices three times between 1500 and 1630. This heavy blow to government finances was compounded by the doubling and redoubling of the size of army. As a result, the Habsburgs were involved in an ongoing struggle for solvency. The government was constantly trying to refinance loans, always at interest rates that spiraled ever upward. It was all the government could do to pay the interest on past debt. Taxes were steadily increased in many imaginative ways, but rarely did they fall on the shoulders of those who could most easily bear them, and they always tended to hurt commerce.

The Habsburgs simply had too many enemies to fight and too many fronts to defend. They had to maintain their strength, regardless of the cost, as the Turks still had an army in Hungary, only 150 miles from Vienna. While other countries enjoyed periods of peace and recovery, it was the Habsburgs' fate to have to turn immediately from a struggle against one enemy to a new conflict with another.[83]

Vienna is so beautiful today that it is hard to imagine what it must have looked like after the Thirty Years War. Austria had not suffered as severely as Germany, but its treasury was exhausted, its armies were in disgrace, and the Peace of Westphalia had lowered the prestige and power of the emperors.[84] The hidden victim of the war was Christianity. Protestantism had been strengthened in Germany but weakened along the Danube. Though the Reformation had been saved, both Protestantism and Catholicism suffered from skepticism encouraged by the brutality of war and the cruelties of belief. An increasing number of people turned to science and philosophy for answers, and the Peace of Westphalia ended the reign of theology over the European mind. It left the road obstructed but passable for the entrance of the Age of Reason.[85]

Hardly had the dust settled from the Thirty Years War when came the horrifying bubonic plague of 1679, cutting down the population like ripened wheat. It is scarcely possible to imagine the suffering of those trapped in Vienna during the plague, and it is understandable that their reactions were irrational. Popular shields against infection ranged from the reasonable, such as isolation of victims, to the bizarre and superstitious: An English traveler, Edward Brown, reported seeing a man drinking the blood from a newly decapitated head in the hope of immunization.[86] Since the movement of air was thought to disburse the infection, church bells were rung constantly, and birds were encouraged to fly around rooms. Stinking goats were tied within dwellings in the belief that their smell would drive out the disease, although it more likely drove out the inhabitants.

Preacher Johann Megerle exploited the climate of fear by claiming the plague was caused by "the Jews, the gravediggers, and also by witches."[87] Of course, his accusation that the plague was caused by the Jews was unsupportable, since almost all of them had been forced to leave Vienna nine years earlier. The death toll ultimately rose to 75,000.

The horrors of the plague had barely faded when Vienna faced the greatest test of its history: the Turkish Siege of 1683. For three hundred years, Austria had been the defender of the Christian West against invasion from the Muslim East, but now rumors had begun to warn of greater aggression from the Turks. The Habsburgs were distracted by the ambitions of their old adversary, Louis XIV, the king of France. The Turkish sultan, Kara Mustafa, felt that the conflicts between the Habsburgs and the French Bourbon and between Catholicism and Protestantism offered him the opportunity to take Vienna and perhaps all of Europe. In Austria it was suspected that the Turkish strategy was planned by French and Italian experts in the pay of Louis XIV, who thought the Turks could be useful in weakening his Habsburg rivals.[88]

At the time, the Habsburg emperor was Leopold I, a man educated by the Jesuits and initially trained for the priesthood. He was inclined toward peace but forced into wars by the aggression of Louis XIV. Between wars, he found time for poetry, art, and music. He composed music and encouraged the performance of opera in Vienna. He labored dutifully in administering his empire, but he was not an effective or efficient ruler. He lacked the vision of his Habsburg forebears, and he was a bizarre mixture of picayune obsessions and wasteful extravagance.[89]

Mustafa assembled men and supplies from Arabia, Syria, Russia, and Turkey, and on March 31, 1683, they began their long march to Vienna. The Christians could muster only around 74,000 men to defend the West against the Turkish army of 140,000, and Leopold was more interested in saving his own skin than in defending his empire. On July 7, he traveled to the Austrian town of Linz, a safe distance from the advancing Turks, and en route, he was jeered and even spat on by the peasants. To his credit, before he left the capital, he sent a messenger to the king of Poland begging him to come at once.

On July 14, the Turks appeared at the city walls and began shelling the city with cannon. Even today, Turkish cannon balls decorate some of the famous old coffee houses in Vienna. As July turned into August, the city had only enough ammunition and supplies to hold out for six weeks more, but on September 5, the Polish cavalry arrived 3000 strong, followed two days later by 23,000 Polish infantry. They caught Mustafa's army by surprise and cut them to pieces in their trenches. Those on the Austrian side were re-inspired by the feeling that they were saving Europe and Christianity, and to their joy, the next dawn showed that the Turks had fled, leaving behind 10,000 dead, most of their materiel, and sacks of something new and strange: coffee beans!

Mustafa's army had already been on the verge of disintegration. After two months of fighting, his soldiers had seen none of the booty that had been promised to them. They had laid waste to the surrounding countryside, so it was becoming difficult to find enough food. The men were disillusioned by the behavior of corrupt senior officers who were more interested in collecting girls to be traded as slaves than applying themselves to the siege. Many officers had adorned their trenches with tapestries and tiles, and Mustafa himself had equipped his tent with baths, fountains, gardens, and concubines.[90] With the arrival of the Polish reinforcements to Vienna, it was over for the Turks.

The defeat of Mustafa's besieging army turned the tide in central Europe, and over the next few years, the Turkish armies were steadily pushed back. Freed from the pressure of Turkish aggression, Austria and Germany could now turn to face the threat of the ambitious Louis XIV. Austria was able to manipulate the economies of Hungary and Bohemia to its own advantage, and its upper classes began to enjoy a new affluence.

Splendid palaces rose for the aristocracy, and beautiful churches honored triumphant priests and monks. Vienna built the Belvedere Palace for Eugene of Savoy, who had successfully resisted the Turks. Architect Johann Fischer van Erlach designed three of the city's grandest buildings: One of these was the expansion of the Hofburg Palace begun in 1279. After 1683, it was decided that additions were needed to celebrate the Turkish defeat. Another was the Royal Library, built between 1723 and 1726. It is one of the most beautiful historical libraries in the world, housing 8 million books, including 200,000 printed between 1501 and 1850. The third impressive structure was the new summer home of the Habsburgs, the Palace of Schonbrunn, a 1,441-room building that remains one of the most important cultural monuments in the country. The palace was designed to rival Versailles in Paris, and its name means "beautiful spring."[91]

The defeat of the Turks was the signal for the flowering of a frontier wilderness into the glory of the Italian-inspired Baroque Period. All of the Habsburg lands were ultimately stamped with a cultural unity that would help the country emerge as a great European power. Proud and splendid, Austria was now ready to move into its greatest century.[92]

CHAPTER 3

The Age of Benevolent Absolutism

I am now, my dear sister, safely arrived at Vienna; and, I thank God, have not at all suffered in my health, nor (what is dearer to me) in that of my child, by all our fatigues. We traveled by water from Ratisbon (in Bavaria), a journey perfectly agreeable, down the Danube, in one of those little vessels, that they, very properly, call wooden houses, having in them all the convenience of a palace, stoves in the chambers, kitchens, etc. They are rowed by twelve

men each, and move with such incredible swiftness, that in the
same day you have the pleasure of a variety of prospects; and,
within the space of a few hours, you have the pleasure of seeing
a populous city adorned with magnificent palaces, and the most
romantic solitudes, which appear distant from the commerce of
mankind, the banks of the Danube being charmingly diversified
with woods, rocks, mountains covered with vines, fields of corn,
large cities and ruins of ancient castles.[93]

Lady Mary Wortley Montague (1689-1762) wrote this letter in 1716 during her travels with her husband, Edward Wortley, British ambassador to the court of Turkey in Constantinople. When the ambassadorship failed, Wortley was recalled to London in 1719, but Lady Mary continued to write letters. After her death, a collection of her letters was finally published in 1763, and several editions sold out quickly. Lady Mary's writings struck at the conventions that had imprisoned her sex, and Samuel Johnson and Edward Gibbon were among her delighted readers.[94] With an eye for detail, Lady Mary gave the following description of Vienna:

This town, which has the honor of being the emperor's residence,
did not at all answer my expectations, nor ideas of it; the streets
are very close, and so narrow, one cannot observe the fine fronts of
the palaces, though many of them very well deserve observation,
being truly magnificent. They are built of fine white stone, and are
excessive high. For as the town is too little for the number of the
people that desire to live in it ... You may easily imagine, that the
streets being so narrow, the rooms are extremely dark; and, what

is an inconvenience much more intolerable, in my opinion, there is no house has so few as five or six families in it ... Their apartments are adorned with hangings of the finest tapestry of Brussels, prodigious large looking glasses in silver frames, fine Japan tables, beds, chairs, canopies, and window curtains of the richest Genoa damask or velvet, covered with gold lace or embroidery.[95]

In the earlier part of the eighteenth century, Lady Mary's Vienna was a city of extremes, with enormous wealth for the upper classes and grinding poverty for those at the bottom of the heap.[96] The term *Baroque*, often associated with the architectural style of palaces, churches, and monuments, ultimately referred more broadly to Vienna's golden age of exuberance. It was a way of life that encompassed art, music, dress, and other expressions which appealed to the city's love of beauty and sensuality. Later in the century, the liberal politics of the emerging *Enlightenment* movement would find its way from France and Prussia all the way to the seat of power in Austria, but it would be slow to take root.

Despite great poverty among some, there was relatively little crime during Lady Mary's time in Vienna, as people found contentment in simple pleasures like exchanging visits, cooling their feet in one of many shady parks, promenading on tree-lined streets, picnicking in the countryside, or thrilling to ferocious and ugly fights between famished animals. Dancing was a prettier pastime, and this included the famed minuet, where a man and woman rarely touched each other, every movement was governed by tradition and rule, and each step was taken with restraint and grace.[97] On January 1, 1717, one of Lady Mary's letters expressed her view of Viennese dancing:

> *The balls are in public places, where the men pay a gold ducat*
> *at entrance, but the ladies nothing. I am told that these houses get*
> *sometimes a thousand ducats in a night. They are magnificently*
> *furnished, and the music good, if they had not that detestible [sic]*
> *custom of mixing hunting horns with it, that almost deafen the*
> *company.*
>
> *... The ball always concludes with English country dances,*
> *to the number of thirty or forty couple, and all so ill danced, that*
> *there is very little pleasure in them. They know but half a dozen,*
> *and they have danced them over and over these fifty years: I would*
> *fain have taught them some new ones, but I found it would be some*
> *months labour to make them comprehend them. What completed*
> *the diversion, was the excessive cold, which was so great, I thought*
> *I should have died there. It is now the very extremity of the winter*
> *here; the Danube is entirely frozen, and the weather not to be sup-*
> *ported without stoves and furs; but however, the air so clear, almost*
> *everybody is well, and colds not half so common as in England.*[98]

Viennese royal splendor was beginning to rival that of Paris.
Schonbrunn, the summer home of the royal family, included 495 acres
of gardens laid out to emulate Versailles, with towering hedges, fanciful
grottos, symmetrical ponds, graceful statues, and countless botanical
specimens. The immense palace had been left unfinished in 1705, but
work would be resumed in 1744 and completed in 1780.[99]

The elaborate style of dress among the Viennese nobility in Lady Mary's
day was captured in her description of preparing for her appearance at court:

I will keep my promise in giving you an account of my first going to court. In order to that ceremony, I was squeezed up in a gown, and adorned with a gorget and the other implements there unto belonging; a dress very inconvenient, but which certainly shows the neck and shape to great advantage. I cannot forbear giving you some description of the fashions here, which are more monstrous, and contrary to all common sense and reason, than tis possible for you to imagine. They build certain fabrics of gauze on their heads, about a yard high, consisting of three or four stories, fortified with numberless yards of heavy ribbon ... it certainly requires as much art and experience to carry the load upright, as to dance upon May-Day with the garland. Their whale-bone petticoats outdo ours by several yards, circumference, and cover some acres of ground. You may easily suppose how this extraordinary dress sets off and impresses the natural ugliness, with which God Almighty has been pleased to endow them, generally speaking."[100]

There was no rich middle class in Austria to challenge the omnipotence of the aristocracy or dilute its blue blood. Marriage was a matter of protocol, and unwritten law allowed for mistresses and lovers within the same class.[101] As Lady Mary wrote:

But what you will think very odd, the two sects that divide our whole nation of petticoats are utterly unknown in this place. Here are neither coquettes nor prudes. No woman dares appear coquette enough to encourage two lovers at a time. And I have

not seen any such prudes as to pretend fidelity to their husbands,
who are certainly the best natured set of people in the world, and
look upon their wives' gallants as favorably as men do upon their
deputies ... 'tis the established custom for every lady to have two
husbands, one that bears the name, and another that performs the
duties. And the engagements are so well known, that it would be a
downright affront, and publicly resented, if you invited a woman
of quality to dinner, without, at the same time, inviting her two
attendants of lover and husband, between whom she sits in state
with great gravity. The sub-marriages generally last twenty years
together, and the lady often commands the poor lover's estate, even
to the utter ruin of his family ... a woman looks out for a lover as
soon as she is married as part of her equipage, without which she
would not be genteel.[102]

Austria and the rest of the Habsburg Empire did not rush to adopt the liberal political and social changes beginning to take hold elsewhere in Europe. Though Eugene of Savoy had successfully defended the Habsburg throne from Turkish aggression, the ambitions of Louis XIV were still menacing, and Prussia was becoming a power to be reckoned with. The Habsburgs continued to think defensively, feudal lords controlled serfs, and torture was still used in imperial prisons as a means of extracting confessions. Surrounded by lordly palaces, elaborate operas, and magnificent churches dispensing hope of a better life in the next world, the lower classes lived in abject poverty.

Following the death of Josef I in 1711, his brother, Charles VI, succeeded to the Habsburg throne at a time when Austria, with a population of six million, appeared to be thriving. Land owned by the nobility or the clergy was worked by serfs and kept intact through *primogeniture*, also practiced in England, where a family's whole estate went to the eldest son. Younger sons were employed by the army, church, or government.[103]

Charles VI wanted desperately to avert a war of succession that he saw as inevitable if he had no male heir; so in 1713, he summoned his privy counselors and announced the *Pragmatic Sanction*, declaring that if he died without a son, the empire would be ruled by any daughter that he had. Hoping that a son would still be born, making it unnecessary for the other European powers to agree to the sanction, Charles kept it a state secret for as long as he could.[104] With the birth of his third daughter in 1724, however, it became clear that the Pragmatic Sanction would have to be publicly announced. After some foot-dragging by France, the sanction was collectively approved by the other European states, and Charles believed that this would keep the Habsburg Empire together without a war.[105]

Next to the Habsburg throne and his eldest daughter, Maria Theresa, Charles VI loved music, and during his reign, Vienna became the music center of the Western world. Music was so important in the city that in some operas many of the singers were members of the aristocracy; and in one performance, the principal role was sung by the Archduchess Maria Theresa herself. Following the lead of the nobility, most Viennese households contained a harpsichord, and everyone in the family learned to play at least one musical instrument.[106] Charles took great pride in his daughter, and his heart was set on her succession to the Habsburg throne.

On February 12, 1736, Maria Theresa married Francis of Lorraine, with whom she had fallen deeply in love while in her early teens; he was to remain the only love of her life. While she rarely recorded her own private thoughts, Sir Thomas Robinson, an English traveler to Vienna, wrote of her, "She sighs and pines all night for her duke of Lorraine. If she sleeps it is only to dream of him, if she wakes it is but to talk of him."[107]

If she had not become a ruling queen, Maria Theresa would have probably devoted her entire life to serving Francis, as she believed that this was the proper role for a woman.[108] But on October 20, 1740, the male line of the Habsburg family died with Charles VI, and at just twenty-two, Maria Theresa became ruler of an empire. Her husband showed little ability or interest in ruling, but her two sisters had married much stronger men of Saxony and Bavaria, and they were both interested in the Habsburg throne. If not for the Pragmatic Sanction, a domestic war among the siblings might well have ensued. Charles VI had shown significant forethought in working to prevent a war of succession at home and abroad, yet Frederick of Prussia wrote of him:

He had received from nature the qualities that make a good citizen, but none of those that make a great man. He knew German law well, and several languages; he excelled above all in Latin. He was a good father, and good husband, but bigoted and superstitious like all princes of the House of Austria.[109]

In spite of Frederick's opinion, Charles actually demonstrated great statesmanship in proposing the Pragmatic Sanction, and it would remain the firm basis of Maria Theresa's claims regarding her right to rule. She was no early believer in women's rights, but she clearly considered herself the legitimate heir to her father's throne because he had no male heir, and he had declared her to be his successor in the Pragmatic Sanction. Based on her father's official word and will, she was convinced that her right to rule was her God-given inheritance from her Habsburg ancestors. Her belief that she was chosen by God to rule made her the unflinching defender of the Pragmatic Sanction. For Maria Theresa, every war would be a holy war.

The young queen was horrified to learn that, along with the throne and the Habsburg Empire, she had inherited massive debt. Charles had spent copious amounts on food, wine, and an extensive collection of exotic parrots that required expensive special care. The Imperial treasury contained only 100,000 florins, and Charles' widow was trying to claim this as her own. Because of poor harvests for several years, there was a serious food shortage, and riots had broken out in Vienna and in rural areas.

Adding to Maria Theresa's financial woes, rumors abounded that the Turks would soon attack Vienna again. But her army was in disarray, and her generals were incompetent. Her Council of State was a collection of old men not eager to recognize a woman as their sovereign. Many of them were deeply shocked when she took an active interest in governing the empire, especially in military matters. It was difficult for them to even recognize the queen at the conference tables or in the throne room. The high-level opposition to Maria Theresa's rule was so strong that it began to infect public opinion, and many ordinary citizens became disturbed at the thought of a woman on the throne.[110]

A new dynamic had threatened the European balance of power when Frederick II of Prussia became king five months before Maria Theresa's own accession. Frederick was determined to make a name for himself as a great commander and statesman on the European stage through the pursuit of a glorious foreign policy. When Maria Theresa became queen, he offered to recognize and defend her, but only if she would cede to him the greater part of Silesia, or much of the modern eastern Czech Republic.[111] Remembering her father's desire that the empire would never be divided, Maria Theresa rejected Frederick's terms. On December 23, 1740, he invaded Silesia, and the young queen found herself at war with the greatest general of her time, a man Voltaire called "Frederick the Great."[112]

Frederick's timing was perfect: Austria's traditional ally, Britain, was bogged down in a costly war with Spain, and another ally, Russia, was in the throes of a succession struggle.[113] Maria Theresa's fighting forces were ill-prepared and ill-equipped compared to the armies of all the other European powers, and Frederick quickly occupied most of Silesia.

More dangerous to Maria Theresa's empire than her domestic ills and the threat of Prussia was the disjointed relationship between her three kingdoms: Austria, Hungary, and Bohemia—the southern part of today's Czech Republic. Each of the kingdoms raised and supported its own army, so the empress could not freely move troops from one area of her empire to another. Instead, she was forced to go before the assembly of each kingdom to request military and financial support for her campaigns. Maria Theresa realized that she would have to replace this feudal system with "benevolent despotism" to bring the entire empire firmly under her own central authority. Unless she could achieve such unity, she could not provide an adequate defense or implement political reform.[114]

By August 1741, Maria Theresa was surrounded by enemies. Her most likely ally, Russia, was at war with Sweden, so she turned to one of her own kingdoms, making a personal appeal to Hungarian feudal lords. They had suffered under Leopold I and had little reason to help his granddaughter; but they were touched by the queen's beauty and moved by her tears. She urgently addressed them in Latin, confessing herself abandoned by her allies and declaring that her honor and throne now depended upon the valor and chivalry of Hungarian knights and arms. In response, the nobles cried out, "Let us die for our king!" ... or so they called the queen.[115]

In spite of Hungary's support, the tides of war turned against Maria Theresa, and in July 1742, she reluctantly ceded to Frederick the Austrian Netherlands and part of Silesia. She never ceased to be bitter about the terms of the peace, and she would always maintain a deep loathing for Frederick. For the twenty-five-year-old Maria Theresa, hatred of her enemies had become a driving motivation, and she now turned that hatred toward France, another formidable foe.

With weakened finances and military forces, the queen needed another ally, so she looked toward England. King George II shared her desire to prevent France from becoming too powerful, but the young empress still stood against Prussia, and King George was from Hanover. Because his alliance with Austria would make him a threat to his own homeland, he responded cautiously to Maria Theresa's call for help.[116]

Despite early setbacks against Frederick the Great of Prussia, Maria Theresa was ultimately able to mobilize a large army, and in 1743, a British-Habsburg army crushed the French and routed Bavarian troops. If she had failed to assert her independence immediately after becoming the Habsburg queen, the Pragmatic Sanction would have meant less to the other European powers. She would have been considered an insignificant ruler, and a 500-year-old dynasty might have come to a premature end. By facing her enemies and effectively mobilizing support, the young Habsburg monarch had weathered her first significant challenges.[117]

After eight years of bloody fighting, the War of the Austrian Succession (or War of the Pragmatic Sanction) finally ended in 1748 because of financial exhaustion on all sides rather than anyone's distaste for war. It was a sorry end for Maria Theresa. Her hated enemy, Frederick, had successfully maintained his claim to the Austrian Netherlands and a portion of Silesia, and it was the only appreciable gain that any of the warring nations could show. The great powers of Europe would remain at peace for the next eight years, until the labor of women could replenish the ranks required for another round in the game of kings.[118]

As ruler of the Habsburg Empire, Maria Theresa wielded much political power, but she also had great personal power. She was said to have all the charms of womanhood, with fine features, white teeth, brilliant blue eyes, ample blond hair, refined manners, and graceful movements. Even more appealing were her qualities of intelligence, determination, and vitality. During her long reign, she gave birth to sixteen children, giving them as much attention as she could without neglecting her official duties; sometimes this required nursing an infant while conducting meetings with her ministers.[119]

Undaunted by hard work, Maria Theresa rose at 8:00 AM and kept a rigid daily schedule, allocating the first hour to dress, eat breakfast, and attend Mass, the next half hour to her children, and the next three hours to the affairs of state. From 12:30 to 1:30 PM, she had a mid-day dinner, forbidding any serious discussion during that time because she felt it was bad for the digestion. Immediately after dinner, she rested before turning again to affairs of state from 4:00 to 8:30 PM. After this, she amused herself until midnight with cards or other games.[120]

In the early 1750s, a radical current of thought would prove to be more devastating to the Habsburg rulers and all the monarchs of Europe than the old winds of war. The new political, cultural, and social movements were collectively known as the *Enlightenment*. Its roots were in the thinking of the *Philosophes* and the *Encyclopedists* of France, who drew substantially on the writings of British philosophers such as John Locke. Locke's theory of the natural rights of individuals inspired the development in England of an impressive system of civil and political liberties. By promoting the concept of fundamental human dignity and embracing social, political, and scientific progress, philosophers of the Enlightenment were laying the foundation for Western contemporary freedoms and the end of all absolute monarchies.[121]

Maria Theresa and her councilors must have felt the hot breath of Voltaire and the Encyclopedists on their necks as they began to make small concessions such as opening to the public the Prater—lands that for centuries had been the private hunting grounds of the Habsburg family. The empress also had her own ideas of reform and did her best to improve the lot of her people according to her views of what that meant.

Maria Theresa enjoyed gala performances at the court theatre, but she was not interested in serious drama or literature. She actively disapproved of the intellectual pursuits encouraged by proponents of the Enlightenment, considering them to be a waste of time or even dangerous because they promoted anti-religious sentiment. The queen warned her daughter, Marie Antoinette, never to read anything that had not been approved by her father confessor. She feared her brilliant contemporary,

Voltaire, whose non-acceptance of the existing order was expressed in biting irony; as she wrote to Dr. Gerard von Swieten, "I dislike everything that goes by the name of irony, and consider it incompatible with Christian, neighborly love. Why should anyone waste time reading or writing such things?"[122]

For a long time, Maria Theresa had been troubled by what she considered to be the low moral conduct of many of her subjects, and in 1753, she founded the *Chastity Commission* to supervise the morality of people in Vienna and elsewhere in Austria. Working closely with the police, the commission employed secret agents to investigate the personal activities of men and women whose reputations did not please the empress. Maria Theresa gave orders that these agents were to enter private homes wherever and whenever necessary to search for wrongdoing.

Of course, the public was very interested in the activities of the morality police, and good citizens who led dull, exemplary lives listened eagerly to gossip about anyone caught sinning. When the police rounded up and jailed members of a group called the Fig Leaf Brotherhood, Maria Theresa had the captives chained to the main city gate to be jeered at, with nothing to eat but morsels of food given to them by people passing by. This idea proved less than successful, for people felt more pity than contempt for the poor victims, who received plenty of food and a great deal of sympathy.[123]

Maria Theresa was troubled by the liberal views of her son, Josef, whose ideas of reform were more far-reaching than her own. Though he was her undisputed heir, she feared that he would prove unfit to rule, and she expressed her concerns in a letter she wrote to him outlining the three fundamental principles of government, stating, "Firstly there should be no free exercise of religion; secondly there should be no destruction of the nobility ... for which I see neither the necessity nor the justice; and thirdly the nonsense about liberty in everything should be stopped. I am too old to accommodate myself to such ideas."[124]

When her husband, Emperor Francis I, died in 1765, Maria Theresa was broken in body and spirit, and she joined his mistress in mourning him: "My dear Princess," she wrote, "we have both lost so much." She cut off her hair, gave away her wardrobe, discarded all jewelry, and wore mourning clothes until her death in 1780. She turned the tasks of government over to her son and spoke of retiring to a convent.[125] She reconsidered her withdrawal in 1769 when, to her shock, she learned that Josef had spent three days in Silesia in a friendly discussion with her old enemy, Frederick of Prussia. Both men felt it was time to put aside their differences in a protective accord against the rising strength of Russia. In reporting on the meeting, Josef wrote to his mother; "After supper we smoked and talked about Voltaire."[126]

In 1780, at the age of sixty-three, Maria Theresa had become over-weight and asthmatic; and the stress of two wars, sixteen pregnancies, and incessant worry had weakened her heart. In November of that year, she was caught in a heavy rain while riding in an open carriage, but still insisted on spending the rest of that day working at her desk, despite the pleas of her aides. All of this contributed to her final illness, and she spent her last hours sitting in a chair. Josef tried to make her more comfortable, saying, "Your Majesty lies in a bad position." She responded, "Yes, but good enough to die in."[127] And die she did, on November 19, 1780.

Maria Theresa's reforms relating to taxes, education, justice, and the army were more limited than those that would be sought by her son, Josef, but they helped to form the foundation for a modern Austrian state. She even tried to set an example of household thrift, but without much success.[128] The fact that she held her empire together against the rising tide of Prussia is all the more remarkable, given that she was by nature not a statesman, politician, or military strategist. Until the end of her life, she believed that a woman's place was in the home and that she was in her position only because God had chosen her for high office. This belief had informed all of her decisions and fueled her determination to remain in power.[129]

At Maria Theresa's death, her son became Josef II, sole ruler of Austria, and he used his power to immediately order many social and political reforms. At the age of forty, he was in the prime of life and quite handsome when he covered his bald head with a wig. He had an alert, active mind and took an eager interest in science, economics, history, and the law, but he had little understanding of human nature. The motivation behind his reforms was always benevolent, but he failed to anticipate the reaction people might have. When he erred, it was usually through haste rather than any ill intent.[130]

Unlike the Age of Voltaire or the Napoleonic Era, the Josefine years are relatively unheard of. But Josef's reign is deserving of serious consideration, since nine years prior to the French Revolution, he tried to establish by decree the reforms that France would later make through a campaign of terror. His reign was the Austrian Monarchy's version of the Enlightenment, with top-down reforms intended to liberate thought, study, and expression from the hand of a church that in most countries still controlled or restricted what was studied, said, and written. The Austrian Monarch was determined to ensure, by decree, the basic human right to intellectual freedom.[131]

Seeking to limit the power of the church, Josef closed seven hundred monasteries, seizing their property to support state schools and other charitable institutions.[132] The emperor had been educated by Jesuits, but he found religious observance irksome, and he resented the importance attached to the supernatural world. Some thought him an atheist who was deeply influenced by Voltaire, but he also believed in religious liberty. On October, 12, 1781, he issued an Edict of Toleration, ending the most severe restrictions on Jews, allowing them to be admitted to schools, the university, the civil service, and the professions. But the ban on synagogues remained, and only wealthy Jews could live in the old city.[133]

Under the edict, Protestants were free to worship in their own churches, schools, and property, and they were allowed to enter the professions of medicine or law and hold political or military office. New Catholic bishops were required to take an oath of obedience to secular authorities, and no papal regulation or decree could be valid in Austria without government permission.[134] Aligning his policies with the ideas of the Enlightenment, Josef treated the church principally as a source of education, charitable activity, and social control. The dissolution of the Jesuits marked the symbolic triumph of the Enlightenment in Austria.

All of these measures aroused the ire of Catholic clergy throughout Europe, and many prelates begged Josef to rescind his decrees or face the threat of hell. In 1782, Pope Pius VI took the unusual step of leaving Rome to cross the Apennines and the Alps in the middle of winter to see Josef in Vienna. During the pope's stay, great crowds gathered daily at the Hofburg Palace to seek the papal blessing, and Josef described the scene by remarking, "It is no exaggeration to say that at one time there were at least 60,000 souls, that was a beautiful spectacle; peasants and their wives and children came from twenty leagues around. Yesterday a woman was crushed right beneath my window."[135]

Josef was moved less by the pope's arguments than by seeing with his own eyes the evidence of religious power on the human mind, but he continued to close monasteries, even during the time that Pius was his guest. After a month of failed attempts to change Josef's mind, Pius sadly returned to Rome.[136]

Josef's ideas were a mix of radical reform and adherence to tradition: He abolished some of the worst abuses of the feudal system in 1781 by granting to serfs the right to change residence or occupation, own property, and marry by mutual consent. Even a special attorney was provided to the peasants to protect their new liberties.[137] But, while he encouraged capitalist industry, he opposed the introduction of new machines, fearing that they would deprive people of work. He abolished or reduced internal tolls on the Danube but retained high protective tariffs for Austrian goods. He eased up a bit on censorship but used it to suppress material likely to undermine his own decrees.[138] Criticism and lampoons were allowed, even if they made fun of Josef, but they had to bear the author's real name, and they were subject to libel laws.

No one could question the humanity of Josef's motives in using the wealth of closed monasteries to support hospitals, charities, and schools, including schools for girls. He also promoted the development of one of the most advanced medical centers in the world.[139] His policies constituted the core of an enlightened despotism in which reform and modernization were imposed from above upon often hostile and usually unappreciative subjects.[140] Josef firmly believed that only an absolute monarch could break the chains of dogma and protect the simple weak from the clever strong.

In France, the revocation of the Edict of Nantes of 1685 had ordered that the Catholic Church would be the nation's only religion and imposed on French subjects an absolutist state. But this edict had been followed in 1687 by the revelation of Sir Isaac Newton's law of gravitation demonstrating how much could be added to knowledge of the natural world through reason, observation, and experiment. More advances could be expected if work of this type was encouraged, even if it appeared to contradict the Bible or theology.[141] Liberal French philosophers would soon influence their nation to the point that France would be given credit for giving birth to the Enlightenment and the stirrings of modern democracy.

Although Josef embraced the basic elements of the Enlightenment, such as the power of human reason, unlike the French, he put aside all thoughts of democratic reform because he did not think his people could be trusted to make the right choices.[142] He thought democracy would actually lead to a closed society controlled by landlords and bishops who would defy any change that did not give them an advantage.

Josef's own people, who initially loved him, began to turn against him as he made changes that affected their traditional customs and cherished beliefs. Priests denounced him as an infidel, nobles hated him for freeing the serfs, peasants wanted more land, and the urban poor were still near starvation. Josef's ambitious reforms had trampled on high and low alike, and everyone cursed his high taxes. On January 30, 1790, under pressure from all directions, Josef rescinded most of the reforms he had decreed since the death of his mother, Maria Theresa.[143]

Josef had tried to use reform to alleviate all of society's ills at once, never learning that politics is the art of the possible, not the perfect. Convinced that imperial power was sufficient to change every aspect of communal life, he had attempted to use it to create an ideal state. He failed to realize that the state had to exist before a central government could be effective,[144] thus affirming Frederick the Great's comment about his rival, "He always took the second step before the first."[145]

Was Josef II a failure? He commanded reforms without taking the necessary time to convince others of their merits, and he sought to accomplish in ten years what ultimately required a century of education and economic change to achieve. In full faith and trust, he had accepted the thesis of the *Philosophes* that a monarch of good education and goodwill would be the best instrument for enlightenment and reform. But he lacked the philosopher's capacity for doubt, and he tried to eliminate too many evils at once. His people, deeply rooted in their privileges, prejudices, customs, and creeds, also failed him. They preferred their traditional church, priests, and tithes to his new taxes and sweeping reforms. Blind to the social progress Josef was trying to promote, they simply could not trust a man who laughed at their beloved legends and humiliated their pope.

Though most of Josef's reforms were formally rescinded in 1790, many of them had a lasting effect. The closed monasteries remained closed, and the church remained subject to the laws of the state. The stimulus to commerce and industry persisted, and brick began to replace wood in Vienna's houses. The population of Josef's empire rose from 18.7 million in 1780 to 21 million by 1790.[146]

Depressed by what he saw as failure to reach his goals, however, Josef made a will and composed his own epitaph to read, "Here lies Josef, who could succeed at nothing." He begged for death, and it came for him on February 20, 1790, when he was forty-eight years old. Vienna rejoiced at his passing, and Hungary gave thanks to God. But with the French Revolution of 1789, the old world was passing away, and Josef had helped Austria to move, *without* violent revolution, from being a medieval state to a modern nation that could share in the diverse cultural vitality of the nineteenth century.

Maria Theresa's more famous offspring, Marie Antoinette, known to the French as Madame Deficit, paid the price of losing her head in 1793 for not understanding that her mother's Europe was no more. And, while the Habsburg dynasty in Austria found itself threatened from within by the revolutionary ideas of the Enlightenment, it found itself threatened from without by the revolutionary French armies.[147]

In 1805, Vienna was occupied by Napoleon. In 1809, Austria stood completely alone as she prepared to fight Napoleon again on the banks of the Danube. The Habsburg Archduke Charles was able to raise an army of only 155,000 to face the French army of 188,000, but he was fighting on his own turf eleven miles northeast of Vienna at the small village of Wagram, on the same field where Austria had soundly defeated the Turks in 1683. Napoleon had suffered a humiliating defeat in 1808 through the capture of an entire French army by a weaker Spanish force, and the feeling in Austria was that the fortunes of war were turning against him.[148]

In July 1809, massive French and Austrian armies fought each other for two days, without pause. In the bloodiest battle seen in Europe up to that time, 45,000 men were killed or wounded on the Austrian side, and 37,000 on the French side.[149] Both armies were too exhausted to continue fighting, and both retreated. Even though the battle could be seen as a stalemate, Napoleon knew he had come close to being routed, and his army needed a breathing spell to prepare for a planned invasion of Russia. The Battle of Wagram was a high-stakes game, with Napoleon needing Vienna as a supply base for his campaign against Russia, and Charles seeking a victory that would make Austria, not Prussia, the leading German power in central Europe.[150]

The Battle of Wagram is today considered the last campaign that Napoleon won, but it also created a political door that would be pushed open by the Austrian Foreign Minister, Prince Klemens von Metternich. During the next four years, Metternich skillfully guided Austrian diplomacy through a maze of challenges to make his country a significant ally of those able to tip the balance of power enough to soundly defeat Napoleon in 1813.[151]

Europe had experienced periods of relative unity and peace at the zenith of Rome's power and during the early Middle Ages when Charlemagne attempted to unite the continent under a common religion and social structure before 1517, when Martin Luther nailed the *Ninety-five Theses* to the church door in Wittenberg. Napoleon envisioned a political unification of Europe, but his hopes proved to be premature. According to Goethe, "Napoleon was the expression of all that was reasonable, legitimate and European in the revolutionary movement." But even if Goethe was right, there are loyalties and habits men will not forsake in the name of reason, and Napoleon's failure reflected the failure of all eighteenth-century leaders to achieve a united Europe.[152]

Austria's Metternich had his own dream of European unity, and he wanted to realize it by bringing the leaders of Europe to a peace conference in Vienna. He knew that the expense of hosting such a conference would strain the balance sheet of a country that had declared bankruptcy in 1811, and new banknotes issued had already lost four-fifths of their value. But Vienna was the geographical heart of Europe, and with a population of 250,000, it was behind only London and Paris in size. Besides, it had a reputation for being a happy, musical, and beautiful city. The Austrian emperor, Francis I, agreed with Prince Metternich, and both men believed that their country would gain lasting goodwill from their important and powerful guests.

Kings, queens, princes, and diplomats poured into the city in the fall of 1814 for the *Congress of Vienna*. More than two hundred states and princely houses sent delegates to settle unresolved issues remaining after years of war. The city they beheld reflected, in part, the foresight of Josef II, who had decreed that a tree must be planted for every one cut down.[153]

The city proper, one traveler noted on entering Vienna's gates, seems like a royal palace: Grand baroque mansions lined the narrow, twisting lanes that snaked their way through the old medieval center. Spires, domes, towers, and neoclassical columns carved in bright white-stone, each roof and facade looked more sumptuous and elaborately adorned than the next. Rows of large bay windows predominated, overlooking one of the greenest capitals in Europe.[154]

Every evening at the Hofburg Palace, some forty to fifty banquet tables were set at an exorbitant cost to the host country. The elaborate affairs involved as many as eight courses, typically including soup, hors d'oeuvres, and trays of food served by wigged and liveried servants on tables decorated with gold, crystal, and gigantic gilded centerpieces that held bountiful flowers and numerous candles. The menus consisted of ham, venison, pheasant, partridge, and oysters with Chablis, boiled beef in Rhenish wine, roast beef with Bordeaux, and delicate dessert wines from the imperial vineyards in Hungary. Fruits, sweet cakes, and a variety of pies, cheeses, and jellies often followed, and some 600 cups of coffee were provided in mammoth kettles. Ice cream, however, was served only when Emperor Francis was present.[155]

The Congress of Vienna was not all frivolity, for with the presence of the most powerful and intellectual people in Europe, the conversation was stimulating and substantial. But a contemporary satirist characterized the gathering this way:

Who skirt chases for them all? Alexander of Russia. Who thinks for them all? Frederich Wilhelm of Prussia. Who speaks for them all? Fredrick of Denmark. Who drinks for them all? Maximilian of Bavaria. Who eats for them all? Fredrick von Wurttemberg. Who pays for them all? Emperor Franz.[156]

The skirt-chasing, thinking, talking, drinking, and eating all ended on March 7, 1815, when Prince Metternich was awakened at 5:00 AM with a dispatch marked URGENT. He did not open it immediately but went back to sleep until 7:30 AM. When he finally read the dispatch, he would never forget it; it was a letter from the commissioner on the island of Elba saying that Napoleon was nowhere to be found and asking if anyone had seen him.[157]

When Metternich reported the contents of the letter, everyone immediately knew that Napoleon's presence on the continent was dangerous, and leaders quickly left Vienna to organize their homeland defenses for an anticipated battle. A decisive fight between the French emperor and a coalition of European powers took place on Sunday, June 18, 1815, near the small Belgian village of Waterloo. The battle resulted in a thorough defeat of the French and an end to the career of Napoleon Bonaparte.

The Congress of Vienna had fulfilled Metternich's hopes by creating a forum where heads of state came together to work out their differences and form important alliances. This was the first time that leaders of the world met in a time of peace for the purpose of maintaining peace, and it generated a spirit of cooperation that has not been surpassed by subsequent conventions or organizations, including the United Nations. It helped to establish a peace that lasted longer than any of the delegates could have imagined.[158]

Tensions would arise throughout the nineteenth century, but the riots, rebellions, civil wars, and conflicts that took place in this nationalistic age would fail to reach a level sufficient to drag all of the great European powers into full-scale international war. The Congress of Vienna had ignited a spirit of European cooperation that would last one hundred years. No other peace conference in history can claim such success.[159]

CHAPTER 4

The Situation Is Hopeless but Not Serious

The French Revolution of 1789 loosened the bonds of feudalism and promoted individual rights, feeding a growing hunger throughout Europe for freedom of movement, enterprise, worship, thought, speech and press, as well as greater access to economic opportunity, education, health, and justice.[160] But in central Europe, especially in the backward lands of the Habsburg Empire, agriculture was still the undisputed engine of economic growth, and farm production continued to depend on serfs to work vast lands belonging to feudal lords. Half of the arable land in Hungary was not yet cultivated, and the population density was less than twenty people per square mile. The army could not even find workers with enough skill to build basic structures, because houses were still built of straw.[161]

Serfs were the descendants of nomadic tribes that had taken part in the siege of Vienna in 1683, German chieftains made leaderless in battle, or mercenaries stranded too far away from home to return.[162] The lands they worked were entailed estates known collectively as the Habsburg Empire, and the Habsburgs were, in this sense, landlords rather than rulers. Some of them were benevolent, some incompetent, and some greedy; all were intent on exacting the best possible return from their tenants so they could exhibit their great wealth to the rest of Europe.[163]

Though they were bound to the land, serfs were not owned, like American slaves whose families could be torn apart when one of them was sold. Estate lords did have the legal right, however, to force their serfs to sow, reap, down trees, and transport goods over long distances. Serfs also had to pay inflated prices for beer, wine, and bread, even when these items were produced on the estate. And they had to use money from the sale of the crops they produced to pay rent to the lords for the privilege of being exploited.[164]

The founding fathers of America sidestepped the troubling issue of slavery, and it would take a tragic civil war to end the practice in the New World. Enlightened thinkers of Europe saw that serfdom also denied the equal rights of men, and they believed the system was economically damaging as well. But it was such an entrenched aspect of property rights that no one dared to suggest that it be eradicated. Not even Adam

Smith, the greatest economic thinker of the day, dreamed that anything resembling the Industrial Revolution was possible.[165]

Napoleon had instituted progressive reforms in promoting morality, modernization, codification of law, the end of feudalism, the growth of industry, and the establishment of a stable currency. He had also encouraged science, art, education, and the beautification of cities. So according to some historians, Europe advanced half a century during Napoleon's fifteen-year rule.[166] But once Napoleon was safely out of the way, his ideas of reform were the farthest thing from the minds of European powers. After twenty-six years of fighting for their very existence, they were exhausted, and their main goals were to restore order, maintain the stability of their monarchies, and ensure that France was effectively restrained.[167] Toward this end, they sought to end individual liberties they associated with disruptive excesses among their people.

Though there was relative peace during the hundred years following the 1815 Congress of Vienna, the consensus established at the Congress among the European leaders was gradually unraveling. This happened in different places at different times and at different speeds, but pressure for political and social change finally came to threaten the stability of Europe.[168]

As Emperor of Austria and the senior monarch at the Congress of Vienna, Franz II had agreed with his brother monarchs in Prussia and Russia that they would each assist each other at any sign of revolutionary violence. But there was no energy anywhere for revolution, and Franz was no tyrant; he was a kind father, an adored uncle, with a good-humored steadiness that was just what his people needed. His Vienna was the city of Beethoven and Schubert; on the surface, life was quiet and orderly.[169]

Under Franz, the Austrian nobility lived in a closed circle, associating with each other and marrying only within their class. The monarchy allowed the aristocrats to exploit the peasants, and the aristocracy sustained the monarchy. Because the earlier attempts at centralization and reform by Maria Theresa and her son, Josef II, had threatened the aristocrats, during the nineteenth century, they did whatever necessary to protect their economic privileges and retain their independence.[170]

The visitor to modern Vienna is overwhelmed by the number of palaces, great and small, used today for public offices or museums. But before the 1848 revolution, life in these palaces was remote, indeed, from the emperor's ordinary subjects. In May of each year, the emperor took his traditional drive through the Prater, and citizens by the thousands would come out to watch the parade of elegant carriages elaborately decorated in brilliant paintwork and polished leather, drawn by high-stepping horses groomed to glistening perfection. When the show was over, the emperor and the attending aristocracy went back into their palaces where they belonged.[171] Like the palaces that filled the city, the Baroque Age itself was grandiose but superficial. In the world of the Habsburgs, life was sometime more like theater than reality. Even if a situation held the potential for dire consequences, no one seemed overly concerned."[172]

In Baroque Vienna, members of the middle class paid high rents to live in apartments or small houses on narrow streets. Many were officials of the government, and all were poorly paid.[173] Vienna was also a city of craftsmen: coach makers, glove makers, instrument makers, and, especially, piano makers. During the week, a craftsman earned good money, but on Sundays he spent it all on music and dancing at parties held in the open air among the hills and vineyards on the city's outskirts. To have a good time, one only needed wine, sausage, and someone to play the piano. Dancing provided the safe outlet for any surplus energy. Franz Schuselka, a rebel writer at the time, wryly remarked:

> *The people of Vienna seem to any serious observer to be reveling in an everlasting state of intoxication. Eat, drink, and be merry are the three cardinal virtues and pleasures of the Viennese ... For the Viennese the only point of anything, of the most important event in the world, is that they can make a joke about it.*[174]

Just as self-censorship was breaking down among writers such as Schuselka, censorship imposed by the authorities was all-powerful, so critics of the system had to get their works published in places such as Hamburg and smuggle them back into Austria. Politics was a forbidden topic, and all intellectual ideas were suspect. Even newspapers reported mostly what was going on at the theatre, what was said during café chatter, or what everyone was eating or drinking. News articles were similar to those we might find today in reviews of new films, television shows, or restaurants.

It never occurred to Emperor Franz II that his people were neither guttersnipes nor potential assassins. He reportedly opened an address to a group of educators with the words, "I do not need scholars, but well-behaved citizens." This observation summed up the Austrian atmosphere in the era of Austria's influential prime minister, Prince Metternich. The curtailment of cultural, intellectual, and political expression seemed the only way to suppress the revolutionary impulses that were spreading throughout the rest of Europe.[175]

A distinguished member of the army's general staff, General Von Moering, attacked the system in his book, *The Sybilline Book of Austria.* Von Moering claimed that the regime was rotten because it trusted only the privileged nobility and treated the masses as beasts of burden valued only as taxpayers or fighters in the army. The Habsburg aristocracy could not understand the desire of the people to be free, and this was to be their ruin. After Maria Theresa's failed attempts at the centralization of government, the continued independence of her kingdoms meant that people did not develop any feeling of nationalism toward Austria as a whole. Instead, Bohemians turned into Czechs, Magyars into Hungarians, and Venetians into Italians. A common patriotism had even been actively discouraged within each kingdom of the empire, so there was not a solitary citizen who was proud of being an Austrian.[176]

As the nineteenth century progressed, people throughout the empire had competing ambitions that were often incompatible with the survival of the dynasty. The growth of towns produced class conflicts not only between towns and the great estates but also within the towns themselves, where urban nationalism had an intellectual flavor. The nationalistic ideas of the intellectuals appealed to the masses, but the masses repudiated intellectual values.[177]

By the 1830s, revolutionary discontent in Europe was growing, but many thought that allowing the monarchies to just disintegrate would be the first step toward establishing a just and equitable European society. They envisioned a world where princes would rule no more, and private citizens would cultivate their own gardens, living side by side in peace and harmony. Others thought the end of the monarchies would bring bitter and bloody fighting among forces vying to take their place.

Most German states remained calm, but revolts occurred in Italy, Belgium, Luxemburg, and the United Netherlands because of increasing unemployment in these areas. Even in Britain, unrest bubbled up as the demand grew for franchise reform. Austria would see no open revolt until the 1840s, when it became apparent that factories were too few to employ the farm workers flooding the cities in search of jobs. Unemployment was the cause of widespread revolts rather than the Industrial Revolution, as is popularly assumed.[178] It was, in fact, the first crisis of capitalism, and when it hit, it hit hard.[179]

When Franz II died in 1835, he was followed by the charming but feeble-minded Ferdinand, of whom Lord Palmerston, the British Prime Minister said, "A perfect nullity the next thing to town idiot." The Viennese knew Ferdinand was a fool, but they adored him anyway. On one occasion he exclaimed, "I am the emperor, and I want dumplings!" His people had in him a benevolent monarch with a good-natured temperament, so what more could they want? Those who wanted more must be wicked, because the monarch was set over them by God. The Habsburgs were there to command, the people to obey.[180]

Vienna's population had more than doubled since 1815, including immigrants from the Austrian countryside, and the city's poverty-stricken people faced severe unemployment. The economic situation led to a declining standard of living, class conflict, and a sense of alienation. Contributing to the fiscal crisis was the fact that huge sums were needed to fund new railroad construction that began in 1842. And raising taxes was not possible unless accompanied by constitutional concessions obnoxious to the regime.

Under Emperor Ferdinand, Prime Minster Metternich found himself locked in an ever-tightening vicious circle of domestic unrest and fiscal constraint. There had been a poor harvest in Europe in 1845 and 1846. In 1847, these woes were compounded by a credit crunch, skyrocketing unemployment, and rising interest rates. The only alternative, borrowing on the international money markets, depended on Habsburg credibility. In the late 1840s, the Austrian state found itself being slowly strangled in a fiscal-political vise like the one that had destroyed the French regime in 1789. The established order had been eroded by the fiscal disorder, even before protestors took to the streets.[181]

At the time, the Austrian bureaucracy was fairly honest and quite hard-working, and it probably did more good than harm. But it was also slow, generated mountains of paper, regarded the creation of new bureaucratic posts as its principal purpose, and forgot that it dealt with human beings. Administration had taken the place of government.[182]

Observing the political, economic, and social conditions in Austria and other European states in the 1840s was a radical young German journalist named Karl Marx. In this environment, he began to develop his materialist conception of history as a process of ongoing class conflict. With like-minded Friedrich Engels, he explained his ideas at length in *The German Ideology,* a book published early in the twentieth century. The only solution Marx and Engels saw to the injustice within the prevailing capitalist system was communism, an ideal to which reality would have to adjust itself. And to realize this ideal, European workers would have to recognize that they had more in common with each other than with their oppressors. Only a month before demonstrations broke out in a number of European countries, *The Communist Manifesto,* by Marx and Engels, was published in February of 1848. It began with these words:

A specter is haunting Europe, the specter of communism. ... The communists bring to the front the common interest of the entire proletariat, independent of nationality. ... Indeed in this interconnected world a new geopolitics which pitted the common interest of the exploited against their oppressor is the only answer. It would render state and national conflict redundant because in proportion as the exploitation of one individual by another is put an end to, the exploitation of one nation by another will also be put an end to.[183]

The Habsburg emperors and Metternich had successfully kept the lid on discontent in Austria until political frustration and economic malaise brought matters to a head in 1848. Although students and workers had more radical agendas, the bourgeoisie (middle class) revolution had fairly moderate aims, including the end of absolutism. They believed this would result in freedom of the press, representative assemblies, and an elementary bill of rights. The early demonstrators even did their best to exalt poor Ferdinand, to whom they always referred with proper respect.[184]

On March 13, 1848, the celebrations at carnival time had never been more exuberant. Crowded public balls had been held in endless succession, night after night, and Franz List was visiting the city, playing to packed audiences. The day began quietly enough, with demonstrators declaring, "Viennese! Liberate your old Emperor Ferdinand from the bonds of his enemies! All who deserve the prosperity of Austria must desire the overthrow of its rulers." They were referring to Prince Metternich and his system of government, but Prime Minister Metternich had already written his letter of resignation and slipped away into the night to find sanctuary in England.[185]

The Austrian revolution of 1848 did not start with a riot, as many did. Students merely stood around on that cloudy, mild March day, wondering what to do next. It might have come to nothing, except for a young doctor from the General Hospital, Adolf Fischhof, who had brought with him a prepared speech. Fischhof suddenly found his courage and cried, "Gentlemen listen to me!" By then, the crowd was eager to listen to anyone, and the doctor was hoisted onto waiting shoulders. For the first time in decades, the voice of dissent was heard in the streets of Vienna.

Fischhof was not a great speaker, but he was a sincere, good man who was overtaken by events of his time. He would soon return to his doctoring, but on March 13, he expressed as well as anyone might what was already on the minds of many of his listeners. As people heard his words, their hearts beat with fear, but also with sudden hope, because they wanted to apply some of the wild, free spirit of the French Revolution to their own land. They were not looking to tear down the fabric of centuries, and the demands Fischhof read out were modest enough: a free press, trial by jury, a representative assembly, freedom for teaching, strength through union, and tolerance in all parts of the empire. He was voicing, for the first time in the Habsburg Empire, the doctrine of the rights of man.[186]

When violence did take hold, idealism and reason were trampled by the mob. Shooting started, and a government minister was lynched. Workmen from the suburbs battered down the gates of the inner city with lamp posts they had torn down. Some were less interested in the establishment of a central European League of Nations under a benevolent national monarch than they were in joining Germany under the black and yellow flag.[187]

In many countries today, we have a free press, trial by jury, a responsive government, a representative assembly, and a measure of academic freedom. But do we know how easy it would be to lose these rights? Looking back at 1848, we can see how Fischhof was asking for too much idealistically and too little materially. It was not Metternich, as Fischhof believed, who kept people apart in the Austrian Empire. On the contrary, people needed a Metternich, a Maria Theresa, or a Josef II to hold them together.[188]

After the 1848 rebellion, "the masses" no longer accepted their prescribed role. Their traditional view of life was undermined by the revolutionary ideas that had spread to the empire from France—a nation with more writers than readers.[189] The rebellion meant different things to different people, but one of the strongest popular responses was the rise of a still greater level of nationalism within the empire's various kingdoms. The rulers of Vienna heard people cry, "Hungary for the Magyars!" "Bohemia for the Slavs!" "Italy for the Italians!" and "Austria for the Germans!" But they had no concept of the intensity of the nationalistic passion swelling within the empire.[190]

The situation took a strange twist when the British Prime Minister, Lord Palmerston, wrote to his ambassador to Austria:

There is a general fight going on all over the continent between governors and governed, between law and disorder, between those who have and those who want to have, between honest men and rogues, and as the turbulent, the poor and the rogues of the world, though perhaps not the most numerous, are at all events the most active, the other classes require for their defense to be led and headed by intelligence, activity and energy, but how can these qualities be found in a government where the sovereign is an idiot?[191]

Palmerston needed a strong Austrian Empire to maintain the balance of power on the continent, so he persuasively recommended the abdication of Emperor Ferdinand and the accession of the son of the emperor's brother.[192] Prince Metternich had hoped to use poor Ferdinand to make himself the virtual ruler of the empire, but the events of March 13 had ended that hope, and there was no one to speak against Palmerston's suggestion.

With the abdication of Emperor Ferdinand, his nephew, Franz, became the new emperor at the age of eighteen. When he assumed the throne, he added to his own name the name of his hero and grandfather, Josef II, and so became Emperor Franz Josef. A slender and handsome young man, he looked brave and splendid in the military uniform that he always wore. He saw himself as a divinely appointed ruler, responsible to none but God, and charged with the sacred duty of restoring the dynasty and maintaining its position in Europe. But he began his reign under turmoil and bitterness, and his rule was sustained by the bayonets of the army. He had a throne, but he lacked an empire.[193]

Franz Josef would prove to be a complete failure as a military commander, and he had no interest in culture. He faced the complex challenges of his time with a mediocre intellect, little imagination, and an ignorance of history. But in spite of everything, he had a unique gift for ruling the Austrian Empire, and for sixty-four years, he wielded this talent as few others have, before or since.

One of the greatest challenges Franz Josef faced was the nationalism within the empire's kingdoms regarding language, independence, privileges such as bureaucratic jobs, and various historic claims of the older nations.[194] Austria and Hungary were the dominant political units, but the Slavic minorities within the empire comprised 46 percent of the population. German-speaking Austrians represented 23 percent, and Hungarian Magyars only 20 percent.[195]

Three factions competed for influence within the empire: The first promoted the supremacy of Vienna in the Germanic community; the second wanted an equal partnership between the two capitals of Vienna and Berlin, and the third wanted to see Berlin the unchallenged center of the German-speaking world, even if it meant they had to sacrifice their identity as Austrians. In the end, the people themselves would have to resolve the problem of their divided allegiance. The nation of Austria had to come from the head as well as the heart, as unified patriotism was not handed down from Austrian forefathers as a birthright.[196]

Unity within the empire was fractured not only by division between the kingdoms but between town and country, liberal and radical, and Protestant and Catholic. In response to the rebellion, attempts were made to buy off the peasantry with concessions so they would support conservative policies. Conservatives in Prussia, Austria, France, and all across Europe also rallied by establishing newspapers of their own to go on the offensive to keep their countries from becoming battlegrounds for foreign forces as they had seen happen during the Thirty Years War.[197]

Franz Josef added to his burdens when, on April 24, 1854, he married sixteen-year-old Elizabeth of Bavaria, perhaps the most beautiful young woman in Europe, with all the pomp and splendor expected of the dashing young emperor. As one of Elizabeth's contemporaries wrote, "She had the finest forehead, with straight, dark eyebrows over wonderful eyes, extravagantly long and lustrous hair. Her face was an oval set on a fine neck, her nose strong and straight if a shade too long."[198] Like the late Princess Diana of England, Elizabeth was on display and in demand, dressed for public appearances from the moment she emerged from her bedroom each morning until she went to bed. While this was normal for European courts of the period, it was hard for Elizabeth to bear. She just wanted to be alone with her husband, and when she could not be with him, she simply wanted to be alone.[199]

Emperor Franz Josef needed a sensible wife who could help him compensate for his own limitations as a ruler. But Elizabeth could not be sensible, and her effect on Franz Josef was to magnify his shortcomings. "Sisi," as Elizabeth was called, was like a moody, stubborn child who was more interested in the perks of her position than in the welfare of her husband or his subjects. She was capable of dazzling gaiety when things were going well for her, but she exhibited extreme self-absorption when she perceived the smallest slight. Since she found herself in a world where she received continual rebuffs, she could seldom function as a real partner for Franz Josef. This was tragic for an emperor in dire need of support from a mature marital relationship.[200]

In addition to his personal problems, Franz Josef also faced international challenges. As Chancellor of Prussia, Otto Von Bismarck was determined to dominate German-speaking areas of central Europe. Franz Josef's belief that he could control Bismarck led to his defeat in 1866, when Bismarck lured Austria into a trap in order to unify the whole of Germany, excluding Austria. Bismarck's gains were solidified when Germany defeated France in the Franco-Prussian War of 1870.[201]

Within Austria, Franz Josef tried to centralize the administration of his ungovernable state, but in 1867, he gave up this unachievable goal. The Habsburg lands were divided into the Empire of Austria, with its capital at Vienna, and a Kingdom of Hungary, with its capital at Budapest, each with its own premier and parliament.[202] The Budapest parliament was elected according to a system that maintained the supremacy of the Magyar landed gentry, but it shared with Vienna a common army, a unified foreign policy, and a shared financial burden. Both governments were ultimately responsible to Franz Josef.

Religion was still a force within the empire: Hungarians tended to be Protestant, many Serbs were Orthodox who felt a kinship with Russian Catholics, and Bosnia had a large Muslim population. Most Austrians were Catholic, but Jews also played a key role in Vienna's cultural life, courtrooms, banks, and hospitals.[203]

Following the horrors of war with Prussia, the years after 1867 were filled with natural disasters and every kind of bad weather, causing harvests to fail all over the empire. Then, when Austria's fortunes took a major turn for the better, with years of bountiful harvests and a better economy, the empire abandoned its attempts to subdue Prussia and concentrated on increasing trade and industry and constructing new railways. The economy grew rapidly until 1873, when a financial crash coincided with an outbreak of cholera.[204]

Also in 1873, Vienna held its first and only World Exhibition to celebrate its industrial achievement and stimulate trade. Their desire to show off Austria to the world unleashed a frenzy of greed among hoteliers, causing wild stock market speculation and soaring inflation. All of this came home to roost just eight days after the opening of the exhibition, when the Austrian stock exchange went into a meltdown.[205] A reporter with a popular newspaper wrote, "Since yesterday a thief is once again called a thief, and not a baron. Never has a more beautiful storm cleansed a more foul air."[206]

European royalty and others who witnessed the 1873 financial disaster in Austria were deeply concerned that it would spread to their own countries. Though capitalism was so new that the word *depression* did not yet exist, it was indeed what they feared, and they were not wrong. The collapse of the Vienna stock exchange contributed to a widespread financial crisis.[207]

In spite of this concern, the city fathers decided to make 1873 the year when Vienna's city walls, initially built to thwart the advance of the Turks, were torn down and replaced with a beautiful boulevard called the Ringstrasse. It was the finest avenue in Europe at the time, lined with rows of trees that gave the Hofburg Palace a new skyline. The cholera outbreak spurred improvements of Vienna's infrastructure with respect to sewage, clean water, and other public services to promote a safer environment.[208] To take people's minds away from cholera and financial collapse, Johann Strauss performed "Die Fledermaus," one of the most popular operettas of 1874. The improvements and distractions were all designed to make Vienna the crown of the empire, but the city remained on the brink of disaster.[209] Vienna was like a star that shines brilliantly just before it explodes in death.

Bismarck had predicted that "some damned foolish thing in the Balkans" would ignite the next war.[210] And by 1875, new trouble was brewing in the eastern part of the empire that would grow into the Turkish-Serbian War. Turkey had expected help from Austria against the threat from Russia, but Franz Josef wanted to avoid war with Russia.[211] Russian interest in the Balkan states had grown tremendously during the nineteenth century, and they were ready to wage war with Turkey. Austria was concerned that the breakup of Turkey would expose its southern flank to Russia. The German emperor, William I, received a letter from the Russian tsar, Alexander, accusing him of plotting intrigue against Russian interests and supporting Austria against Russia at every turn. Bismarck now realized that Germany had more to lose by being tied to a strong Russia than to a weak Austria.[212] A mood of Russophobia was sweeping through Europe.

European states increasingly sought to form alliances with each other to attain the security that they could not achieve singlehandedly. In 1879, the Triple Alliance between Germany and Austria-Hungary provided that either country, if attacked by Russia, would come to the other's aid. The net result of the Triple Alliance was to force Germany to support Austrian policy in the Balkans and force Austria to support Germany against France. It was the pivot on which swung the jaws of the monstrous trap which would crush the body of Europe just thirty-five years later. The reason for the treaty was to maintain the peace of Europe, but it was signed by two monarchs who valued honor above peace.[213]

In 1882, Italy joined the Triple Alliance, pledging that Germany and Italy would support each other in the case of aggression by France. But Italy had her feet firmly planted on both sides. After developing better relations with France, she would join the Triple Entente, an agreement between England, France, and Russia made in 1907, making things even more complicated. An *entente* is less specific in its terms and less binding in its obligations than an *alliance*, but the Triple Entente was clearly a rival with the Triple Alliance, and it represented a series of agreements between the powers that provided for mutual military assistance in case either France or Russia were attacked by Germany alone or with Austria-Hungary.

By 1887, the whole character of the Austrian Empire had changed. Franz Josef was fifty-seven years old, presiding over a state that had little in common with the Austria he inherited. He remained behind the times: Instead of reading the newspapers, he saw brief summaries prepared daily by his aides. If he had read the daily news, he would have seen that the lives of people in the Austrian half of the empire were no longer regulated by the central government but by factions and interest groups who were viciously banging away at each other, almost as though the emperor no longer mattered. It was also reported that 25 percent of the members of the Austrian Parliament were actively engaged in bribes, speculation, and other forms of corruption, including the upper house.[214]

Everyone knew that Berlin was the true powerhouse now and that Germany was undeniably the senior partner in the military alliance between Germany and Austria. While Berlin dressed itself in military uniforms, Vienna was putting on fancy dresses. Berlin turned its energy to the thrill of power, wishing to impress others with its might, but Vienna was a more modest, capable of laughing at itself. This was described in the writing of Karl Kraus, a journalist, critic, playwright, and poet who made popular the Viennese art of satire. He was not wrong when he said, "In Berlin things are serious but not hopeless, in Vienna they are hopeless but not serious."[215]

Much of Germany's rise in power could be traced back to the Congress of Vienna held in 1815, when Prussia had been granted valuable territory that laid the foundation for spectacular economic growth. Also, Prussia had been given command of all the major rivers of Germany plus the Saar region, where Europe's richest coal and iron deposits were later discovered. When the Industrial Revolution arrived, German states were unified under Prussian leadership, making Germany a major European power. Centuries of disunity and strife had bred in the German people a feeling of political insecurity, so they were inclined to trust their nation's welfare to the leadership of the military and the landed gentry that had secured Germany's unification in 1870. There was widespread acceptance of militarism and authoritarianism.[216]

Minorities living in Austria-Hungary and Russia, however, became increasingly restless, though their goal was not independence but an increase in their civil rights. In Austria-Hungary, the Croats and Slavs were particularly sensitive to the success of nationalism in the Balkans. Closely akin to each other in language and aspirations, Croatian and Serbian minorities joined with the Bosnians and Herzegovinians in ongoing resistance against restraints imposed by the Austro-Hungarian regime.[217]

At the start of the twentieth century, nationalism within countries was the movement that provided Europeans with a sense of community, tradition, moral standards, a legal framework for business transactions, and a motivation for political activity. National feeling satisfied the people's desire for kinship and gave them the feeling of security that comes from belonging to an organized society.[218] For centuries, the peasants of Europe had been guided in their habits and beliefs by local customs and traditions administered by the church. But in the latter half of the nineteenth century, millions had left villages that had been home for generations for new lives in urban environments. Tradition and belief were replaced by education, followed by a decline of faith in the church.[219] Because it provided them a new identity, nationalism developed a stronghold on the people of Europe at the beginning of the twentieth century.

Unlike nationalists, socialists believed that the interests of the individual could be better achieved through international cooperation than through rivalry. The most influential of the socialist writers were Marx and Engels, and the principal tenet of Marxism was that the socialist party should achieve political victory and enlist the power of the workers to form a more just society. Socialists favored a steeply graded income tax to provide the financial means for social security, public education, public housing, and ownership by the state of all means of production. Workers would join trade unions to solve their economic problems, gaining power through the organization of political parties. Success of socialist strategy rested on the solidarity of international workers, or the proletariat. This was expressed in the concept of the General Strike through which workers would paralyze the capitalist war machine.[220]

With the European world turning into a bubbling cauldron of instability, Emperor Franz Josef still had to contend with his Sisi, the Empress Elizabeth. He never understood the hopeless incompatibility between his wife and his mother or his own problems with an immature wife whom he nevertheless adored. By 1898, Elizabeth was quite out of her head. Her beloved brother, Rudolf, had committed suicide amid a scandal, and she had dressed in black for the following ten years. Her restlessness resulted in obsessive traveling, and she spent much of her time on the English seacoast.[221] Sir Compton Mackenzie saw her there when he was only four years old, and he later recalled a "tall, slender woman dressed in brown alpaca, who sat on the bench alone, with a small lace parasol, staring out to sea, then writing, then staring out to sea, then writing, then staring out to sea again. This was the Empress of Austria."[222]

In September of 1898, Sisi's wanderings had taken her one afternoon to Lake Geneva, where she and her lady-in-waiting were to take a steamer; but as they walked from their hotel, a young man hurried toward them and stabbed the empress violently in the breast. She fell to the ground but got back up, said it was nothing, and resumed her walk to the ship. Upon setting foot on the deck, however, she collapsed again and died.[223] Her killer was a twenty-six-year-old anarchist who belonged to no party and was acting completely on his own. The act had no political effect except to bring the people of the empire closer to Franz Josef.

We who are living in the twenty-first century are proud of the great advances we have seen in our lifetime in the areas of communication, technology, and healthcare. But looking back to the turn of the twentieth century, we also see major advances, such as the airplane, automobile, telephone, home comforts, and the expanded availability of electricity. Travel became cheaper and safer; no longer just for wealthy tourists, but for anyone in search of new adventures. By 1913, a trip around the world, once fraught with danger, could now be sold to the curious traveler as a cruise to be completed in the lap of luxury. The Hamburg-America line offered a round-the-world cruise on the *S.S. Cleveland* from New York to Europe and then, via the Suez Canal, to India, Burma, the Philippines, Hong Kong, Hawaii, and San Francisco for as little as $650. The opening of the Panama Canal in 1914 allowed travelers to complete their trip entirely by sea.[224]

During the relatively stable hundred years following the Congress of Vienna, Europe became the center of a newly interconnected world, crisscrossed by railway lines and telegraph wires. The continent was the quintessential model of interdependence, with each country relying on its neighbor for resources, markets, and access to the rest of the world. A popular book at the time was *The Great Illusion*, by Norman Angell, which spelled out the persuasive argument that Europe's economies were so intertwined that war was futile.

With a population of just two million, Vienna had fallen behind Paris as Europe's pleasure capital. It did not have the drive and energy of Berlin and, instead, the city seemed elegantly shabby. "Vienna has no nightlife," complained the *Wiener Montage Journal.* "The Viennese are already asleep by ten." And Herman Bahr wrote in 1906, "In Europe one knows Vienna as the place where it is forever Sunday. This reputation of a happy city swaying with dance, of harmless people, a little dissolute, not very active, not very efficient, but of good and kind people, has been retained in the wider world."[225]

Vienna was then, and still is, a city of cafés. Remember, coffee beans were discovered by the Austrian army after the failed Turkish siege of 1683. The coffeehouse was a refuge from dark and under-heated Viennese apartments; what made it more important was that it was a place to exchange a wide variety of intellectual ideas. The columnist Alfred Pogar captured the atmosphere when he said, "A coffeehouse is where you can go when you want to be alone, but for that you need to have people around you." And though there was always a diverse group, each café had its own style and special clientele, be it theatre people, politicians, journalists, or the professions. In the early twentieth century, many a literary Bohemian seemed to live permanently in the coffeehouse, leaving only to sleep in a nearby small hotel and surviving by sponging off friends and fellow patrons.[226]

Because administration of the city was sloppy in those days, Vienna was a good place to hide out and meet interesting people. And the year 1913 brought together people who would later change the world. In January of that year, a man with a dark complexion and a large peasant's mustache disembarked from the Krakow train at Vienna's North terminal station carrying a basic wooden suitcase. His passport bore the name Stavros Papadopoulos, and the person he had come to meet wrote years later, "I was sitting at a table when the door opened with a knock and an unknown man entered. He was short ... thin ... his grayish-brown skin covered in pockmarks. I saw nothing in his eyes that resembled friendliness."[227] The writer of the above lines was the editor of a radical newspaper called *Pravda* (Truth), a dissident Russian intellectual named Leon Trotsky. And the man traveling as Papadopoulos is known to the world as Joseph Stalin.

Living precariously as a journalist, Trotsky described Vienna as "a center of political and intellectual interests, a love of music, speaking four European languages, and various European connections." In 1913, a young Adolf Hitler was also in the city, trying to become an artist at the Vienna Academy of Fine Arts. Transported by the operas of Richard Wagner, as performed by the Jewish composer and conductor, Gustav Mahler, he spent time painting many views of the opera house.[228] While no one knows if Hitler bumped into Trotsky and Stalin, we do know that he lived not far from the Café Central on the Ringstrasse, a place which they both frequented, where cakes, newspapers, chess, and, above all, talk, were the passions.[229]

Presiding in Vienna's rambling Hofburg Palace while all of this was going on, was the aging emperor, Franz Josef, who had reigned since 1848. He was a man entirely unwilling to have his habits altered with the passage of time: He thought the telephone a nuisance, lit the palace with kerosene lamps instead of electricity, and, as a stickler for court etiquette, gloried in his old-fashioned ways. "You see in me," he said to Theodore Roosevelt, "the last monarch of the old school."[230]

Franz Josef would not be able to maintain his old-style empire while the rest of the world changed around him. Dissatisfaction was spreading not only throughout the Austro-Hungarian Empire but also throughout the empires of Germany and Russia. All three were threatened by the unrest of their minorities who, in Austria, were populated by the Slavs but dominated by the less-numerous German and Hungarian Magyars. And all three were troubled by persistent demands for greater democracy that became louder when nationalism and democracy found a common voice.[231]

While not exactly a melting pot, Vienna fostered its own kind of cultural soup: Said one writer, "Officers in the Austro-Hungarian army had to be able to give commands in eleven languages besides German."[232] By 1913, the Austrian parliament had become something of a circus: Ten languages were spoken, yet there were no interpreters. Desks were rattled, insults exchanged, and a fist fight often followed the throwing of an occasional ink stand. Tourists came to visit parliament just to gawk at the spectacle, and one of these was a young Adolf Hitler, his fists clenched in excitement. In 1914, the Vienna satirist Karl Kraus called the scene a proving ground for world destruction. It would have been a miracle to hold together the empire's various lands under any political structure, much less the chaotic system of the early twentieth century.[233]

The Turkish Empire was also passing through a transition. The more westernized elements of the ruling class, known as the Young Turks, were preparing to take action to restore the constitution of 1876, which provided for an elected parliament. But more zealous individuals had formed a secret society in Serbia known as the Black Hand, which trained men in the art of bomb throwing, blowing up bridges, and other skills that might prove useful in an emergency. The membership was so secret that individuals were designated only by number.[234] The Serbian government began to work with the Black Hand to plan a confrontation with Austria-Hungary. This plan was supported by Russia, who regarded Austria-Hungary, along with its ally Germany, as an obstacle in the way of Russian designs on the Dardanelles Straits.[235]

The heir apparent to the throne of Austria-Hungary, Archduke Franz Ferdinand, was a man of ability and intelligence who was a strong advocate of settling differences by peaceful means. In 1914, he went to Sarajevo, Bosnia—today's Yugoslavia—to make an inspection of the two army corps stationed there. Amid popular acclaim, the archduke and his wife made a shopping trip through the bazaars of Sarajevo the day before official activities were scheduled for June 28. The archduke's party were in an open touring car proceeding along the main boulevard to the city hall when a man suddenly stepped forward and threw a bomb that landed on the folded-down top of the archduke's vehicle. It bounced onto the street, seriously injuring the occupants in the next car.

After making sure that the wounded were taken to a hospital, the archduke proceeded to the city hall, where he made a speech with the mayor. His next stop was to be at the governor's residence for lunch. Because of the bomb incident, the route to the luncheon was changed, and everyone was informed except the archduke's chauffeur. As his car stopped to turn and follow the new route, a young assassin pulled out a revolver and shot the archduke and his wife at close range, killing them both.[236]

News of the assassination aroused heartfelt sorrow in the capitals of Europe. And in July, Austrian leaders resolved to undertake a punitive war with Serbia, as they were sure that Serbian government officials had been involved. Austria sent such an onerous ultimatum to Serbia that Winston Churchill wrote of it, as only he could, in his *World Crisis*:

It was the Austrian note to Serbia. We were all very tired, but gradually as the phrases and sentences followed one another, impressions of a wholly different character began to form in my mind. This note was clearly an ultimatum; but it was an ultimatum such as had never been penned in modern times. As the reading proceeded it seemed absolutely impossible that any State in the world could accept it ... and a strange light began immediately, but by perceptible graduations, to fall and grow, upon the map of Europe.[237]

On July 28, 1914, Austria declared war on Serbia. The wires of Europe were hot with telegrams between Berlin and London, and the German Kaiser sent a personal appeal to the Russian tsar. But no statesman could stop the events for which the seeds had been sown throughout the previous decade. The leaders of Vienna hoped the war with Serbia would remain localized, though they knew there was danger of Russian intervention. They took the fatalistic attitude that if Russia did march, they would have done so sooner or later anyway, and if a wider war did break out, they were certain to have Germany's support.[238]

The Austro-Hungarians were determined to use the assassination of Archduke Franz Ferdinand for military resolution of the impossible relationship with their southern neighbor, allowing them to reassert their position as an independent great power. They thought a strike against Serbia would break the encirclement which had been tightening around the monarchy.[239] The truth was that Austria-Hungary was the only great power who could gain nothing from a war in 1914, yet she alone was hell-bent on war.[240] An Austrian housewife, Anna Eisenmenger, wrote of the war fever in her country:

The people were all in the highest spirits, and when a military train decorated with fir branches and crammed with soldiers pulled into the station it was greeted with rousing cheers and shouts of "Down with Serbia." My husband pointed to the noisy, yelling crowd. "There you have it!" he said. "War psychosis!" And he leant back his head against the cushion and closed his eyes. Liesbeth and I exchanged smiling glances. At that time I did not realize that his brain had remained cool and clear in contrast to all those who were shouting and bawling around us, obsessed by feverish enthusiasm for war.[241]

The War of 1914 cannot be accounted for by examining any one failure of statesmanship. Because of the rivalry between the great powers and their existing alliances, it developed into a conflict of unprecedented scope involving the whole European continent, with all of the countries fighting for their version of a balance of power. Newly published daily newspapers added to the momentum for war, because their editors discovered that sensational news would sell more copies of their papers. Thus, the people of Europe read a constant stream of articles that exhorted them to embrace a narrow nationalist doctrine instead of providing them with a broader political analysis. This prepared them to accept, as a matter of course, the unrestrained hatred promoted by the press.[242]

When the call to war came, Marx thought the workers of Europe would align themselves with their own class instead of their country and become the force that would topple capitalism. But he was disappointed to see that the working class went off to war willingly, even eagerly, just like the upper class.[243]

Understanding of the events surrounding the First World War is critical to understanding the Second World War, which was merely an extension of the first. The truce that existed between the two wars was needed simply to allow women to produce another generation of fodder for the guns of Europe.

The First World War didn't have to happen. Before 1914, European countries had been showing real signs of working well together. In 1900, Europe had responded to China's Boxer rebellion with a successful international relief expedition carried out jointly by British, Russian, French, Italian, German, and Austro-Hungarian armies, along with Japanese guardsmen and U.S. Marines. In the field of literature, names such as Tolstoy, Victor Hugo, Balzac, Zola, Dickens, Shakespeare, Goethe, Molière, and Dante were familiar to every European high school student. Europe could act together when it chose, and it could think and feel together. The educated classes held much culture in common through an appreciation of the art of the Renaissance, the architecture of the Middle Ages and the classical revival, the music of Mozart, Beethoven, and grand opera, and each other's modern literature.[244]

The mystery is this: Why did such a prosperous continent at the height of its success as a source and agent of global wealth and power choose to risk it all in the lottery of a vicious local conflict? Why, when the conflict could have been brought to a quick and decisive conclusion, was hope for international peace dashed to the ground and countless young men committed to pointless slaughter? The First War was not only tragic, but unnecessary, because the chain of events that led to it could have been broken at any point during five weeks following the initial crisis. Had sound leadership, prudence, or common goodwill found an adequate voice, ten million human beings would not have lost their lives, and millions more would not have survived with emotions tortured by the horror they had witnessed.

In addition to massive loss of life, a benevolent and optimistic culture on the European continent was sacrificed. The war left a legacy of political rancor and international hatred so intense that no explanation of the causes of World War II can stand without reference to these roots.[245]

It has been noted that there were great technological advances not only at the turn of the twenty-first century but also at the turn of the twentieth century, including the invention of machine guns and barbed wire used in the First War. What kind of military leaders would send young men into trenches to face barbed wire and machine guns? And they didn't encounter these things only in the first battle and then come to an understanding that they needed to quickly change their tactics; the leaders of war kept on sending young men to be maimed and killed in the same way for four years.

Those who could influence the events of 1914 through 1917 seemed to suffer a sort of paralysis of the brain that manifested itself in a total incapacity to exhibit common sense. Only real leadership could have convinced those in power to use their heads, and there was certainly no such leader in Austria-Hungary. There was only eighty-four-year-old Franz Josef, sunk in a fatalism so deep that he rationalized the very end of his empire with this stark comment: "If we must go down, let us go down as gentlemen."[246]

CHAPTER 5

Starving with Full Barns

The First World War ended when the guns fell silent on November 11, 1918. But for Austria, it all but ended in November 1916, when Emperor Franz Josef died. The 86-year-old emperor developed a fatal case of pneumonia just one month after his premier, Count Karl von Stürgkh, was assassinated by radical socialist Friedrich Adler. The old emperor's long reign had begun with the Revolution of 1848, and it closed while yet another revolution was brewing in his tottering empire.

More than two million people had immigrated to the United States from Austria-Hungary from 1900 to 1910, but the outflow of disenchanted people ceased when the U.S. imposed stricter immigration quotas.

The unrest caused by societal and economic ills that had been siphoned off by the New World was now left to grow and fester.[247] During the winter of 1918 to 1919, Austria experienced a relatively tame uprising when previously loyal troops went over to the revolutionaries, but there were neither barricades to man nor gunfire to run toward. This was surprising, given the empire's military defeat and deprivations such as the shortage of food and fuel, but the breakup of the Habsburg Empire was the end result of a process that had been in motion for a long time.[248]

Before the assassination of the emperor's heir, Archduke Franz Ferdinand, in 1914, tensions had already been growing between the two members of the dual monarchy, Austria and Hungary.[249] Minorities within the empire's eastern countries were striving to achieve a more modern way of life by means of self-determination, and as the rule of the Austro-Hungarian government evolved into a military dictatorship and economic hardships increased, they were actively demanding independence. For the dying empire, the political settlement laid down for postwar Germany and Austria would be one of the most significant results of the war.[250] From its ruins emerged a collection of small territorial nation states, born as the victorious Allies determined new borders. But few of the new states enjoyed democracy for long. Many of them are still governed by clans, sects, families, or the military, who suppress any group that challenges the ruling power.

Seeds of future wars are often planted in peace treaties of previous wars, and this was true in the Treaty of Versailles of 1919 that closed the "War to End All Wars." The carving up of the Ottoman Empire bore no relation to the pre-existing loyalties of people who identified them-selves in religious rather than national terms. The imposition of national boundaries led to the kind of chaos we have more recently witnessed in Iraq, where Sunni and Shiite Muslims fight for dominance, or in Syria, where a minority Islamic sect has maintained power since the rise of the Assad family. Europeans define themselves in national terms, but for followers of Islam, God has laid down laws to be interpreted by leaders to whom the people must submit, wherever they live.

Another key element of the Treaty of Versailles was the insistence by the Allies on making Germany and Austria repay the costs of the war to France and England. Reparations included all military expenses and civilian damages, including the payment of pensions that more than doubled the amount Germany and Austria owed. Payback was required even as the people of Vienna were starving, and Allied relief agencies were rushing food into the city.[251] A few months after the treaty was signed, the noted economist, John Maynard Keynes, pointed out the impossibility of carrying out the treaty's economic clauses when he said, "No one has yet devised a scheme for killing the goose and still managing to collect the golden eggs."[252]

In January 1918, months before the end of the war, American president Woodrow Wilson announced to the world his famous Fourteen Points. They were designed to prevent the emergence of a German-dominated bloc of Europe and to establish a new order based on democracy and self-determination. Point Ten spoke for the autonomy of the peoples of Austria-Hungary along national lines. But Wilson completely misunderstood the former Habsburg Empire's minority populations, whose varying traditions were alive, important, and irreconcilable.[253]

Wilson's lack of understanding produced most of the errors committed in the name of self-determination. America was impatient with Europe's inability to arrange internal borders as easily as she had arranged her own, but the United States did not have to deal with groups of people who already had entrenched traditions, and it had wide-open spaces on which to draw new boundaries. In Austrian Europe, distinctive peoples had too much history and too little space.[254]

On September 10, 1919, almost as an afterthought, the Allies specifically addressed the Austrian problem with the Treaty of Saint Germain-en-Laye. This treaty not only dismantled the Habsburg Empire but whittled Austria itself down to a fraction of its enormous prewar territory. Austria was given a small portion of West Hungary, an area inhabited mostly by Germans, from which Vienna had always received its supply of vegetables and milk. But Hungary refused to remove its own soldiers from the area, as did the Czechs and the Serbs; so the arbitrary borders drawn cut off the new Austria from much-needed food and coal from these regions. The Treaty of Saint Germain was modeled closely after the Treaty of Versailles, and from the beginning, Austria could make only modest payments toward its required reparations.[255]

Once a sprawling empire, Austria was reduced to a tiny mountainous country where only half the land could be cultivated. It no longer had access to the fertile lands of Czechoslovakia or the breadbasket of Hungary, and its only major city, Vienna, faced massive unemployment and a severe housing shortage. The city's postwar population ballooned to 2.4 million, too many people for the nation's small agricultural area to support. To make matters worse, the Spanish influenza that had swept through Europe and even America at the end of the war was cutting a swath through Vienna. The weakened condition of the population made them especially vulnerable to the ravaging disease.[256]

Once an imperial capital, Vienna was a dismal place as it faced the bitter winter of 1919. Cold and hungry people, including exhausted and angry soldiers, were easily inflamed by any talk of the poor conditions in what was left of their country. The depreciation of the Austrian krone happened far before that of the German mark and with less chance of recovery.[257] To alleviate the severe conditions, there was a sensible proposal to unite Austria with democratic Germany, whose farmlands could have fed Vienna's starving population. But the Allies did not want a defeated Germany to acquire territory as a result of losing the war. Instead, they insisted upon the creation of an independent Austria, even if it presented a financial liability to the rest of Europe.[258]

The Treaty of Saint Germain had made of Austria a Republic, and the revolution of 1919 forced a parliamentary system for which the county was ill prepared. It was designed to give little authority to anyone, so all business had to be done by committee. Such a system was decidedly unwieldy in a country that had more government employees in its population of 6.5 million than a country with a population of 50 million might have. Tax collection was entirely inefficient, and government agencies ran at a huge loss. Less than half of the railways users paid the full fare, and the bankrupt country was supplying goods such as cigars at far below cost of production. Ministries, railways, and the post office all needed drastic pruning and reform. Excessive expenditure on wages that rose automatically with the cost-of-living index could be supported only by printing money, creating constant pressure to print more.[259]

These and other problems in Austria, and later in Germany, added fuel to the fire that was burning in response to the Allied demand that the two countries pay steep reparations for the cost of the war. England

and France blamed Germany and Austria for the loss of ten million lives, so it seemed only reasonable that they pay. But the decision had been made with little thought about the long-term interests of the whole of Europe. How would the two bankrupt nations pay reparations to the other nations without simply printing more money? The only way to square the circle on debt payments was for American banks, awash with potential credit, to lend Germany and Austria the money needed to pay their war debts. The similarity of this practice to the modern strategy of running up debt on one credit card to pay off another is striking.[260]

The United States played a major role in this merry-go-round by insisting that that the European Allies repay *their* war debts to the U.S., making them even more determined to demand reparations from Germany and Austria. Germany and Austria then borrowed money from the U.S. to make the required payments. Instead of fostering a healthy exchange of goods, there was a vicious circle of contrived and ultimately disastrous transfers of credits.[261] Austria's economy sank faster than Germany's, though it would manage to stabilize sooner.

Money is no more than a medium of exchange, and it can be used as such only when its value is acknowledged by more than one party; the wider the acknowledgement, the more useful money is. Once Germans and Austrians learned their money had no value except for papering walls, there was no means to measure the worth of anything, and this discovery shattered their societies.[262]

Due to severe shortages of food and supplies, prices in Austria had risen steeply during the last year of the war, and they continued to rise with new restrictions imposed by the Treaty of Saint Germain. For many, the only source of food was the black market, and wheat flour was unattainable at any price. Some indefinable substitute could be purchased from an illicit dealer at fifty times the 1914 price.

Hyper-inflation is defined as occurring when prices rise 50 percent or more in one month. It was a natural reaction of most Austrians to assume that goods were becoming more expensive, not that their money was falling in value. So as prices went up, people demanded more money to buy what they needed rather than asking for stable purchasing power.[263] As they lost trust in their currency, they spent money faster, until people could no longer purchase basic necessities. It was clear proof of the modern adage: "If you want to destroy a nation, corrupt its currency."

In 1925, an American silent film was made in Vienna called *The Joyless Street*, starring Greta Garbo in her first feature role. In one scene, a butcher insults and taunts women he finds unattractive or unwilling to accept his advances and refuses to sell them meat. In another, a group of gluttonous foreigners are gaily enjoying Vienna's nightlife when they are attacked by an angry, starving crowd of locals. It is a faithful reflection of the postwar Vienna we are about to enter.[264]

The diary of Frau Anna Eisenmenger takes us into war-torn Vienna by providing a vivid firsthand account of what it was like to live through those days. The Eisenmengers were an upper middle-class Viennese family, and when Anna began writing, her husband, Victor, was a doctor who was also the director of a hospital department. The couple had four children: The eldest, nineteen-year-old Karl, was in his first year of medical studies. Otto, seventeen, and Ernst, fifteen, were still in school. Erni was the pride of his family: a talented pianist who was described by his mother as having beautiful dark blue eyes and a sunny and sweet disposition. Anna wrote that everyone felt Erni had a bright future as a musician. The Eisenmengers' only daughter, eighteen-year-old Liesbeth, had just married a soldier, Lieutenant Rudi Stark, much to the displeasure of her father, an avowed pacifist. A grandson, Wolfgang, was born a year before the outbreak of the war. Wolfi was pale and delicate during the difficult war years, but he was always lively and cheerful—a welcome source of gaiety in the home.[265]

Like many middle-class Viennese, the Eisenmengers were a musical family, and each of them was proficient in playing several instruments. They had their own family band, and Erni was already showing real talent, not only as a musician but also as a composer.[266] The family home was a six-room flat near the center of the city, with a kitchen, maid's room, bathroom, bedrooms, and sitting room. A large drawing room overlooked the garden and contained the piano, serving as the entertainment center for the whole family.[267]

Frau Eisenmenger dedicated her diary to "All the Women in the World," as the war had decimated the male population, and she felt it was left to women to keep society alive. As years passed, stresses of the war took their toll on Anna's family: Her husband died of heart failure from overwork and insufficient nourishment, after his sixty-year-old sister, "Aunt Bertha," had moved into their home to help care for him. Otto was in the army on the Russian front in 1915 when the family received the news that he was missing in action. No further word was ever received. Karl left medical school to join the army Ambulance Corps. He was decorated twice, but he received a severe head wound, and though it had appeared to heal, he was now easily impatient and sometimes even violent for no reason. The youngest, Erni, had joined the army in 1917, but with the help of his brother-in-law, now Major Rudi Stark, he had been assigned to a relatively safe artillery regiment.

Anna began writing as she heard news of the assassination of Archduke Franz Ferdinand and his wife on June 28, 1914. She left her diary during the war years but picked it up again in October 1918, just a month before the armistice. The blockade that the Allies had placed on goods going to Germany and Austria was taking a heavy toll, and Anna wrote on October 25, 1918:

Liesbeth's cough is worse, and Wolfi is begging for milk; it is now a week since we had the 1/4 pint of milk due us on our ration cards. I resolve to hamster (hoard food) ... Now at the end of the fourth year of war, when the Central Powers ... are like a besieged fortress cut off from all external supplies and without any hope of breaking through the hunger blockade, I am no longer disposed to sacrifice any more members of my family to the Moloch (sacrifice) of war.[268]

She didn't know it then, but Anna's nightmare was only beginning. Like her neighbors, she had just begun the illegal practice of hoarding food and fuel. As portrayed in the movie, *The Joyless Street*, Anna found that, to feed her family any meat at all, she must join the daily queue. On November 8, 1918, she wrote:

Kathi (housekeeper) woke me and reminded me that I wanted to take my place in the queue for horse flesh at 7 o'clock this morning ... The cavalry horses are being slaughtered by the military authorities for lack of fodder, and the people of Vienna are for a change to get a few mouthfuls of meat of which they have so long been deprived.

"Oh, Kathi if only it weren't horse flesh!" I sighed. "But, Frau, we must be glad that we can get any meat at all. It's a fortnight since we last had any in the house, and the young gentlemen need some strengthening food once in a while." A soft steady rain was falling as I left the house before 7 o'clock and the meat distribution did not begin until 9 o'clock. I hoped to get well to the front of the queue ... The police were examining the ration cards of all people in the queue to see whether they were entitled to horse flesh. I estimated the crowd waiting here for a meagre midday meal at two thousand at least ... No one seemed to mind the rain, although many were wet through ... Slowly, infinitely slowly, we moved forward ... The crowd became very uneasy and impatient and, before the police guard could prevent it, those standing in front organized an attack on the hall which the salesmen inside were powerless to repel. Everyone seized whatever he could lay his hands on, and in a few moments all the eatables had vanished, as though devoured by a hungry swarm of locusts ... The crowds waiting outside, many of whom had been there all night and were soaked through, angrily demanded their due, consisting on this occasion of a scrap of horse flesh, and refused to budge from the spot ... I fled into the adjacent public park but was driven out again, and at length I reached home, depressed and disgusted, with a broken umbrella ... My own state of mind made me realize, however, how easy it must be to upset the moral equilibrium of whole classes of the population who have been forced out of their ordinary habits of life by this unhappy war and now fall easy prey to the political agitator. After four years, I have to mourn a terrible war sacrifice: My husband and Otto dead ...;

Rudi a cripple with only half a leg; Karl utterly changed owing to his head wound and perhaps not sane; Liesbeth weak and ailing for lack of nourishing food; Wolfi, small and in constant danger of infection; Aunt Bertha bedridden with bone softening due to under-nourishment, the hospitals are full to overflowing and no longer take civilians unless their lives are in danger.[269]

Anna's bank manager had advised her to convert all her Austrian kronen into Swiss francs. But private dealings in foreign currencies were illegal, and she decided that breaking the law against hoarding was risk enough. By the end of 1918, however, all kronen had to be overprinted as Deutschösterreich, and Anna took what remained of her money, twenty thousand kronen, to be stamped at the bank, recording in her diary the first evidence of the ruin before her:

In the large banking hall a great deal of business was being done ... All around me animated discussions were in progress concerning the stamping of currency, the issue of new notes, the purchase of foreign money and so on ... I went to the bank official who always advised me. 'Well, wasn't I right?' he said. 'If you had bought Swiss francs when I suggested, you would not now have lost three fourths of your fortune.' 'Lost!' I exclaimed in horror. 'Why don't you think the krone will recover again?' 'Recover'! he said with a laugh. 'Just test the promise made on this kronen note and try to get, say, twenty silver kronen in exchange.' 'Yes, but mine are government securities; surely there can't be anything safer than that?' 'My dear lady, where is the State which guaranteed these securities to you? It is dead.'[270]

Confidence or lack of confidence in their country's currency determines how quickly people pass it on. And a good place to get rid of kronen was to purchase stock on the exchange. Yes, there was risk, but as long as companies were selling and growing, the market adjusted the value of shares to correspond to inflation. The stock market almost automatically maintained the value of investments, and if an investor was lucky, and a company did well, his money increased.[271]

Price manipulation and speculation were rampant in the stock market. In *The Joyless Street,* the value of money was falling rapidly, and Garbo's father had a pension worth less with every passing day. He cashed in his entire pension to invest it in the market on a tip that a certain stock was sure to keep going up. But, as you can guess, he lost everything, forcing our heroine into prostitution. She was saved at the end of the movie by, who else?—a good American soldier!

Things began to get steadily worse for Anna Eisenmenger, and on October 27, 1918, she received a letter reporting that her youngest son, Erni, was lying wounded in Innsbruck. His life was not in danger, but his injury was to his eyes. Especially because of his musical gifts, when she received this news, Anna felt "a vague, terrible anxiety—for Erni's big, blue, childlike eyes." He was soon transferred home to be cared for by his family, and Anna writes movingly of the moment when she first sees her beloved son:

On the way to Erni's room I heard the notes of the piano. I stood still and listened. I heard Erni's favorite melody from Mozart's C Sharp string quartette. On the tips of my toes I stepped to the door of the sitting-room and opened it quietly ... Erni, with a black bandage over both eyes, was seated at the piano. He looked very pale. His face was turned upwards, and an ecstatic smile played over his soft, childish lips ... He told me how he and his men were repelling an aeroplane attack ... when a bomb dropped and exploded near them and killed seven of his men, while he himself was wounded in the left eye by a small splinter. The Dr. said that the optic nerve was injured and that he had practically no hope of saving his sight.[272]

Anna's woes didn't end with the injury to Erni's eyes. She describes a journey with her eldest son, Karl, to a small rural village south of Vienna to barter with a farmer friend for some food.

In the whole of Vienna there is no milk to be had on our ration cards. I resolved to go with Karl to the farmer at Laxenburg ... We found the streets filled with excited crowds. Several times we saw officers being mishandled in order to force them to take the imperial eagle from their caps. "Karl, go and help him." "I shouldn't dream of doing such a thing. It's these great men who have grown fat on the War and looked after their own safety ..." Karl's conduct appalled me and turning to Karl I said: "What right have these young hooligans to rob officers of distinctions which it is only their duty to wear?" "Oh, mother," said Karl, "the difference between officers and soldiers has vanished with the War, just as in future there will be no privileged social class. No emperor, no princes, no counts, no barons." "Tell me Karl," I said, "where did you get hold of these anarchistic or nihilistic ideas?" "My ideas are neither anarchistic or nihilistic. I am a communist."[273]

The war had hit the middle class hardest, destroying their savings, including the war bonds that people had purchased out of a sense of patriotism. Former civil servants and officers had become the poorest of the poor. They were too proud to press their claims and could get no employment. It became a common daily occurrence in Vienna for an elderly person or retired official of high rank to collapse on the street from hunger.[274]

Frau Eisenmenger's diary contained repeated regrets about the deceits into which life was forcing her, and she was resentful about the unfeeling behavior she saw in others. When her grandson, Wolfi, developed scurvy due to an almost complete lack of fresh milk, she wrote on December 15, 1918:

I was struck by the number of pale, ragged children who kept asking me for bread. They were the result of the closing of the schools for lack of coal ... Milk is only attainable for children up to one year of age, and even for these the quantity is insufficient—to say nothing of the quality ... What has become of humanity and love for one's neighbor? The hunger blockade is maintained in order to punish us. Yet the bulk of those who have to suffer this heavy punishment are poor helpless beings who were humbly and harmlessly following the path that life has marked out for them. The growing lack of consideration for one's fellow men ... impresses me painfully. I can understand however, that the instinct of self-preservation in people whose very existence is threatened should overcome all moral laws ... It has become common for better and more warmly clad people to be robbed of their clothes in the street, and obliged to go home barefoot.[275]

The key to survival was in material assets such as jewelry, food, and above all, cigarettes, and the black market ruled. Anna wrote on November 27, 1918:

*It was my husband's supply of tobacco which did me good ser-
vice ... He had feared that the quality of these good cigars might
suffer from the War. He had, at the beginning of the War, before
tobacco was rationed, laid in a large supply of good Trabucco cigars.
After his death I did not know at first what to do with the piles
of cigar-boxes. Our house-porter asked me mysteriously whether
I would give his son a few cigars in exchange for some pork and
lard. Pork and lard! I could hardly believe my ears. I went to the
house-porter's flat, and there I found Schani, his son and a butcher's
apprentice, cutting up half of a fat sow. When I asked him where
he got this treasure, he answered evasively: "We didn't go to war
in order to starve afterwards. Everyone has to help himself as best
he can." At that moment I understood the acts of criminal violence
now so frequently perpetrated against persons and property just for
the sake of one satisfying meal.*[276]

Also in November, Anna recorded that the krone was worth twenty-five Swiss centimes the Christmas before, but it was now worth only half a centime. Her shares of stock were going up, however, and gambling on the stock exchange had become the fashion, as it seemed the only way to avoid losing all of one's money.[277] On January 1, 1919, Anna wrote:

*The State still accepts its own money for the scanty provisions
it offers us. The private tradesman already refuses to sell his*

precious wares for money and demands something of real value in exchange. The wife of a doctor whom I know recently exchanged her beautiful piano for a sack of wheat flour. I too have exchanged my husband's gold watch for four sacks of potatoes, which will at all events carry us through the winter ... My farmer had hidden the sacks of potatoes under straw on top of which he placed some apples. The apples were duly stolen, but the potatoes reached me safely ... I had to give the porter half a sack as hush money. When the farmer's eyes rested on the beautiful grand piano at which Erni was seated, improvising, he took me aside and said: 'My wife has been wanting one of those things for a long time. If you'll give it to me, you shall have all you want for three months.' [278]

It's easy to say that inflation wiped out the middle class in Austria, but these are just words until the impact is understood. For instance, there was a long-established tradition that no middle-class Austrian girl could marry without a dowry, and if her father didn't have the money, a young woman saved for years until she had enough. When money became worthless, it destroyed the traditions surrounding marriage, including the idea of remaining chaste until marriage. During the inflation, virginity didn't matter anymore, and, in that sense, women were liberated.[279]

When food imported using foreign exchange ran short, and Austrian farmers were increasingly unwilling to part with produce for worthless Austrian paper money, people experienced what some called "bei volley Scheuern verhungern," or starving with full barns.[280] If they had no access to agricultural produce or foreign-exchange goods, they stood in long food lines, turned to hunting, or slowly starved.

As the situation worsened, the educated classes became increasingly hostile to the postwar Austrian government. Those who lost their fortunes or their savings in the stock market did not understand the complex forces underlying the sinking economy. And since most Austrians associated the stock exchange with Jews, they were receptive to widely circulated propaganda promoting reactionary ideas, including virulent anti-Semitism.[281]

Inflation had become like an addiction that inflicted greater damage as it strengthened its hold. Finally, it reached a point where Austria had to go into detox or die.[282] As Anna wrote:

Prices rise from day to day, so that the State has been obliged to put 10,000 kronen notes into general circulation. 10,000 kronen—that is equivalent to two years' income from my capital. Never before have I had a note for so large an amount. Nor had I ever dreamed it possible that one could purchase so little for 10,000 kronen.[283]

By late 1921, the fall of the krone was gathering speed, and food was scarcer than ever. It was not uncommon to see a housewife doing her daily shopping for milk and bread with a bushel basket full of kronen. If she left the basket unattended, the basket would most likely be stolen and the money left scattered on the sidewalk.

With the continual rise in prices came growing resentment and even hatred against all who were thought to have profited from Austria's misfortunes, including the speculator on the stock exchange, and inevitably, the Jews. On December 2, 1921, an unarmed crowd of thirty thousand wrecked and looted food shops, restaurants, and cafés everywhere and attacked the hotels in the city's main quarter. At the Bristol Hotel, the mob found the former president of the Austrian Reparations Commission, ransacked his apartment, and robbed him of all his effects.

Demonstrators wanted all gold to be taken into State hands, even if it belonged to the churches and monasteries. They further demanded State control of the securities market and insisted that the government seize all foreign currency, which most shops, in self-defense, had begun to require for any purchase. The Austrian chancellor was forced to give in on all these matters, but the demonstrations were only a precursor to even darker days: The British Commercial Attaché in Vienna wrote, "I fear these disturbances presage collapse."[284]

The capacity of Austrians for long suffering had already proved remarkable, and the December riots seemed to lessen the intensity of fear and anger for most Viennese. For a time, the country settled back into a state of lethargy; but to her neighbors, especially Germany, Austria seemed to be heading toward disaster at an alarming pace. Only eighteen months earlier, the krone was 800 to the British pound, but it was now at 3,000, and still falling.[285] On November 25, 1919, Frau Eisenmenger wrote:

The large numbers of unemployed, their passions fermented by the Communists, are seething with discontent ... A mob has attempted to set the Parliament house on fire. Mounted policemen were torn from their horses, which were slaughtered in the Ringstrasse and the warm bleeding flesh dragged away by the crowd ... The rioters clamored for bread and work ... Side by side with unprecedented want among the bulk of the population, there is a striking display of luxury among those who are benefiting from the inflation ... New nightclubs are being opened, in spite of the difficulty of obtaining supplies, and the gains of their owners are so enormous that they are indifferent to the penalties often imposed on them by the police. These clubs have the effect of greatly intensifying the class hatred of the proletariat against the bourgeoisie. Even the most respectable Austrian citizen now breaks the law, unless he is prepared to starve for the sake of obeying it.[286]

Even during the inflation, the individual who was prepared to improvise and think outside the box could end up not just surviving but thriving. Inflation was paradise for anyone who owed money, including highly leveraged businessmen and mortgagees whose contracted payments were shrinking by the month, or even by the week. Times were good for those agile enough to move between money and goods and back as required, especially if they had access to foreign currencies or a friendly banker.[287]

By the same token, times were bad for creditors of all kinds, savers, and investors who depended on a fixed return. Large numbers of the old Austrian middle and upper classes suffered a drastic fall in their standard of living. The State and other employers demanded currency to respond to the constant rise in prices. And since private banks could not meet the demand, they resorted to the rationing of check cashing. While checks remained frozen, their purchasing power dried up. In factories, offices, and companies, employees who had been paid monthly or weekly were now paid twice and then thrice weekly, and finally daily or twice daily. Business came to a literal standstill.[288]

Coal had been available during the war, but the Czechs had stopped exporting coal to postwar Austria and Germany. Anna complained,

"A new struggle, which we were spared during the war, is being imposed upon us housewives: the struggle against the winter cold in our homes."[289] A decree was issued that no one could purchase more than one half centum weight (cwt) of coal per week, and it could be used only for cooking, not for heating the home. As winter tightened its icy grip around the city, the temperature plunged below freezing, and the decree was completely ignored. Anna had always saved coal during the summer so she would have plenty for the colder months, and she had managed to save about one and one-half tons of the precious fuel in her cellar. If the authorities found out, however, her supply would be confiscated, making for a difficult and dangerous winter.

Anna had to act quickly to hide her coal, as she knew that cellars were going to be searched by the Volkswehr, the People's Defense forces. She wrote on November 20, 1918:

I came to an understanding with our good-natured house-porter, promising him 2 cwt. of coal if he would quietly transfer on to the verandah the stock of coal in my cellar. The other people living in the house must not see it, for how often it had happened that an envious and less fortunate neighbor had secretly given information to the authorities! At 11 o'clock at night, when everyone else was asleep, I began, aided by Kathi and the house-porter, to transport to our verandah the supply of coal in the kitchen ... As we live on the third floor, we had to go up and down four storeys each time, for there is no lift in our house ... At 4 o'clock we had almost all the coal on the verandah. But both I and the porter were utterly worn out ... That I should one day, in order to escape freezing in my own

home carry up my coal and thereby constitute myself a criminal,
was something that no one had prophesied at my cradle.[290]

Anna's timing was good. Two days later, three soldiers of the Volkswehr searched her house and strode through each room of her flat. The sight of bedridden Aunt Bertha, blind Erni, and poor crippled Rudi may have induced them to make no more than a superficial investigation, for they found nothing suspicious and went on their way.[291]

Early in the hyper-inflation period of 1919 to 1920, farmers had bumper harvests, so the starving Viennese headed out to the rural countryside to buy food, only to find their paper kronen worthless. They were then forced to beg or barter, and many a precious family heirloom or fine piece of jewelry was surrendered in exchange for food.

Fear and insecurity grew stronger among those who had already known too much of both. Contempt of government and disrespect for law and order became the norm. Contemporary newspaper articles reported that things could not go on like this, but they did.[292] It was a dire prelude to the Great Depression, although preceding it by several years. Inflation brought out the worst in people everywhere. As the days, weeks, months, and years wore on, people became increasingly desperate, and violence sometimes accompanied the forays of city dwellers to rural Austria.[293] Despair was complete, and Austrians waited for the sky to fall, as though it had not already done so a dozen times.

For Anna, life began to get a bit better as 1920 began. She still had some of her husband's fine cigars, and her daughter, Liesbeth, had found a job at the American Mission. She was even able to rent a room in their house to a coworker of Liesbeth's, an American who paid his rent in *dollars!* But Christmas 1919 was not as merry as those of the past had been:

I turned over the pages of my diary and found the last Christmas festival before the terrible World War. How many things have happened in these last years! Then: A silver fir as high as the room, eagerly and tastefully decorated by my four children and bearing seventy little white wax candles. Now: A meagre little fir tree, hardly as high as the table, procured with difficulty in exchange for some expensive cigars. Hung with decorations preserved from pre-war days, but only lit with a few unsightly tallow stumps cut from one of the rationed candles. Then: The traditional Vienna Christmas menu; fried carp with potatoes and bean salad, and a poppy and nut pancake concocted with special care. With it beer and light Moselle wine. Afterwards, punch, pastries and fruit. Now: Christmas was accompanied by a sharp frost and icy winds. The little iron stove, even supplemented by the oil stove, could not bring the temperature of the room above 11 degrees. We were therefore all obliged to wrap ourselves up warmly so that there was no question of festival attire ... The preparation of the Christmas menu was fraught with difficulties. At great pecuniary sacrifice I bought a few Portuguese sardines at an exorbitant price along with 4 oz. of rice each. A good loaf baked by the farmer's wife at Laxenburg and presented to me as a Christmas gift, together with 8 oz. of butter, heightened the enjoyment of what was to us an unusually varied supper. [294]

In April 1922, the German foreign minister, Walter Rathenau, said that Europe had committed two errors: The first was the sham of disarmament, since only Germany and Austria had disarmed so far, and the second, debt. The whole of Europe was being strangled by an infernal circle of debt because everyone needed temporary loans to get through the crisis. "We are living in our own fat. Our property is a bubble. Our companies pay dividends but in fairy gold."[295] By August of that year, the collapse of government authority in Austria was inevitable and imminent. An alarming picture of national selfishness, bred by inflation and economic uncertainty, was painted by Mr. O.S. Phillpotts, Commercial Secretary at the British Legation in Vienna:

The Austrians are like men on a ship who cannot manage it, and are continually signaling for help. While waiting, however, most of them begin to cut rafts, each for himself, out of the sides and decks. The ship has not yet sunk despite the leaks so caused, and those who have acquired stores of wood in this way may use them to cook their food, while the more seamanlike look on cold and hungry. The population lack courage and energy as well as patriotism.[296]

Something had to change. Refusing to wait passively for the approach of ruin, Chancellor Ignaz Seipel resolved to trade part of his country's independence for survival. "Now was seen," said one commentator, "the hitherto unparalleled spectacle of an Austrian chancellor touring Europe offering his country to the highest bidder."[297] Dr. Seipel's tour included each of Austria's neighbors, followed by a September visit to the

League of Nations in Geneva. To this body he made a moving appeal, arguing conclusively that, without financial help, Austria would collapse. In exchange for help to put her house in order, Vienna would agree to accept whatever discipline the League required.

The League of Nations was receptive to Seipel's plea, because the idea of Austria's union with Germany, Bavaria, Italy, or the Danube states appeared to be the only alternative, and the specter of any of these options was like a pistol to the head of the League. The very thought of Austria becoming a protectorate of Italy convinced France to go along with the decision to provide financial aid.[298]

The Austrian krone had reached its low point on August 25, 1922, but now it finally began to rise, as the Geneva talks had engendered confidence. The Geneva Protocol guaranteed first that Austria's political and territorial integrity would be preserved; second, that Britain, France, Italy, and Czechoslovakia would underwrite an Austrian loan of 650 million gold kronen; and third, that Austria would improve her financial situation by setting up new bank notes and ceasing to discount treasury bills. The plan would be guaranteed by investing absolute financial power in a *Commissioner-General,* who would be appointed by the League. From September 15 to the end of the year, prices in Austria fell, but the country was still living on credit inspired by the hopes aroused in Geneva, and the government was walking the thinnest of tightropes.[299]

By the end of 1922, Austria was in the hands of Dr. Alfred Zimmerman, the League's Commissioner-General. Arriving in Vienna in the middle of December, Dr. Zimmerman began at once to create and maintain the economic conditions which the Geneva Protocol demanded. Under

Zimmerman, Austria began to regain a stable currency, and the speed with which stability was restored indicated the extent to which Austria's problems had been psychological and administrative. According to some, distrust in themselves and in their government and an almost childlike reliance on foreign help and control had always been an essential characteristic of the Austrians.[300]

Among all the former Central Powers, only Austria's finances were plainly on the mend. And, as public confidence returned despite continued unemployment, some of the great quantity of hoarded foreign currency began to flow back into the market. Here, at last, was a base which the country could build on.[301] But there was still no real degree of prosperity for the average citizen. Stabilization had brought little relief to middle-class families dependent on fixed incomes or to unemployed workers. For many, the first year of stability had actually imposed a deeper, more devastating social chafing than ever.[302] About a year after Dr. Zimmerman's arrival, Anna Eisenmenger wrote on December 21, 1923:

Foodstuffs which three years ago were entirely unobtainable in Vienna and the rest of Austria can now be bought everywhere. But who can buy them? Whose income has kept pace with the tireless activities of the banknote printing-press? Although my holding in shares is worth at today's quotation more than ten million kronen, I am at my wits' end to know where to find money to buy food ... Today the value of our krone is quoted in Zurich as .00705 centimes. [303]

As part of the stabilization of the currency, kronen had to be exchanged into schillings; and in her final entry, on January 2, 1924, Anna described the devastating effect this had on her savings:

It is a drastic change. For fifteen thousand kronen we get one schilling! Thousands of Austrians have been reduced during the last days to beggary. All who were not clever enough to hoard the forbidden stable currencies or gold have, without exception, suffered losses. An old married couple with whom I have been friendly for years, had a holding of government stock amounting to two million pre-war kronen, which brought them in interest eighty thousand pre-war kronen a year. They were justly regarded as rich people. Today their stock brings them in eight new schillings a year. Panic has seized the stock exchange ... My millions have dwindled to about a thousand new schillings. We, too, belong today to the new poor. The middle class has been reduced to a proletariat. I too, can escape from starvation only if I find new sources of income. More fighting daily, repeated, exasperating, demoralizing offensive and defensive fighting of man against man. I feel that my strength is deserting me. I cannot go on.[304]

Throughout the inflationary troubles of Europe, America played the role of Uncle Shylock, refusing to forgive the debt of the other Allies and insisting on normal commercial terms. Because of their anxieties about a future German resurgence, the French also stiffened, demanding the repayment of German debt. But in the end, no one ever really got their money, not even the Americans, because Germany used American loans it received to pay reparations to the French and British, who used that money to service their debt to the United States. With the advent of the Great Depression, all the major powers effectively defaulted.[305]

So who did well in Austria during this postwar era of extraordinary inflation? Those who owed money saw their debt rapidly liquidated. Banking mushroomed, so people who worked in them profited. Investors in stock that increased in price with inflation did better than those with fixed investments. Farmers paid off mortgages and other debts by selling produce to desperate city dwellers and middlemen on the black market.[306] But no one who *lost* their money ever got it back — not the holders of war bonds, the savers, the professors, the civil servants, or the small business people whose earnings dwindled to nothing. Creditors lost almost everything. Forced to sell all their items of material value to survive, the losers had nothing left to fall back on when the economy fell into depression just five years later.[307]

In periods of hyper-inflation, necessity becomes the sole criterion of value, the basis of everything from barter to behavior. Human values begin to more nearly reflect animal values as people adopt attitudes of dog eat dog or survival of the fittest. On the field of war, a comfortable pair of boots may be the most valuable item, and on a sinking ship, a place in a life raft is worth more than untold millions. If life is secure, people may turn to non-essential luxuries, but when life is threatened and conditions are harsh, values change. Without shelter or clothing, it is difficult to sustain life, and without food, it is harder still. More valuable than food is water, and most precious is air, in whose absence life cannot long exist.

During Austria's postwar experience, many valued a kilo of potatoes more than the family silver, and a side of pork above the grand piano.

A prostitute in the family was better than an infant corpse, and theft preferable to starvation. Warmth was finer than honor and food more essential than freedom.[308] As Frau Eisenmenger had written on April 6, 1919, "A housewife who has had no experience of the horrors of currency depreciation has no idea what a blessing stable money is, and how glorious it is to be able to buy with the note in one's purse the article one had intended to buy at the price one had intended to pay."[309]

Before the war, Europeans had been actively cooperating to promote their own and each other's prosperity as an international community of nations. As stated in the previous chapter, all trade and communications passed through Europe in 1913, and it had become the crossroads of the world. The war, hyper-inflation, and a subsequent deep depression ended all of that, and Europe fell into a more cynical age of nationalism, with predictable results.

By 1926, in spite of a more stable currency, unemployment in Austria remained a major problem, and most citizens of Vienna were still hungry. Once again, a union between Austria and Germany was proposed—a customs union that would allow German agricultural goods to be freely imported into Austria to help feed the hungry. The proposal went nowhere until 1931, when the financial structure of Austria again came to the brink of ruin. The proposal for a customs union resurfaced, but sharp opposition from France forced the idea down again.

France put severe pressure on Austria by withdrawing its short-term deposits from Austrian banks, and this action played a major role in the May 11, 1931 collapse of the Kreditanstalt, one of the biggest international banking houses in Central Europe. The Kreditanstalt held two thirds of all Austrian assets and liabilities, and its bankruptcy brought with it bank failures in neighboring states. When the bank could not cover its losses, the Austrian government had to lend support.[310] When even this proved insufficient, a loan from the Bank of England prevented complete collapse.

Austria's financial crisis ignited a political crisis, and the entire structure of European finance was called into question. Fear aroused by the Austrian bank failure was soon felt in Germany, where foreign investors were beginning to withdraw capital.[311] Next, unemployment began to spiral, not only in Europe but also in the United States. Many historians believe that the European geopolitical crisis of the early 1930s caused the Great Depression, and not the other way around.[312]

The worldwide depression strengthened a trend that began with World War I: Instead of taking a common view of problems and solutions, each European state approached its economy in isolation, seeking to meet its own needs. This resulted in a plethora of differing policies, all of them increasing the powers of the State and all attempting to make each nation independent of the international economy and immune to its pitfalls.[313]

High tariffs were the first measure to which most states turned to protect the value of their own industrial products and raw materials, but high tariffs maintained artificially high prices. Austria, the only one of the smaller states that had to import large quantities of foodstuffs, had the lowest tariffs of all, but even this tiny country introduced a tariff-protection system in 1930. As the principal international creditor, America remained the most adamant in insisting on repayment of the Allied debt while refusing to lower its own tariffs.[314]

By 1933, Europe was finally beginning to see signs of economic recovery, and nations began to find ways to progress by acting together, as they had done before the war. It was decided that they should meet to find a definitive solution to the recent economic crisis, so during the summer of 1933, the World Economic Conference was held in London with sixty-four countries attending, including America and the Soviet Union. The immediate object of the conference was threefold: to lower tariffs, create an international monetary standard, and reduce restrictions on commerce and loans imposed during the crisis.[315]

Things got off to a bad start when the United States supported free discussion on all items of concern except for the question of war debts, which it refused even to allow on the agenda. American President Franklin Roosevelt, new to his office, saw U.S. domestic recovery as his chief problem. Stabilizing the dollar in relation to European currencies, which most delegates desired, would have meant surrendering the useful weapon of currency manipulation in dealing with America's economic problems, and President Roosevelt was unwilling to do this. His decision contributed powerfully to the failure of the conference to achieve its goals.[316]

The United States was not alone in blocking progress: No compromise could be reached between any of the nations on the issue of tariff reductions, the cooperation of central banks, or the resumption of international lending until a satisfactory monetary standard was agreed upon and currencies were stabilized. Until this occurred, there could be no real revival of international trade. A return to a system of greater international exchange would have meant major sacrifices for each country, and none of the participants would risk alienating important domestic groups that might combine to overthrow them.[317]

The self-interest displayed at the World Economic Conference had an unintended consequence that the delegates could not anticipate. In the early 1930s, no one realized that the drive toward economic nationalism would deepen the trend toward political authoritarianism and eventually confront them all with the dilemma of facing economic disaster or war.[318] Failure to establish an international economic structure threw each country back on its own resources. Before the depression, a high standard of living had been sought through the international exchange of goods and services, but now each country was left to protect its own incomplete resources in a broken system.[319]

A good case can be made for the view that the World Economic Conference of 1933 was the last chance the European states had to return to a policy of international economic cooperation. Measures resulting from the conference led not to gradual equalization but to greater competition, and the collaborative spirit of the previous generation of leaders was shattered.

It is difficult to avoid the conclusion that the worldwide depression was as important as World War I in changing the face of Europe. The First War had resulted in vast destruction and intensified many inherent tendencies within European societies. But it was the Great Depression that dealt the final blow to the easy way of life and cooperative attitudes that Europe had experienced at the start of the twentieth century. From 1930 on, a new political movement began to make its presence felt, starting with small disturbances that became frank terrorism, followed by widespread political unrest.[320] Nazism was rising, and another great war would soon threaten the security of all nations on the earth.

CHAPTER 6

The Hardest School

History is the story of greatness, genius, triumph, and tragedy—love, hatred, or even indifference, but it is always the story of people. And history is most compelling when it reveals how ordinary events can have extraordinary consequences that have lasting effects on the entire world. One such event took place in a small Austrian village in the late spring of 1876, but few took notice.

Thirty-nine years earlier, on June 7, 1837, Aloys Schicklgruber was born in the little village of Strones, near the Austrian border with today's Czech Republic. The village was surrounded by rolling hills whose graceful slopes were carpeted by green forests dotted with neatly-cultivated fields worked hard by generations of frugal people. Maria Anna Schicklgruber was forty-two and single when she gave birth to a son, registered as "Illegitimate." His father's name was left blank, though he was probably the son of a man from Maria's neighborhood.

By this time he was five years old, the boy's first name was spelled "Alois," and he was still using his mother's maiden name, even though she had married an itinerant miller, Johann Georg Heidler. Maria died five years after the marriage, and Georg promptly abandoned the family to resume his rambling ways. Ten-year-old Alois was taken in by Georg's brother, Johann Nepomuk Hiedler, but at the age of thirteen, he packed his small knapsack and left home to work his way to Vienna. After being apprenticed to a Viennese shoemaker for several years, he enlisted in the frontier guards, which made him a civil servant, when he was eighteen. He studied diligently to pass a civil service examination and became a supervisor when he was only twenty-four. By 1875, at the age of thirty-eight, he was a full-fledged inspector of customs at the west Austrian village of Braunau am Inn near the border with Germany, an exceptional honor for an illegitimate boy from the village of Strones.[321]

No one was prouder of Alois than Johann Nepomuck Hiedler, the step uncle who had taken him in as a boy. No Hiedler had ever risen so high, so Johann actually instituted legal proceedings to have the young man's last name changed to his own. Alois Schicklgruber shared the status of being illegitimate with as many as 40 percent of the population in rural Austrian districts, and it had not kept him from advancing through the civil service, so why did he agree to the change? The talk of the village was that Hiedler had promised to remember Alois in his will, and this theory was confirmed when Alois bought a farm for 5,000 florins just six months after his step uncle's death. During the proceedings for his name change, however, the name "Hiedler" appears to have been misspelled; for when Alois signed the papers to purchase the farm in 1876, he used his new legal name: Alois Hitler.[322]

A man of modest means whose income was similar to that of an elementary school headmaster, Alois was devoted to the civil service, status-proud, frugal, pompous, strict, and humorless. He was respected in his position by the local community, but he had a volatile temper, smoked incessantly, and preferred going for drinks after work to going home. When he became a husband and father, he was domineering, authoritarian, distant, and often irritable.[323]

Alois was known to have an eye for the ladies, and his marriage to an ailing woman fourteen years his senior did not prevent him from siring an illegitimate daughter. He persuaded the family of his sixteen-year-old second cousin, Klara Pölzl, a quiet, sweet-faced girl with dark brown hair, to let her come into the home to provide care for his ill wife. But because Alois was already having an affair with the kitchen maid, Fanni Matzelsberger, Frau Hitler could not accept another attractive young girl in the house, and she secured a legal separation from Alois. He moved Fanni into the home to become his common-law wife. Fanni understood the threat posed by the pretty young Klara and promptly fired her.

When his estranged wife died of consumption in 1881, Alois married Fanni, but she, too, was stricken with tuberculosis and left Braunau to recuperate in the country. Alone with two infants, Alois brought Klara back into the house to become housemaid, nursemaid, and mistress. Klara was so good-hearted that she not only provided excellent care for the children but also did her best to restore Fanni to health, causing

Fanni to accept her rival. When Fanni died in 1884, Klara was already pregnant, and Alois married her at six in the morning on January 7, 1885. There was no honeymoon, as the forty-eight-year-old Alois returned to work after a simple meal. At only twenty-five, young Klara was a model housekeeper who was completely devoted to the care of her two stepchildren.[324]

On April 20, 1889, on a chilly overcast Easter Sunday, Klara gave birth to her fourth child and the first to survive infancy: His name was Adolf Hitler. Two unremarkable events in the family's history would have an impact on this baby's future: One was his father's legal name change in 1876, for it is difficult to imagine 70,000 Germans in the Nuremberg Stadium shouting in all seriousness, "Heil Schicklgruber!"[325] The other was the baby's birth in Braunau, a village so close to Bavaria that Adolf would grow up believing there should be no national border between the peoples of Austria and Germany.[326]

According to Klara Hitler's Jewish doctor, Eduard Bloch, Adolf's mother was a simple, modest, and kindly woman. She was tall, and her dark hair framed a long, oval face with expressive grey-blue eyes. A pious churchgoer, Klara was quiet, submissive, and fully dedicated to running the household. But above all, she loved her children and stepchildren, and they loved her back, especially Adolf. Speaking of the youthful Hitler, Dr. Bloch wrote, "Outwardly, his love for his mother was his most striking feature." Hitler himself said in *Mein Kampf*, "I had honored my father, but loved my mother." His mother may have been the only person he ever genuinely loved.[327]

Adolf was raised by an overly anxious mother in a household dominated by an abusive father against whose wrath the submissive Klara was helpless to protect her children. In *Mein Kampf,* Hitler describes a worker's family whose children witnessed beatings of their mother by their drunken father, and this anecdote may have been based on his childhood experience.[328]

When Alois retired from the customs service at the age of fifty-eight, six-year-old Adolf was earning good marks at a public elementary school near the Austrian town of Linz. But the restless pensioner moved his family from one village to another seven times, and Adolf attended five schools by the time he was fifteen.[329] When it was time to transition to secondary school, the family was living in Leonding, and Adolf and his sister traveled more than one hour each way to attend high school in Linz. This left them no time for out-of-school friendships.[330] A teacher, Dr. Eduard Huemer, remembered Adolf as a thin, pale youth who did not apply his talents and was unable to accept discipline. Huemer further characterized him as high-handed, hot-tempered, and stubborn, with scarcely concealed insolence, a boy who tended to waste time and tried to dominate his classmates.[331]

While Adolf's marks were good in grade school, he spent his years at Linz High School dreaming, drawing, and giving no thought to the kind of career his father had valued so highly. When asked what he envisioned for his future, twelve-year-old Adolf said he wanted to be an artist. His father must have taken this as a rejection of everything he stood for. As Adolf wrote in *Mein Kampf,* "One day it became clear to me that I would become a painter, an artist. My father was struck speechless." Adolf stopped studying because he thought his lack of academic progress would influence his father to let him to devote himself to art, and he left high school without graduating.[332]

In *Mein Kampf,* Adolf praised only his high school history teacher, Dr. Leonard Pötsch, for firing his imagination through vivid tales of German heroism, stirring within him the strong emotions of German Nationalism and anti-Habsburg feelings that were prevalent in his school and in Linz. Listening to the powerful music of Richard Wagner was a near-religious experience for young Adolf, plunging him into fantasies about a larger-than-life, mythical Germanic past.[333]

On January 3, 1903, Adolf's life changed. Just before his fourteenth birthday, his father suffered a lung hemorrhage at the age of sixty-five and died while drinking his usual glass of wine at the Gasthaus Wiesinger. Adolf's conflict with his father about his future was over, and he described the next years as among the happiest of his life. He saw Linz as an idyllic German town, even though it was in Austria, and he loved living there. He contented himself with idling the days away along the Danube and dreaming of becoming an artist. His mother and other relatives urged him to learn a trade, but Adolf relished his freedom to roam the streets of Linz and the surrounding countryside, explaining to his companions the wrongs of the world and how to right them.[334]

In the late fall of 1905, Adolf met someone he could tolerate: The son of a Linz upholsterer, August Kubizek, known as Gustl, a young man with dreams of his own about becoming a great musician. Dressed in their best, Adolf and Gustl attended almost every opera in Linz. Sporting the beginnings of a thin mustache, Adolf looked distinctly foppish in his dark coat and hat, carrying a black cane with an ivory handle. Gustl was adaptable by nature, and Adolf was high strung and opinionated, but their differences seemed to solidify their friendship.[335]

Linz was, in the end, a provincial town, and it was not long before Vienna, the glittering capital of the empire, began to beckon young Adolf, inspiring his imagination and whetting his artistic ambitions. In 1906, just after his seventeenth birthday, with funds provided by his mother and his Aunt Johanna, he set off to spend two months in Vienna. Walking the streets of the great city for days, he was captivated by the museums, theaters, opera, and imposing buildings along the Ringstrasse. He eagerly inquired about how he might become a student at the Vienna Academy of Fine Arts.[336]

Adolf returned to Linz more determined than ever to become an artist, and he insisted that Gustl come with him to Vienna to share his dream. But on January 14, 1907, Klara went to the office of Dr. Bloch, a Jewish physician known as "the poor people's doctor," complaining of pain in her chest. His examination revealed an extensive breast tumor. Touched by Adolf's reaction to the news, Dr. Bloch later wrote: "His long, sallow face was contorted, tears flowed from his eyes."[337] An operation on January 17 improved Klara's health, and by early fall, Adolf was pleading with his mother to allow him to return to Vienna. He wanted to be in the city for an examination, given only in October, which would qualify him for entrance to the Academy of Fine Arts. Yielding to his request, Adolf's mother provided him with enough funds to live in Vienna for a full year.[338]

The entrance exam at the academy included an assessment of Adolf's work, and he sat through two three-hour examinations for which he had to produce drawings on specified themes. Of 113 applicants, only 28 were chosen, and Adolf was not among them.[339]

On October 22, Adolf received word that his mother was dying, and he rushed back to Linz. As Christmas approached, the end was obviously near, and in the dark morning hours of December 21, 1907, Klara quietly passed away. Dr. Bloch came the next day to sign the death certificate, and he would write in a 1941 article for *Colliers Magazine:* "In all my career I never saw anyone so prostrate with grief as Adolf Hitler." Adolf grasped Dr. Bloch's hand, looked directly at him, and said, "I shall be grateful to you forever." Wondering if Hitler remembered that scene, Dr. Bloch wrote, "I am quite sure that he does, for in a sparing sense Adolf Hitler has kept his promise. Favors were granted to me which I feel were accorded no other Jew in all Germany or Austria."[340]

At the time of his mother's death in the winter of 1907, Adolf was eighteen years old, and he had yet to earn a day's income: "I was faced with the problem of somehow making my own living," he wrote in *Mein Kampf.*[341] He had no trade, and he had always avoided manual labor, but with his mother's careful housekeeping and a significant contribution from Aunt Johanna, he still had more than enough money to live in Vienna for yet another year.[342] Undaunted by his lack of prospects, Adolf bid his remaining relatives farewell and declared that he would not return to Linz until he had made good.[343] As he later wrote, "With a suitcase full of clothes and underwear in my hand and an indomitable will in my heart, I set out for Vienna. I too hoped to wrest from fate what my father had accomplished fifty years before; I too hoped to become 'something'—but in no case a civil servant."[344]

On February 17, 1908, Adolf boarded the train to Vienna for the third-class fare of 5.30 kronen. After five hours, the eighteen-year-old arrived in the magical city and obtained a room at Frau Zakrey's establishment, just a few minute's walk from the Westbahnhof train station. The weather was dreary, but Adolf's spirits were high. Five days later, on a foggy Sunday, Gustl arrived, carrying a brown canvas bag. As Adolf walked towards him wearing his best, Gustl thought he already looked like one of the elegant citizens of Vienna, wearing his familiar but good-quality black coat, black hat, and carrying his ivory-handled walking stick. In their room, Adolf spread a newspaper on the table and brought out his meager supply of milk, sausage, and bread. But Gustl shoved these aside, producing from his canvas bag an ample quantity of roast pork, freshly baked buns, cheese, and a bottle of coffee. Adolf wistfully said, "That's what it is like to have a mother."[345]

After the feast, Adolf insisted on taking Gustl on a tour of the city. At the first stop, he introduced his friend, the would-be musician, to the grandeur of Vienna's Opera House. An amazed Gustl wrote: "I felt as though I had been transplanted to another planet, so overwhelming was the impression."[346]

In the first years of the twentieth century, Vienna was radiant with imperial grandeur, dazzling opulence, cultural excitement, and intellectual fervor. Set along the Danube beneath the Wienerwald's wooded hills and yellow-green vineyards, the city was also surrounded by natural beauty that enthralled the visitor and made the Viennese believe that Providence had been especially kind to them.[347] Music filled the air—the music of gifted native sons like Hayden, Mozart, Beethoven, and Schubert. The popular and haunting melodies of the beloved Johann Strauss, Vienna's own "Waltz King," were signature sounds of the city.

In the midst of beautiful surroundings and plentiful cultural niceties in Vienna, people in the city passed days and nights waltzing, wining, and whiling away the hours. They engaged in light talk while listening to music in the congenial atmosphere of the coffeehouse or busied themselves with appreciating the theater, relishing the opera, flirting with attractive companions, or making love. If they weren't actively pursuing pleasure, they were dreaming it.[348]

A city with no common language, Vienna fairly represented the four corners of the Austro-Hungarian Empire. There were Bohemian theaters, Italian operas, French singers, and Polish clubs. Some cafés were German in character, but others might offer newspapers in Czech, Slavic, Polish, and Hungarian, but not in German. And if you happened to be German, your wife might be a Galician or Pole, your cook a Bohemian, your valet a Serb, your coachman a Slav, your barber a Magyar, your tutor a Frenchman, and your nursemaid a Dalmatian! Vienna was the capital of finance, fashion, and culture. A shortage of money could not dim the city's luster in this golden era, and the Viennese exhibited a persistent *joie de vivre* even as the Austro-Hungarian Empire faced impending doom.[349]

After returning to Vienna in early 1908, Adolf slid into a life of indolence and self-indulgence like the one he had begun to follow before his mother's death. His only hope of an art career lay in retaking and passing the entrance exam for the Academy of Fine Art, but he did nothing to improve his chances.[350] After many idle months, he submitted drawings that he hoped would qualify him to reapply for admission in mid-September, but they were so poorly regarded that he was not even allowed to take the examination.

After this crushing blow, Adolf was faced with the problem of how to survive, but he did not tell Gustl or his Aunt Johanna about his rejection by the academy. Instead, he stayed in bed most mornings, hung around the Schönbrunn Palace on fine afternoons, poring over books and fantasizing over grandiose architectural plans, and stayed up late into the nights to draw. Drifting aimlessly, he had no idea what he would do to support himself when his money ran out.[351]

Gustl and Adolf lived in the 6th District of Vienna, close to the Westbahnhof, an unattractive part of the city where soot-covered tenement buildings with dark inner courtyards lined dismal unlit streets. The two lived a Spartan life in a miserable room that stank of paraffin, with crumbling plaster walls and bug-ridden beds.[352] Gustl later wrote that Adolf often went hungry: "For days on end he could live on milk and bread and butter only." He pressed his trousers by spreading them under the mattress so he could go to the Burgtheater or the opera several times a week.[353]

The roommates coexisted in their humble lodgings through the end of 1908. Adolf even thought the relationship was "exclusive," but Gustl invited a young female music student to their apartment, and Adolf flew into a rage, adamantly insisting on the futility of women studying.[354] Because of Adolf's hate-filled tirades at everything and everybody, Gustl began to think his friend was becoming unbalanced. They seemed to reflect an outsized ego, desperate for acceptance and unable to come to terms with his personal insignificance and mediocrity.[355] He had failed to fulfill his dream of becoming an artist, whereas Gustl had succeeded as a music teacher. The relationship had run its course.

Unable to continue paying for the lodging he shared with Gustl, Adolf moved to the other side of Westbahnhof on Felberstrasse, to an even cheaper apartment in a dilapidated building overlooking the railroad yard, where he celebrated his twentieth birthday on April 20, 1909. Month after month, he endured cheerless surroundings, still drifting and dreaming of success. His neighbors recalled only that he was polite and distant, but the cashier of a nearby restaurant, the Café Kubata, was impressed, "because he was very reserved and quiet, and would read books, and seemed very serious, unlike the rest of the young men."[356]

Drawn as he had been initially to Vienna, Adolf began to feel repelled by "the dubious magic of the national melting pot." As success persistently eluded him, he spent time ferreting out the evils of the city, and evils there were: Behind the resplendent royal palace, imposing civic buildings, elegant cafés, spacious parks, and splendid boulevards lay human misery as deep as any in Europe.[357] Vice, prostitution, and other crimes were rampant in areas where people lacked adequate food, clothing, and shelter.[358] Hitler would later tell how his exposure to deprivation and poverty among the outcasts of society sharpened his world view and shaped his political understanding. Using two chapters of *Mein Kampf* to give an account of these years, he wrote, "Vienna was and remained for me the hardest, most thorough school of my life."[359]

With his savings completely depleted, Adolf was forced to leave even the apartment on Felberstrasse in August of 1909. Throughout that autumn, he slept in the open, moving into cheap lodgings only when wet and cold conditions forced him indoors. For at least three months, he disappeared into the underworld of poverty, unable or unwilling to work. He wandered aimlessly, sleeping in parks and doorways, and for a time, his home was a bench in the Prater. Once he found shelter in laborers' barracks, a dirty refuge that he shared with other homeless people. While there, he reportedly could not sleep because of the foul air and the constant noise of a crying child or a drunk beating his wife.[360]

Adolf had been interested in architectural drawing, and despite his lack of a high school diploma, the School of Architecture was still open to him. But he made no effort to apply and still exhibited no inclination toward learning a trade or seeking regular employment. To earn enough to eat, he took odd jobs like shoveling snow, beating carpets, or carrying bags outside the Westbohnhof.[361] During the weeks before Christmas 1909, he reached rock bottom: a foot-sore, thin, and bedraggled Adolf, in filthy, lice-ridden clothes, joined the ranks of the destitute and discarded. At the age of twenty, the would-be artist had found his way to the flop-houses of the homeless, among tramps and winos, in society's basement.[362]

While staying at the laborers' barracks, Adolf met someone who made a living selling addresses of people who might be soft touches for door-to-door begging. He agreed to a fifty-fifty split of the proceeds and set off with special instructions for each customer: He was to greet an old lady with, "Praised be Jesus Christ," and say he was an unemployed church painter. While she usually gave two kronen for such a story, Adolf got only religious platitudes for his trouble. He had better luck asking his Aunt Johanna for money, for she responded with a fifty-kronen bank note. The first thing he bought was a winter coat, as he had a cough that was getting worse.[363]

In February 1910, the money from Aunt Johanna allowed Adolf to move into the Männerheim, a men's home in the 20th District at 27 Meldemanstrasse, near the Danube. The new facility had been built only a few years earlier with private donations, largely from wealthy Jewish families. Residents had private cubicles that could be retained on an indefinite basis, though they had to be vacated during the day. There was a canteen where the men could obtain meals and alcohol-free drinks and a kitchen where they could prepare food. There was also a laundry, a small library, and a reading room and lounge where newspapers were available.[364]

At the Männerheim, Adolf made his second close friend, Reinhold Hanisch, who provided the only testimony about his first months there. Hanisch described Adolf as appearing at the dorm in a shabby blue-checkered suit, tired and hungry.[365] Seeing potential in the skinny, woebegone young man, Reinhold encouraged Adolf to paint postcards and scenes of Vienna that Reinhold could peddle. Adolf painted on a long wooden table in the lounge on the first floor of the men's home, and the two shared the proceeds from Reinhold's door-to-door sales.[366]

Adolf and Reinhold achieved some commercial success when Adolf began painting advertising posters for shopkeepers. One poster promoted "Teddy's Perspiration Powder," one depicted Santa Claus selling bright-colored candles, and another showed St. Stephen's Gothic spire rising out of a mountain of soap.[367] Adolf could complete one painting a day, and Reinhold could sell it for five kronen, making a modest living for both of them. But Reinhold could sell faster than Adolf could paint, and by the summer of 1910, he was increasingly frustrated with his friend's failure to keep up with orders. The partnership disintegrated completely when Adolf accused Reinhold of withholding fifty kronen from the sale of a painting.

Debates in the reading room about Austrian politics were more than sufficient to distract Adolf from painting.[368] And when his Aunt Johanna died, she left him an inheritance that greatly reduced his need to work. It provided enough for Adolf to maintain his life style and practice political oratory on any audience that would listen, either at the Männerheim or elsewhere in the city.[369] Adolf's life receded into relative obscurity after his business with Reinhold ended, but when he resurfaced in 1912, he was still at the Männerheim, having become an established member of the community and a central figure within his own social group.[370]

At the turn of the twentieth century, as noted earlier, Austria's politics were dominated by growing nationalism among minority groups. The long reign of Franz Josef on the Habsburg throne implies stability, but Austria was being rocked by ethnic conflict, and it was struggling to cope with social and political forces that were tearing it apart. Fear and anxiety were in the air because people sensed that their way of life was under attack. Small tradesmen and craftsmen resented the development of department stores and mass production, and the liberal bourgeoisie were threatened by the rise of organized labor, reminding them of Marx's prophecy that they were doomed to come under the rule of the proletariat. Heavy on the minds of many was the thought that the old order was crumbling.[371]

With a population of more than two million, 1910 Vienna was the center for movements that were challenging the ancient autocracy of the Habsburgs. But the new democratic energy was mixed with a liberal dose of fear, giving rise to an increase in the political rhetoric of overt anti-Semitism. During the second half of the nineteenth century, Vienna's population had grown faster than any other major city apart from Berlin, and it included a sizeable Jewish minority.[372] The number of Jews had increased from about 6,000 to 175,318 and from 2 to 8.6 percent of the city's population. Many of them had become an integral part of Vienna's liberal society and assimilated into the city's German culture, but those who had fled from pogroms in Eastern Europe and Russia had moved into poor neighborhoods where doctrines of Marxism and Zionism were popular. This made it possible for politicians and others to blame the Jews for being both capitalist exploiters and social revolutionaries.[373]

There were three major political parties in the Austria of Hitler's day: Pan-German Nationalists, Social Democrats, and Christian Socialists. Hitler took issue with all of them, but he later applied useful political strategies he observed in each one. He would not repeat their mistakes when he formed his own National Socialist Party, and these early lessons would help him to seize control of a nation.[374]

Pan-German Nationalism was led for a time by the aggressive voice of Georg Ritter von Schönerer. Born to wealthy Viennese parents, Schönerer's brand of politics was anti-liberal, anti-socialist, anti-catholic, and anti-Habsburg, but most of all, anti-Jew.[375] Linz was a hotbed of nationalism, but Hitler was not known to be active in Schönerer's movement when he lived there. Still, he probably shared the Pan-German derision of the very state to which his father had devoted his life.[376] Popular support for Schönerer had waned by the time Hitler arrived in Vienna, but he would later use three signature tactics learned from the aging politician: the use of anti-Semitism as a unifying political theme, the breaching of no tolerance for democratic decision-making, and the promotion of an obligatory "Heil!" as a self-aggrandizing salute.[377]

Hitler quickly recognized the failure of the Pan-German Nationalists to appeal to the masses or win support from powerful institutions such as the church, army, or cabinet. But he agreed with them that the Austrian empire was sinking into a "foul morass" that could be saved only if the master race, the Germans, reasserted absolute authority over inferior people such as the Slavs and Czechs, and he advocated the abolition of Parliament and an end to "all this democratic nonsense."[378]

With every fiber of his being, Hitler hated the Social Democrats because they embraced internationalism, equality, universal suffrage, union rights, and separation of church and state.[379] He also abhorred their "disgraceful courting of the Slavic comrade." But he admired their ability to use propaganda to effectively stimulate a mass movement and make use of "spiritual and physical terror."[380] As a quarter of a million workers in red armbands paraded by him for two hours, he was mesmerized by the endless columns of demonstrators marching four abreast. He watched "with baited breath the gigantic human dragon slowly winding by," and realized the value of intimidation, concluding that "the psyche of the great masses is not receptive to anything that is half hearted and weak."[381] No more precise analysis of Nazi tactics was ever written than his response to the display:

I achieved an equal understanding of the importance of physical terror toward the individual and the masses ... For while in the ranks of their supporters the victory achieved seems a triumph of the justice of their own cause, the defeated adversary in most cases despairs of the success of any further resistance.[382]

While he was living in Vienna, Hitler embraced the leader of the Christian Socialist Party as his new hero: the big, blustery, genial mayor of the city, Dr. Karl Lueger. Lueger had won political support with a heady brew of populist and rabble-rousing rhetoric, appealing both to the piety of Catholics and the economic self-interest of German-speaking lower middle-class citizens. Many in the lower middle class felt their very existence threatened by international capitalism, Marxist social democracy, and Slavic nationalism; but they now controlled city politics through their mayor. As Lueger organized a powerful political party, Hitler was watching.[383]

The tactic Lueger used across the board to whip up support was anti-Semitism. As early as 1890, with no dissenting response, he had given a speech quoting a remark made by one of Vienna's wildest anti-Semites, saying the Jewish problem would be solved, and a service to the world achieved, if all Jews were placed on a large ship to be sunk on the high seas. And in 1899, to thunderous applause, he said that Jews were exercising unimaginable terrorism over the masses through their control of capital and the press.[384]

From a family of modest means, Lueger had worked his way through the University of Vienna, and even his opponents conceded that he was a man of considerable intellect who was generous and tolerant in his private life.[385] The eminent Austrian Jewish writer, Stefan Zweig, wrote that Lueger never allowed his public anti-Semitism to stop him from being helpful and friendly to Jews.[386] But, influenced by Schönerer's ideas, Lueger made political capital out of anti-Semitism, and it struck a chord, especially among those who were suffering economically. Whether they were associated in people's minds with main-street financiers or back-street peddlers, Jews became the focus of ever-growing resentment.[387]

Though the two never met, when Lueger died in 1911, Hitler stood among the mourning thousands who watched his funeral cortége pass by. He would later emulate the man who built up his political party by understanding modern social problems and swaying the masses with propaganda and powerful oratory. He most certainly realized enormous political gains from popularizing hatred against the Jews.[388]

A third close friend of Hitler's was Karl Honish, who lived with him in the Männerheim. Honish claimed never to have heard Hitler rail against the Jews, noting that most of Hitler's favorite actors and singers were Jewish, and he had expressed gratitude for Jewish character, of which he acknowledged he had been a beneficiary. Two of Hitler's closer associates at the Männerheim were Jewish: a one-eyed locksmith named Robinsohn, who had helped him financially, and an art dealer, Josef Neumann, who took pity on his tattered attire and gave him a long frock coat.[389]

In truth, we do not know for certain why, or even when, Hitler became an obsessive and passionate anti-Semite. His admiration for Karl Lueger certainly affected his understanding of anti-Semitism as a political strategy.[390] And one of the racist periodicals he was likely to have read, *Ostara*, first appeared in 1905, when he was only sixteen. The magazine was the product of the warped imagination of an eccentric former monk, Adolf Lanz, who embraced homo-erotic notions of a struggle between the heroic and creative "blond" race and a race of dark men who preyed on women of the blond race with primitive lust. The animal instincts of the dark "beast men" were corrupting and destroying the culture of the human race. Lanz advocated the purification and domination of the blond race through the slavery and forced sterilization—even extermination—of the inferior races, the complete subordination of Aryan women to their husbands, and the crushing of corrupting influences such as socialism, democracy, and feminism.[391] *Ostara* also stirred in its readers an intense fear of the limitless power of Jews, their control of money, their ascendency in the world of art and theater, and their "strange attraction to women."[392]

Whether Lanz's ideas had any direct influence on Hitler's thinking is questionable, but he probably read *Ostara* and other racist papers which were prominent on Vienna's newsstands.[393] Anti-Semitic literature was popular in Vienna then, and the young Hitler was an avid reader. He had experienced bereavement, rejection, isolation, and dire poverty, and the gulf between his self-image as a great artist and the frustrating reality of his life as a dropout needed an explanation. The city's anti-Semitic gutter press may have helped him to find it.[394]

Hitler remained at the Männerheim until May 1913, but Vienna had little more to offer him, and he was beginning to look toward Germany when he thought of his future. Some said he wanted to leave Austria to escape military service because the draft board had finally caught up with him. He was not averse to fighting, but he loathed the idea of serving in the eclectic Austro-Hungarian army that included many minorities. Hitler had spent five and a half years loving and hating the glamorous capital of the Habsburgs, and his experiences there would have a lasting influence.[395] It was in Vienna that he had encountered many ideas and techniques he would use to build his own political party and lead it to power in Germany. In *Mein Kampf,* he wrote:

Vienna was and remained for me the hardest, though most thorough school of my life. I had set foot in this town while still half a boy and I left it a man, grown quiet and grave. In this period there took shape within me a world picture and a philosophy which became the granite foundation of all my acts. In addition to what I then created, I have had to learn little; and I have had to alter nothing.[396]

If Hitler's anti-Semitism took root in Vienna, why was it unnoticed by the friends who were closest to him? There is the account of his emotional outpouring of gratitude to Dr. Bloch, the Jewish physician who cared for his mother in Linz. His friend Reinhold Hanisch was adamant that Adolf "was by no means a Jew hater," emphasizing Hitler's friendship with Jews who had given him help when he was down and out.[397] And his friend Karl Honish corroborated this.

Given Hitler's virulent hatred for the Jews, well documented between 1919 and the end of his life, it is hard to believe he was not influenced to become anti-Semitic when he lived in Vienna—one of the most anti-Jewish cities in Europe. We know that he admired Karl Lueger and had seen anti-Semitism used as an effective tool to garner political support; he had read anti-Semitic publications, and anti-Semitic attitudes were generally pervasive in the city. The answer to why his anti-Semitism went unnoticed among his friends and acquaintances could be that it was nearly invisible in a place where anti-Semitic sentiment was so prevalent; his own prejudice may not have exceeded that of the average resident of the city.[398] It is most likely that Hitler developed a deeply personal and systematic anti-Semitism after he left Vienna.

Whatever the case, Hitler went on to develop a burning hatred of the Jews that spread a fire already ignited in central Europe. His dictatorship would lead to a massacre of innocents—men, women, and children—on such a scale that it will leave a scar on the human psyche for as long as humanity exists.[399] The Holocaust demonstrates how a modern society can enter into intense ideological warfare using weapons of fear and hatred to bring about calculated brutality on a level that can hardly be imagined. It is more than the story of one dictator's drive to destroy the

Jews; it reveals humanity's descent into a maelstrom of evil, where heinous acts of murder against unarmed citizens of multiple nations were routinely committed by ordinary people "just following orders," while many looked the other way. It is a reflection of the dark potential of our own human nature.[400]

CHAPTER 7

From Humanitarianism Through Nationalism to Bestiality

In the spring of 2014, the front-page headline of a national U.S. newspaper declared that Eastern Ukraine would begin to register Jews. While this turned out to be a hoax, it is one indication that anti-Semitism still lurks in the hearts of Eastern Europeans. Have we learned nothing from the Holocaust?

Jews have been the scapegoat for any number of human calamities over thousands of years. During the Middle Ages, they were blamed for causing the plague, and in the nineteenth century, for every financial disaster that people perpetuated upon themselves. Anti-Semitism was not invented by Adolf Hitler and the Nazi gangsters who acted out racist ideas expressed by others before them. The murderous "final solution" of the Nazis was fueled by the hatred of centuries.[401] Cranks, demagogues, and even theologians and philosophers had been among those who saw Jews as outcasts who were less than human and capable of perpetrating almost any crime. Underpinning the most radical form of anti-Semitism was a smoldering sense that Jews had no right to exist.[402]

Jews had been settling in Vienna since the early thirteenth century, and the city's Jewish population had become the largest in German-speaking Europe by the time Hitler was rising to power. Anti-Semitism had long been alive and well, and there was no shortage of justifications. One of the few occupations open to Austrian Jews was money lending, which helped to maintain the economy and the lifestyle of the aristocracy, but the practice aroused envy and distaste among non-Jews. The Catholic dictionary defined the term "usury" as requiring interest from a needy man, and Jewish money lenders charged interest. This gave Christians a reason to condemn them, even as they benefitted from the loans. The Church also blamed Jews for rejecting Christ as the Messiah, holding them responsible for the crucifixion of Jesus, or the murder of God.

Though such allegations had been commonplace since the Middle Ages, active persecution increased during historical periods of crisis.[403] When threatened by economic woes, widespread disease, or other societal ills, people readily blamed the Jews for their problems to the point that some committed violent acts against them, untroubled by the consequences of their behaviors.

When the Black Plague ravaged Europe in the mid-fourteenth century, Jews were accused of poisoning the wells to start an epidemic that would stamp out Christianity. In AD 1348, more than 1,400 Jewish men, women, and children were burned to death in the town of Mühldorf in the archbishopric of Salzburg. In the next century, on March 12, 1421, people in Vienna were so disturbed by their indebtedness to Jewish money lenders that they burned to death 214 Jewish men and women who refused to be baptized as Christians. Vienna's poorer Jews were merely set adrift on the Danube to fend for themselves. Jews left alive in the city were imprisoned in the synagogue, where many committed suicide. These and similar events in 1420-21 earned Vienna the title of "City of Blood" in Jewish memory.[404]

With the discovery of the New World in 1492, popular views began to broaden as Europeans were introduced to human beings who lived their lives in a way totally different from their own. Travelers and missionaries brought back stories of a culture whose existence raised doubts as to whether all peoples of the world had evolved from one source, causing some to question the traditional Christian explanation of history.[405]

Beginning with the Renaissance and continuing into the eighteenth century, a rationalistic way of thinking developed with the spirit of criticism being its primary characteristic. Using logic and reason, Rationalists explained human society, natural and historical phenomena, and even the nature of man, concluding that religious views were the products of imagination and delusion.[406] This new perspective provided a basis for portraying both Christians and Jews as superstitious fools. Christians repudiated Judaism as they always had, but they could not ignore it, because it was the ground from which Christianity had sprung.[407]

The Rationalist argument invalidating Christian doctrine was a central factor in changing the status of Jews, but the change was not ultimately favorable. Rationalism benefitted the Jews by encouraging their emancipation in their areas of residence, but from the beginning, opponents fought to delay, obstruct, or limit emancipation based on the ancient Christian doctrine that disparaged the Jews because of their sin of rejecting Jesus as the savior of mankind. And wherever Rationalist criticism successfully undermined Christianity, it struck a blow to all religious teaching and practice, including Judaism, itself a system of beliefs, ceremonies, and rituals. Even when Rationalists were speaking out against only Christianity, the same arguments could be easily used against Judaism, and this gave society one more reason to denigrate the bearers of the religion, the Jews.[408]

Among philosophers who emerged in England and France during the eighteenth century were the Deists. Though their name implies faith in God, Deists launched an attack on traditional Christianity, including its beliefs and rituals. They also rejected Judaism and its biblical literature, as they were the basis for Christian theology. Like the Rationalists, Deists believed that people did not need religion in order to lead a moral life because they could decide to do right by virtue of their own reason and understanding.[409] They condemned equally the Old and the New Testaments and did not regard the Bible as revelation, concluding that biblical morality conflicted with qualities which human reason demanded of a good and just God. As one proof of their thinking, they cited a story found in the Old Testament Book of Judges, in which Jephthah agrees to sacrifice his daughter, his only child, if God will lead him to victory over the Ammonites. Would a good God accept such a bargain? This was among many examples Deists used to support their conclusion that the Bible was based on ignorance rather than revelation.[410]

Deism nourished the views of the eighteenth-century French philosopher Voltaire, who did more than any other individual to shape a brand of Rationalism that moved European society toward improving the status of Jews. During the early 1750s, Voltaire launched a vigorous effort to undermine the authority of the Church and promote tolerance in matters of belief.[411] While his arguments would ultimately lead to improving the situation of the Jews in Europe, Voltaire's Rationalist approach led him to find as much fault with the Jews as the more traditional anti-Semites who were driven by fear, resentment, and dogma.

Voltaire discounted the traditional Christian notion that the Jews were a divinely forsaken community, but he also categorically challenged the foundation of any ideology, philosophy, or religion that was based on the concept of biblical revelation. And though his primary target was Christianity, he attacked Judaism as its source. And he sought to reduce the stature of the Jewish people by arguing that their culture had no value.[412]

In his early works, Voltaire looked at Jewish history in the same way he looked at all of human history. Using the four criteria he developed to inquire into the history and nature of any group within human society, he found the Jewish people deficient: His first criterion was morality, and he concluded that many among the generations of Jews in biblical literature were guilty of cruelty and deceit as well as sexual promiscuity, upon which he frowned sternly.

Voltaire's second criterion was reason. In evaluating the behaviors of past generations of Jews to determine whether they were based on reason or on superstition, he concluded that Jewish ceremonies and rituals served no purpose other than to appease God and that a rational God would not command people to engage in meaningless acts. He also regarded belief in a divine source for things like rain or rainbows as evidence of an intellectually immature people.

His third criterion was contribution to society. He examined biblical history for examples of Jewish contributions in the areas of art, literature, science, and technology to determine if they brought greater elegance, beauty, and functionality to human life. He concluded that Jews were primarily nomadic shepherds or primitive farmers who did not satisfy this requirement.

Voltaire's fourth criterion was the ability to sustain a proper political system. The fact that the Jews were twice exiled from their land was, for him, evidence that they lacked the qualities necessary for sustaining a state. Because Jews were often participants in commerce and money-lending activities, he argued that their chief occupations required far different qualities than those of the soldier or statesman.[413]

Christians could use Voltaire's analysis to bolster their own anti-Semitism. They had long harbored and perpetuated similar views—that the Jews were a people whose anachronistic traditions and strange language and customs alienated them from the broader community, that they had little contact with non-Jews except for business dealings such as usury and trade, and they were devoted to their brethren but hostile to others. These negative views caused Christians to maintain a sense of superiority, if not hostility, toward the Jews.[414]

In spite of his overt anti-Semitism, Voltaire was a harbinger of the modern age, the Age of Reason, and he differed from other anti-Semites in one important way: With the spread of knowledge by philosophers like himself, Voltaire hoped that abuses of the authorities would cease and that the state would be governed by the enlightened principles of humanism and tolerance. Less than a generation after his death in 1778, a fundamental shift did take place. Rationalism swept the countries of Europe to find expression in the French Revolution, and the emancipation of Jews in their lands of residence soon followed.

Jews were tolerated more than before, but they were still on the margins of society. It would prove to be impossible for them to become citizens with equal political rights as long as persistent negative perceptions remained dominant.[415]

During the reign of Maria Theresa from 1740 to 1780, there was only a small population of Jews in Vienna because they had been expelled by Emperor Leopold in 1673. Some Jews had slowly trickled back from Spain, Portugal, Holland, and Italy, and though most of them were wealthy, they had no political status and were completely dependent on the favor of the monarch. Maria Theresa had virtually forced participation in commerce on them by limiting their employment to financial operations such as money lending and jewel trading. Even though she was among the more enlightened rulers, Maria Theresa was a religious bigot who insisted that Jews stay out of sight on Sunday mornings and holidays.[416]

The 1780 accession of Maria Theresa's son, Emperor Josef II, marked the beginning of a new era for Austrian Jews. As an avid reader of Voltaire's philosophy, Josef was the first modern European ruler to rescind medieval laws that had so restricted Jewish life. Though Jews could still not enter the civil service or own land, Josef's Edict of Tolerance in 1782 improved their educational opportunities, and this made them more useful to the state. Under Josef, Austria was the first country to allow complete tolerance in religious affairs, preceding the United States and France.

Josef also made Austria the first country in Europe to grant Jews the status of natural citizens. The very fact that the emperor acknowledged their right to be citizens and permanent residents was revolutionary for the Jews of Austria.[417]

Jewish economic, social, and political gains did not prevent anti-Semitism from continuing to raise its ugly head. On the contrary, the progress of the Jews in a Catholic society served to heighten the hostility of those opposed to the integration of the Jews into that society. Naturalization and emancipation were regarded by Jews and their supporters as lofty ideals whose realization righted grave wrongs committed by blind and ignorant forces for generations. But opponents of the Jews saw these new freedoms as a perilous threat, and they sought to make this clear in no uncertain terms.

Despite the spread of the Enlightenment and Rationalism, many held the traditional Church view that Jews were destined to be oppressed, to suffer, and to experience degradation for the sin of having rejected Jesus. If the Jew had been a thorn in the side of the Christian when on the outer fringes of society, how much greater a threat would he be as a citizen in the very midst of their society?[418] The death of Josef II in early 1790 marked a surge in anti-Semitism caused by the negative public reaction to the gains Jews had made under the liberal emperor. It would result in a complete reversal of many of the reforms in Josef's Edict of Tolerance and end the country's leading role in moving toward the full emancipation of the Jews.

The Congress of Vienna, ending in 1815, had produced a spirit of cooperation among European countries that extended to a more benign political attitude toward Judaism, but books were appearing that focused on Jewish ethnicity and race rather than their religion. In 1818, Ludolf Holst wrote a popular book containing allegations against the Jews disguised as facts. Accusing the Jews of corruption, Holst said they were selling shoddy second-hand clothes imported from England, debasing the currency by "clipping" coins (decreasing the amount of precious metal in a coin), trading in "paper money," and performing fictitious banking transactions.

Holst's methodology was quite simple: He enumerated societal hardships that were the subject of current complaints and blamed them on the Jews: Spiraling prices, unemployment, the decline of morality, and an increase in the number of children's asylums because people could not sustain families. Naturally, no proof was offered, but since the hardships were painfully real, his statements fell on ready ears. Holst used the misery resulting from wars, unstable governments, and economic ills to argue that the Jews had extracted advantages from the suffering of others. He predicted that if the Jews were not stopped, they would take over the livelihood of Christians.[419]

Josef II's Edict of Tolerance had offered unprecedented opportunities for Jews, including admission to the University of Vienna. This allowed them to take an active part in the intellectual life of Vienna and to gradually become prominent in the legal and medical professions. However, by becoming conspicuously successful, they became targets to those looking for scapegoats. In 1842, writer Anton E. von Rosas published a book, *On the Sources of Medical Discontent*, to make the case that the disproportionate increase in the number of doctors who were Jews had caused a general deterioration of the profession. His conclusion read: "The Israelite as he is may and should become peasant, artisan, artist, indeed anything in the world rather than doctor, jurist or theologian for Christians." He was not alone in thinking that a preconceived right of Christians to certain professions was endangered by competition from the Jews.[420]

Adolf Fischhoff, a thirty-two-year-old Jewish medical student, stood on the streets of Vienna to deliver the opening speech of the 1848 Revolution, and Jews were prominent in every phase of the uprising. This caused conservatives to identify them with unwelcome change.[421] Though the imperial government was forced to accept a new constitution granting equal rights to all citizens regardless of religion, it was a concession quickly retreated from when the revolution was suppressed in 1849.[422] Jews were once again forbidden to own land, although they were allowed to retain property they had already purchased, and they could not hold public office, including teaching positions.[423]

Throughout Europe, the Revolution of 1848 was about nationalism, but in the vast Austro-Hungarian Empire, nationalism carried the added dimension of hate. The Hungarians hated the German-Austrians, the Czechs, and the Croats; the German-Austrians hated the Hungarians; the Czechs hated almost everybody, and they were all united in hating the Jews. In theory, nationalism and liberalism implied greater tolerance of minorities, but this was not true in practice. Some saw the Jews as being in league with the government against them, while others feared them as revolutionaries. It became convenient and popular for anti-Semites to accuse Jewish bankers and businessmen of controlling virtually the entire Austrian economy through the banks and the stock exchange.[424]

In 1860, 6,000 Jews lived in Vienna, representing only about 2 percent of the population. Through most of the 1870s, anti-Semitism seemed to be abating, and Jews who spoke fluent German were considered, by themselves and their non-Jewish neighbors, to be German-Austrian. Austria became a country where a young Jewish man could study to become an officer in the army and to accomplish within his lifetime the transition from life in the Jewish ghetto to life as a respected citizen of Vienna, then the most glamorous capital in Europe.[425] With thrift, diligence, ingenuity, and intelligence, Jews gained prominence in nearly every walk of life during these years. They were assimilated into Austrian society at an amazing speed and were soon among the distinguished in letters, music, medicine, history, science, and the theatre. They greatly enriched Austria's culture and contributed significantly to its economic life.[426]

Why then, did Austria, particularly Vienna, become the center of European anti-Semitism? First, Jewish business success contributed to the rise of capitalism in Austria to a greater degree than it did in other countries. Capitalism itself was introduced in Austria mainly by Jews, and to some, Jews appeared to almost embody capitalism, including its elements of undisguised greed and corruption.[427] Jewish money lenders of the Habsburg Court built the Austrian railways and helped to develop Austrian industry and trade on a grand scale. Partly because the majority of the population held a traditional disdain for commerce, work in this sector had been readily accessible to Jews. An alien race had been restricted to less-respected occupations and then hated for it.[428]

The rapidity with which Austria entered the modern industrialized world brought an inevitable clash between traditionalism, represented primarily by the Catholic Church, and secularism. The conflict was far more striking in Austria than in countries like Britain and France, where modernization happened more gradually. The Austrian Catholic Church was still a powerful and authoritative institution, and it bitterly opposed the trend toward liberalism, democracy, Marxism, capitalism, and especially secularism, all of which it associated with the Jews. The small shopkeepers in Vienna hated the city's large department stores, whose owners were mostly Jewish. Industrial workers often despised the Jewish owners of the factories where they worked. While many thought that religious anti-Semitism was becoming obsolete in an increasingly secular world, well-organized political parties were making racial anti-Semitism a strategic part of their propaganda.[429]

A byproduct of growing nationalism, racial anti-Semitism was an invention of the nineteenth century that began to infect much of Europe as a result of the Napoleonic Wars. Frederick Grillparzer, the great Austrian poet and dramatist who witnessed this development during his lifetime, summed up the new nationalism and its unintended consequences in one prophetic phrase: "From humanitarianism through nationalism to bestiality."[430]

The concept of Jewish alienation lay at the bottom of anti-Semitic writings. Theodor Fritsch (1852-1933) was the main exponent of propaganda intended to undermine the position of the Jews by distorting their religion, character, and mentality. An engineer by training, Fritsch joined the anti-Semitic movement at the age of twenty-nine, when he wrote his first anti-Jewish pamphlet. He relied on the slow but methodical indoctrination of the public with anti-Semitic ideas, which he believed could be effectively absorbed and promoted by people of any political party, social trend, or religion. He strove to convince all of his non-Jewish contemporaries, regardless of their convictions, that Jews must be opposed because they were a destructive species who lacked morality.

Fritsch's first pamphlet, produced in 1881, depicted Jews as enemies of mankind: deceitful, parasitic beings incapable of reforming themselves by baptism or any means. He wrote that Semites were degenerate sub-humans compared with physically and mentally superior Aryans. His handbook of anti-Semitism, published in 1896, went through thirty-six editions before World War I, no doubt reaching millions of readers.[431]

Fritsch was one of the first anti-Semites to propose that Jesus was of Aryan descent. Many Passion Plays during this time were cast with Aryan-looking blonds playing the role of Jesus. Eleven of the twelve disciples were also played by Aryans, but, of course, Judas Iscariot was always portrayed by someone who looked more typically Jewish. This increasingly popular version of the Christian story was laying the groundwork for a racist outlook on all of human history, and on the history of the Jews in particular.[432]

Anti-Semitism was quickly moving to a new level, and using the racial factor to interpret Christianity was becoming a central theme for writers like Fritsch and Houston Stewart Chamberlain (1855-1927), an Englishman by birth but a German by choice. His widely read book, *Foundations of the 19th Century*, prophesied German national ascendancy. While Fritsch had emphasized the difference between the lowly, despicable Semites and the gifted, admirable Aryans, Chamberlain believed that positive or negative qualities were not innate to any race. He rather proposed that the qualities of each race were due to the fortunate or unfortunate blending of that race with various virtues or vices. For Chamberlain, this apportioning of virtues had led to the highest standard of human qualities in the Germanic peoples, but the lowest standard in the Jewish people, who had suffered greatly from the consequences of racial bastardization.

Chamberlain claimed that the Jews were morally inferior, lacked cultural development, and had little or no religious sensibility.[433] His derogation of Jews went hand in hand with the glorification of Christians, and he saw the figure of Jesus Christ as a stimulus to having the highest order of religious experience. Since he could not possibly credit the Jews with having produced Jesus, he declared Jesus to have been of Aryan origin.[434] Racists used Chamberlain's theories to say that it was scientifically demonstrable that Jews were sensual scoundrels who preyed on German women, and that they were imitators and exploiters compared with Aryans, who were honest, simple, pious, and creative.[435] More than many other anti-Semitic writings, Chamberlain's book had a broad impact and a lasting effect.[436]

In the 1880s, anti-Semitism became a valuable and persistent propaganda weapon in the capable hands of Georg Ritter von Schönerer, a man described in one biography as the "most prominent propagandist and symbol" of anti-Semitism in his day. The rise of the racist Pan-German movement under Schönerer was just one of the difficulties Emperor Franz Josef had to contend with toward the end of his long reign in the late nineteenth century. He publicly repudiated his loyalty to the emperor and his allegiance to the Catholic Church, since he saw them both as betraying the interests of the German people within the empire to appease the demands of Slav nationalists.[437]

Schönerer believed that race ought to be the criterion for all civil rights.[438] Like a growing number of anti-Semites of his day, he said the fight ought to be not against the Jewish religion but against the racial characteristics of the Jews. And though his was a dominant voice, he was not the only politician who appealed to new groups of voters using anti-elitist and anti-intellectual demagoguery, directly and indirectly targeting the Jews.[439]

Schönerer's influence was bolstered by the broadening of the right to vote in 1882. It is sobering to realize that the steep rise of anti-Semitism after that year was a result of the democratization of Austrian politics. Until then, voting laws had favored the aristocracy and the liberal bourgeoisie, but electoral reform expanded the vote to include all men over twenty-four who paid at least five kronen a year in direct taxes. Overnight, the electorate in Vienna almost tripled from 15,000 to 40,000, and the number of voters increased to 78,000 as the city expanded into the lower middle-class suburbs. The primary beneficiaries of this voter expansion were the anti-capitalist artisans who saw big business and mass production, which they associated with the Jews, as threats to their economic well-being.

Schönerer's popularity had already faded by 1887, when a Viennese newspaper published proof that his wife had a Jewish ancestor. His total support had never exceeded 3 or 4 percent percent of the German-speaking population, but the small number supporting him is far from an accurate reflection of his influence on the increasing anti-Semitism in Austria.[440] From the 1880s until the Republic was formed in 1918, anti-Semitism was a central focus in political life in the German-speaking territories of Austria, especially in Vienna. It is by no means a coincidence that Hitler came from Austria, and that Vienna was the cradle of the brand of anti-Semitism which he espoused and brutally implemented. Without adding anything original to anti-Semitic ideology, Hitler merely amplified and executed the gospel of hatred penned by numerous writers and preached by many speakers well before he came of age in Vienna.[441]

Another of Hitler's predecessors was Karl Lueger, Mayor of Vienna from 1897 until his death in 1910. From Lueger, Hitler learned the technique of inciting racist fear and hatred to promote broad popular support. Lueger's success was greater than Schönerer's because of his superior sense of mass psychology and a determination to win the vote of the peasants, people in the lower middle class, and members of the Catholic Church. Lueger effectively appealed to both Christian anti-Semitism and Austrian patriotism.[442] He was adeptly opportunistic and ready to disavow a principle if it could serve his political purpose: Once a liberal, he later became anti-liberal; he was anti-Semitic, but Jews were never officially persecuted under his administration. When asked why he had so many Jewish friends, he proclaimed, "I decide who is a Jew." He denigrated Jewish peddlers and socialists, but he did not consider wealthy or influential Jews to be Jews at all.[443]

In spite of having a well-run administration that made significant improvements to Vienna's appearance and infrastructure, Lueger's political legacy was disastrous for Austria. To a degree, it was disastrous for the world, as Hitler may have modeled himself after Lueger in using anti-Semitism as a strategy to win the support of the German masses. During the twenty years that the Christian Social Party dominated Vienna, Lueger's opportunistic attitude pervaded the lower middle class. This might explain why the same people who claimed they were ready to die defending their country from the Nazi occupation received Hitler with frantic ovations greater than those they had bestowed on any other human being parading down the streets of Vienna.[444] Austrian essayist Alfred Polgar described this paradox perfectly when he said, "The Germans are first class Nazis, but lousy anti-Semites; the Austrians are lousy Nazis but first class anti-Semites!" His statement summed up the attitudes and behaviors of many Austrians and Germans during the next few years.[445]

Twenty years prior to World War I, prospects for Austrian Jews had looked almost as bright as they had after 1860, when a vibrant Jewish culture began to grow in Vienna. Anti-Semitic statements were still in the air, but active persecution was becoming increasingly rare. By 1910, the Christian Social Party, which had frightened Austrian Jews, had lost its leader, Karl Lueger, and Jews were prospering economically and intellectually as never before. A degree of assimilation was occurring, as intermarriage between Jews and Christians had become fairly commonplace, and some Jews had either ceased practicing their religion or even converted to Christianity.[446] While this may have been an unwelcome trend for Jews concerned about preserving their cultural and religious identity, it appeared to demonstrate that anti-Semitism was on the wane.

It is only through the prism of hindsight that the anti-Semitism of the later nineteenth century or early twentieth century appears as a harbinger of the Hitler catastrophe. Thoughts of eliminating the Jews had arisen among unrestrained anti-Semites long before the racial theories emerged. The negative reaction to Jewish emancipation and progressive success in Vienna and elsewhere was underscored by a thousand years of resentment against Jews and Judaism. Though the intensity of its expression had fluctuated, anti-Semitism had not ended. It remained a latent but mighty force that crystallized first into an idea, next a strategy, then a plan, and ultimately a stark reality: the extermination of Jews by the Nazis.[447]

In the early twentieth century, between 1900 and 1910, the majority of Jews in Vienna were Westernized, pro-Austrian, politically liberal, and prosperous—a people who adhered primarily to Reform Judaism. They represented 63 percent of the city's industrialists, 71 percent of its financiers, 65 percent of its lawyers, 59 percent of its physicians, and more than half of its journalists. A well-known Jewish writer, Jakob Wassermann, observed this when he visited the city in 1898: "All public life was dominated by the Jews, the banks, the press, the theatre, literature, social organizations, all lay in the hands of the Jews." The explanation was easy to find: The aristocracy would have nothing to do with those occupations.[448]

About 25 percent of the Jews in Vienna were recent immigrants from Galicia, today's southern Poland, many of whom were Orthodox Jews. The more assimilated Westernized Jews regarded the *Ostjuden,* or Eastern Jews, with suspicion, if not contempt. Because they were generally less educated and without cultural refinements, their more prosperous brethren sometimes characterized them as loud, coarse, dirty, immoral, backward, or even as being responsible for provoking anti-Semitism.[449]

In 1910, a very real problem in Vienna was a severe housing shortage. There were 1.24 people living in every room within the city, including the kitchen, bathrooms, and front halls. The more recent Jewish immigrants, the *Ostjuden,* were blamed for the housing and economic hardships endured by the entire population. People said that the issue could be solved overnight if only the unwanted immigrants would return to their homeland.[450]

With the beginning of the war in 1914, things got worse. The migration of the Galician Jews to Vienna rapidly expanded, and, in a matter of months, the city's Jewish population increased by 125,000. The new Jewish refugees were mostly penniless peddlers, artisans, and cattle dealers, and they were consistently blamed for the housing and food shortages resulting from the Allied blockade of Austria and Germany. But far worse were the allegations that they were profiteers. Newspaper articles gave the impression that only Jews were involved in illegal activities, while in reality, the number of Jews enriched by the war was tiny compared to the number of Jews impoverished by it. The largest profits were made in the armaments industries and in agriculture, two areas from which Jews were almost completely excluded.[451]

Knowing what we know today about the catastrophe that would engulf the Jews of Germany and Austria, it is easy to say they were living in a fool's paradise. The shots that killed the heir-apparent to the Austro-Hungarian throne on June 28, 1914, brought an almost instant end to a golden age for Viennese Jews. More than four grueling years of war and famine revived Austrian anti-Semitism to the greatest level since the seventeenth century.[452] Anti-Semitism had been festering because the Jews were a minority civilization in a majority environment, but now it was coming to a head. The same point was made repeatedly:

> *The Jew does not truly belong to the country in which he lives, for as the Jew from Poland is not a Pole, the Jew from England is not an Englishman, and the Jew from Sweden is not a Swede ... The Jews are an alien people, they are nothing but guests in the land of their dispersion. So long as they remain Jews their integration with the Christian people of Europe is impossible.*[453]

The outbreak of World War I served not only as a signal for the end of an era but also as a crucial landmark in the development of Jewish history. The war released aggressions and revealed the potential for mass annihilation of human beings on a level never seen before. The carnage that took place on the battlefields was greater than in any other war in human history. For the first time, deaths on an unimaginably large scale occurred in a conflict between civilized societies. The killing, mutilation, and gas poisoning of millions of soldiers on both sides had broken taboos and blunted moral sensibilities.

The harsh realities of World War I stood in stark contrast to pre-war hopes for a Europe whose countries could work together for the common good. The Great War tore at the thin veneer of civilization, and the world was left vulnerable to the disaster that would occur less than twenty years later: the Holocaust—a tragedy that can be understood only by examining historical events in the framework of World War I.[454]

When the Habsburg Monarchy collapsed at the end of The Great War, Austria became an unhappy fragment of a once huge empire, retaining only a remnant of her former greatness. And though it was still the capital city, Vienna was far too big for the new dwarf state of Austria. Austrians longed for their splendid past, disliked the new world as it was, and feared for their future. Their country had become what some historians called "The State nobody wanted."[455]

The Catholic newspaper *Reichsport* placed the blame for Austria's defeat on the Jews, Freemasons, Czechs, and Social Democrats.[456] Questions were raised about the real share Jews had contributed to the war effort, and Jews were accused of shirking their duty, sitting back behind the front lines, and profiteering in the black market.[457] Anti-Jewish propaganda in post-war Austria was unequalled in other European countries for quantity or virulence.[458]

By May 1918, the Austrian Nazi Party was initiated, with a call for the nationalization of monopolies, department stores, and large estates that were not the product of "honest work." This was a thinly disguised anti-Semitic message. The Nazis insisted that the predominance of Jewish banks and bankers in Austria had to be countered, and Dr. Walter Riehl, leader of the new Nazi party, promoted terror on the streets and other violent expressions of racial anti-Semitism.[459] In a speech at a Nazi Party rally on August 31, 1920, Riehl declared: "Our housing shortage could be completely solved if the approximately 200,000 Eastern Jews were expelled because there are about 150,000 Viennese without homes."[460] On April 1, 1921, the Nazi Party considered a resolution supporting the expulsion of all Jews who had immigrated to Vienna after the start of the war. Young people expressed their support by breaking the windows of Jewish stores and attacking Jewish streetcar passengers. Anti-Semitic rallies diminished in 1922, only to reach new heights as hyper-inflation worsened during the early part of 1923.[461]

Hyper-inflation hurt almost everyone, but it had the greatest negative impact on bankers, landlords, merchants, lenders, and savers. Of the twelve Austrian banks that folded in 1920, ten were owned by Jews, but anti-Semites still held Jews responsible for their economic woes.[462] Instead of searching for solutions to societal crises, the majority of Austrians found it easier to blame a familiar scapegoat—a minority group that was perceived as weak.[463]

On November 19, 1923, Nazi students from the University of Vienna invaded the lecture hall of the Anatomy Institute, shouting, "Juden hinaus! (Jews out!)." They gave Jews three minutes to vacate the room. Those who did not leave in time were beaten with rubber clubs and sticks, dragged to the top of the ramp in front of the main building, and thrown off. The police standing nearby did nothing because of "academic freedom," the ancient rule that prevented police from entering a university building.[464]

From the end of 1923 until 1929, there was a period of relative calm, with a general decline in overt expressions of anti-Semitism. First, there was a split in the Austrian Nazi Party between those who were adamantly opposed to Hitler in Germany and those who were fanatically devoted to him, temporarily distracting the Nazis from their anti-Semitic agenda. Additionally, the replacement of the Austrian krone with the schilling in January 1924 had stabilized and improved the Austrian economy despite the high unemployment rate, so there was less blame to place on the Jews.[465]

With savings wiped out by the hyper-inflation, people had nothing to fall back on when the Great Depression hit, and by the early 1930s, the unemployment number had risen to 600,000. The Depression brought anti-Semitism back with a vengeance: Jews already had little political influence, and now they were losing much of their economic clout. By April 1932, an increase in the Nazi Party vote brought with it a more aggressive attitude toward Viennese Jews, and by June of the same year, Nazi youths were openly attacking Jews in the streets. Even people who looked Jewish were targets.[466]

In *A History of the Holocaust*, author Yehuda Bauer claims that the Holocaust can be explained by specific factors operating in German-speaking lands:

I. The lack of national unity that retarded Germany's economic and social development, effectively delaying the rise of a middle class that would have had a vital interest in the establishment of a strong democracy;

2. An increase in German nationalism that always had excluded the Jews;

3. German defeat in World War I that fed the desire of German people to reassert their collective strength, and

4. The economic crisis of the 1920s through the 1930s that destroyed security for individuals and the middle class as a whole.[467]

During The Great Depression, many affected groups blamed the Jews for their financial predicaments. Among them were university students who could not find jobs upon graduation; small shopkeepers who hated the larger department stores, many of which were owned by Jews; industrial workers who felt abused by the factory owners, many of them Jewish; and the Pan-German nationalists, who seized any excuse to justify the idea of a "pure" German Austria. All of these groups believed that their way of life was being fundamentally threatened by the economic calamity that had fallen upon Austria and the world, and they were ready to turn their fear and anger toward the Jews.

In April 1932, political events occurred that increased the risk to the Jewish population: The Austrian Nazi Party garnered 17 percent of the vote throughout Austria. In Vienna alone, the Nazis won 200,000 votes compared to only 27,500 votes two years before. In neighboring Germany, the Nazis won 37 percent of the vote, and a Nazi takeover seemed imminent. Would Austria be next?[468]

Attacks by Nazis on Jewish individuals and businesses in Austria continued throughout the winters of 1932 and 1933. By May, so many stores had been wrecked that non-Jewish businesses displayed swastikas in an attempt to gain immunity from attack. However, not until the Nazis began throwing small bombs into Jewish shops, one of which killed a Jewish jeweler, did the government act by outlawing the Austrian Nazi Party.[469] The Austrian government was under pressure from a number of sources to protect the country's Jews, but it found itself under equal or even greater pressure from Austrian anti-Semites. The government also faced economic pressure from Germany, especially after Hitler gained power in 1933. It therefore tried to steer a middle course by tolerating expressions of political and economic anti-Semitism from lower level officials while not sanctioning it at higher levels.[470]

It is doubtful whether any other single issue in Austria, even the hated Treaty of St. Germain, appealed to so large a cross-section of the population as anti-Semitism. Austria's Christian Social Party was primarily concerned with defending Christianity and the Socialist Party with defending the interests of the working class against the capitalists, but all the major political parties were anti-Semitic. What made the Austrian Nazi Party unique among them was its willingness to use violence against the Jews.[471]

By the early 1930s, Austrian Jews were too splintered, and their Christian allies too few to be effective against the onslaught of anti-Semitism. But just when the Nazis in Austria and Germany were gaining popularity and anti-Semitic violence was reaching unprecedented proportions, the Jews of Austria gained an unexpected ally: The Christian Social Party's new chancellor—thirty-nine-year-old, four-foot, eleven-inch Engelbert Dollfuss. Although Austrian Jews found it difficult to agree on many things, they agreed on giving almost unqualified support to the young chancellor. Their support never wavered, even when Dollfuss dissolved Parliament and forcibly prevented it from reconvening.[472]

From 1933 on, Jewish satirist Karl Kraus was concerned about the threat to Jews from Nazi Germany, and he was convinced that the Social Democrats in both Austria and Germany failed to see the danger represented by the rising power of the Nazis.[473] Kraus watched with mounting disgust the suicide of Austrian democracy under Dollfuss, but he was one of those who supported the chancellor as the only person who could effectively defend Austria against the outlawed Nazi Party.[474]

Dollfuss acted in the spirit of his predecessor, Karl Lueger, but without Lueger's cunning. He broke his oath to the Constitution by abolishing democracy, crushing his socialist opponents, and even dissolving his own party to make room for a perfect fascist state in which he would play the role of dictator.[475] But on July 25, 1934, as he worked in his office, Dollfuss was assassinated by a group of Austrian Nazis. The Jewish newspaper *Die Stimme* memorialized Dollfus as "the only statesman in the world who defended humanity and morality against the Nazis."[476]

The successor to Dollfuss, Kurt von Schuschnigg, presided over a semi-fascist Austrian state. While he launched no official campaign of discrimination against the Jews, the government's power base consisted of pseudo-military organizations such as the Heimwehr, a racial anti-Semitic group. The writing was on the wall, but the world seemed blind. Beginning in 1935, the leader of German Jewry tried to inform the international community of their worsening predicament, but there was little response. Slowly, the Jews of Germany and Austria began to realize that to physically and spiritually survive in an immoral environment, they would have to depend largely on themselves.[477]

Anti-Semitism permeated Austrian public life, and the activities of the illegal Nazi Party grew bolder with every passing day. Secret S.A. and S.S. cells, along with special terrorist commando groups, were actively spreading fear.[478] The vice-mayor of Vienna made several speeches advocating that Jews be banned from trade unions and that their businesses boycotted by Christians. In 1934, a large number of contracts with Jewish physicians who had been working in city hospitals were not renewed. Officially, fifty-eight physicians had lost their jobs because they belonged to the Social Democratic Party, but fifty-six of those released were Jews. Most were not even active in the party, joining only because doing so had been a prerequisite for obtaining the job.[479]

Even for Jews who could see the increasing danger, emigration from Austria was not an easy or simple solution. The chief obstacle was the unwillingness of other countries to accept Austrian Jews, motivated by fears of immigrants swamping the labor market during the world economic crisis. Farmers and miners might be accepted, but middle-class and professional people were not. Immigration to the United States had been limited in the early 1930s, especially after September 8, 1930, when President Herbert Hoover announced: "If the consular officer believes that the applicant may probably be a public charge at any time, even during a considerable period subsequent to his arrival, he must refuse the visa." Consuls who denied immigration to Jews for ethnic or religious reasons frequently cited this directive as the official reason.[480]

When the annexation of Austria as part of Germany occurred on March 13, 1938, many Jews were relatively recent arrivals, having come during the past one hundred years from Polish Galicia or Czech lands. The overwhelming majority lived in Vienna, and most were engaged in trade, small business, and the professions. As late as 1937, Jewish participation in the Viennese economy was significant:

TRADES AND PROFESSIONS	JEWISH REPRESENTATION
Advertising	90%
Furniture Manufacturing	85%
Newspaper	80%
Shoemaking	80%
Lawyers	62%
Physicians	51.6%

While they were well represented in the trades and professions, many Jews lived in great poverty in the slums of Vienna, and 35 percent of Jewish workers were unemployed. After the post-war dissolution of the Habsburg monarchy, dislike of the stranger had increased.[481] The storm clouds were gathering, and the signs were there, but no one wanted to read them. Stefan Zweig, the Austrian Jewish novelist, playwright, journalist, and biographer, was one of the most popular writers in the world during the 1920s and 30s, and he aptly summed up the attitude of the majority of many Viennese Jews:

My house in Salzburg lay so close to the border that with the naked eye I could view Berchtesgaden Mountain on which Adolf Hitler's house stood. This proximity to the German border, however, gave me an opportunity to judge the threat to the Austrian situation better than my friends in Vienna. In that city the café observers and even men in government regarded National Socialism as something that was happening 'over there' and that could in no way affect Austria ... Not even the Jews worried, and they acted as if the canceling of all rights of physicians, lawyers, scholars, and actors was happening in China instead of across the border three hours away where their own language was spoken. They rested comfortably in their homes, rode about in their cars. Moreover, everybody had a ready-made phrase: 'That cannot last long' ... It was the self deception that we practiced because of reluctance to abandon our accustomed life.[482]

CHAPTER 8

Finis Austriae

In Vienna, the New Year has always begun with Carnival Time, and 1938 was no different. Though pressures on the government from neighboring Germany and from Nazis within Austria were increasing each day, the people of Vienna were in a mood to celebrate. They came out in droves to attend the opening ball held outdoors at the neo-Gothic Rathhaus, or city hall, except for the aristocrats, who would attend the ball scheduled near the end of the festivities, just before Lent. At the opening event, revelers ate gallons of goulash, drank huge quantities of wine and beer, and waltzed with abandon until the early morning hours, under the colors of the Austrian flag—red-white-red banners waving over a large parquet dance floor. For one night, at least, no one cared whether the government or the Nazi street mobs were running the country. For one night, it was clear who ruled: the waltz king—Johann Strauss.[483]

The Nazi Party had been outlawed, but Austrians were not going to be able to ignore the Nazis for much longer. On Saturday, February 12, Georg Klaar and his friend Fritzl Pollack entered the Reiss-Bar, a popular establishment well located near Kärntnerstrasse, a high-end shopping street off the Ringstrasse. The tony bar was just the kind of place that appealed to the two young men-about-town. At five o'clock in the evening, the seventeen-year-old youths were the only customers, but they didn't mind. They knew that the impressive burgundy leather wingback chairs and the long, shiny mahogany bar would soon be filled by sophisticated men and glamorous women. A waiter, the only other person in the bar, switched on the radio and turned the dial to a light music station, and Georg and Fritzl prepared to relax. But in the middle of a waltz, the music suddenly stopped, and the young men looked up in surprise to hear the voice of a familiar radio newscaster:

Radio Vienna here. We break off for an official announcement. Following an invitation from the Führer and Reich-Chancellor, Adolf Hitler, Chancellor Dr. Kurt von Schuschnigg, accompanied by Dr. Guido Schmidt, Minister of State for Foreign Affairs, arrived in Berchtesgaden this morning where talks between the German and Austrian leaders are taking place. We are now returning you to the studio for the second part of our afternoon music transmission.[484]

Georg and Fritzl looked at each other, paid for their drinks, and walked out onto the street, unsure of what they would find. There was no sign of any Nazi sympathizers, but the young men decided to head home to be with their families. Georg's father was not nearly as alarmed as he had expected. Ernst Klaar said he had talked with friends who had convinced him the situation was serious, but not hopeless, and that Chancellor Schuschnigg was the right man to negotiate with Hitler. After all, the German Führer had invited the Austrian leaders for a visit to work out their differences, and the government's propaganda made it sound like a cozy afternoon tea-party. The *Wiener Zeitung,* the official government newspaper, used terms like "a friendly discussion ... amiable atmosphere ... frank talks man to man ... and no sensational development." Everything had apparently been lovely in Hitler's mountain garden.[485]

On Monday, February 14, the Austrian government held the final New Year's ball for its most prominent citizens. It was the most lavish and sumptuous dance ever held at the Hofburg Palace, the Habsburg residence in Vienna. Gold-laced diplomats, government ministers, leading bankers, and bejeweled ladies chatted and smiled as they waltzed through the Imperial halls. How many of the important guests were unconcerned about the current political events, and how many harbored hidden feelings of sadness and fear, or even thoughts of treason?[486]

Reports of the last New Year's ball in 1938 reminded Georg Klaar of stories he had heard from his grandmother, Julie, about living with her parents at one of the city's finest addresses, Opernring 3, and gazing out of her window at the elegant attendees of the final ball in 1873. As a young girl, Julie had looked from her window across Opera Square to the corner where the upper end of Kärntnerstrasse meets the Ringstrasse, a wide, tree-lined boulevard that still exemplifies the beauty of the splendid old city. The Ringstrasse is shaped like a horseshoe with its two ends resting on the bank of the Danube canal, and within its two arms stand baroque palaces of the now long-vanished nobility, elaborate old churches, and wide squares through which Mozart, Hayden, Beethoven, and Schubert once strolled.[487]

The Ringstrasse was the creation of Emperor Franz-Josef, who in 1858 wanted a capital worthy of his great empire. With unbounded confidence in the future and no inhibitions about the display of wealth, Franz-Josef had ordered the destruction of the old wall that had held off the Turks in 1683 to make way for an expanded city. Blocks of apartments for the rich shot up with amazing speed, flanking the grandest of all European boulevards. Official buildings vied with private houses for opulence and high style. The Opera House was built as an Italian Renaissance palazzo, the university as a French castle, the new town hall as a neo-Gothic cathedral, and the parliament building as a Greek temple.[488]

Young Julie had dreamed of her own future as she watched fine carriages driving up the ramp to the main entrance of the Opera House to unload their cargo of beautifully dressed society ladies and their handsomely attired husbands, lovers—or both. The men usually wore white tie and tails, though some of them were dressed in the impressive uniforms of the Imperial Army: The dragoons wore white tunics with gold lace, their blood-red trousers disappearing into the glistening leather of their black boots, and the hussars wore short, fur-trimmed, gold cloaks nonchalantly thrown over one shoulder. All of the military men wore jangling spurs with saber scabbards that glinted in the gaslight of the outdoor candelabras. For Julie, it was a scene of incredible richness and splendor.[489]

As a young girl enthralled with the view from her window, Julie could not know that, underneath the elegant façade of Viennese society, decay was already festering. She was not aware that murderous hatred had already wormed itself into the soul of her lovely city or that it would condemn her to die amid poverty and terror. It is easier to identify with Julie's comfortable early life and its suffering end than it is to comprehend that millions of others died similarly during the Holocaust, each with a story and hopes for the future. The death of one is a tragedy, but the death of one million can become a statistic.[490]

In his autobiography, *Mein Kampf*, the chief architect of the Holocaust, Adolf Hitler, was clear about his own views on Austria: He opened his first chapter with these words:

In my earliest youth I came to the basic insight, which never left me but only became more profound, that Germanism could be safeguarded only by the destruction of Austria ... Even then I had drawn the consequences from this realization. Ardent love for my German-Austrian homeland, deep hatred for the Austrian state.[491]

At first, Hitler did not have sufficient control of Germany's army to carry out his plan to annex Austria. Both the army and the foreign office were conservative, and they were initially able to keep a rein on Hitler's growing ambitions. In Austria, the comforting school of thought that said "Hitler cannot last long" held fast for some time. But on Saturday, February 5, the news from Berlin was that Hitler had sacked the men who had built up German military strength, including the Commanders-in-Chief of the Army and the Armed Forces. And the "little corporal" of the Great War had made himself Supreme Commander of the Armed Services by abolishing the Ministry of War.[492] Rather than the conservatives getting rid of Hitler, he had gotten rid of them. The *new* comforting school of thought was that "Hitler cannot last long because he has now over-reached himself."[493]

Hitler's political and military housecleaning marked a turning point in the evolution of his Third Reich. The key conservatives who had blocked his desire to embark on risky international adventures were swept away in one winter's weekend, and those who had acted as a brake on Nazi excesses had been replaced by younger, more compliant men. With significant opposition eliminated, Hitler's immediate goal was to gain control of Austria.[494] This would give the German Reich a substantial demographic and economic boost, and it would expose Czechoslovakia to attack.[495]

Months before Austria was annexed by Germany, an American historian and war correspondent, William L. Shirer, returned to Vienna with his Austrian-born wife, Tess. The Shirers had arrived at Christmastime in 1937 to find a city that had become a sad place during the years they had been away. Shirer would write that dilapidated classical buildings had paint peeling from their walls, and the city looked "terribly poor … The workers are sullen, even those who have jobs, and one sees beggars on every street corner." William and Tess were also astonished at the degree of anti-Semitism they encountered in Vienna.[496] Working as a journalist and radio reporter for CBS, Shirer was the only American broadcaster in the city when the *Anschluss* took place in early 1938, and his autobiography, *A 20th Century Journey*, provides a firsthand account of the opening act of a drama that would engulf the world.

Soon after World War I ended, there was considerable enthusiasm for the idea that Austrians should "come home to their German brothers and sisters," but the Allies would not allow it, as the French did not want

Germany to become larger as a result of losing the war. After the Allied blockade caused the hyper-inflation, and Vienna was starving, there was another proposal to integrate the two countries, but this effort failed as well. After Hitler came to power in 1933 and promoted the union of Austria and Germany in *Mein Kampf*, the *Anschluss* became an almost mystic vision for all Pan-Germans: Industrialists thought it would mean larger markets, professionals thought it would create broader career opportunities, and the unemployed, numbering 600,000 of Austria's 6.5 million people, hoped it would bring them regular work.[497]

Here our story takes a strange twist: One of the conservatives who had stood in the way of Hitler's dreams of the *Anschluss* was the German Minister to Austria, Franz von Papen. When he was about to be sacked, von Papen made an effort to keep his job by proposing that he could arrange a face-to-face meeting between Hitler and Austrian Chancellor Schuschnigg for the purpose of solving numerous problems between the two countries.[498] Chancellor Schuschnigg was a sensitive man of integrity who had a strong desire to preserve Austria's independence, but he would be dealing from a weak position. Austria's ally, Italian dictator Benito Mussolini, had been keeping an army division on the Austrian border to inhibit Hitler's ambitions, but there was growing evidence that Mussolini was preparing for a complete reversal of policy.[499]

Hitler accepted von Papen's suggestion, and Schuschnigg reluctantly agreed to a meeting in Germany, hoping to gain time until the international situation improved in Austria's favor. But neither Britain nor France was showing interest in defending Austrian independence.[500] France was in the middle of a cabinet crisis, and Britain's Neville Chamberlain considered direct negotiations with Hitler as the best means of assuring peace.[501]

In an effort to strengthen his position, Schuschnigg laid down certain preconditions for the meeting, requiring Hitler's assurance that he would stand by the agreement of July 11, 1936, in which Germany promised to respect Austrian independence and not interfere in her internal affairs. Hitler quickly confirmed his adherence to the agreement, stating that he merely wanted to discuss some points of misunderstanding between the two countries, and Schushnigg took him at his word.[502] As a devout Catholic, an intellectual, and a decent man with little driving ambition, the Austrian chancellor was ill-suited to face his ruthless opponent.[503]

On the morning of February 12, 1938, on the outskirts of Berchtesgaden, Schuschnigg and Dr. Schmidt were met by a half-track vehicle that carried them up the mountain to Obersalzburg. Wearing black trousers and the brown tunic of a storm trooper, and flanked by three generals, Hitler greeted his Austrian visitors with an outstretched hand. The genial host then led the chancellor into his study on the second floor. Once inside, Hitler abruptly shed his affability, and Schuschnigg was not prepared for what followed. As a man of impeccable Old World Austrian manners, he had just begun talking about the fine weather, when Hitler cut him short:

We did not gather here to speak of the fine view or of the weather. You have done everything to avoid a friendly policy ... The whole history of Austria is just one uninterrupted act of high treason ... I have a historic mission and this mission I will fulfill because Providence has destined me to do so ... who is not with me will be crushed.[504]

Determined not to lose his temper, Schuschnigg responded by saying that Austria's entire history had been an essential and inseparable part of German history. But once again, Hitler cut him off: "Absolutely zero, I'm telling you, absolutely zero. Every national idea was sabotaged by Austria throughout history."[505]

Hitler threatened and badgered Schuschnigg to turn over control of Austria to the Nazis or face an invasion by the German Army.[506] He further demanded that the government lift the ban against the Austrian Nazi party, give amnesty to all Nazis in prison, including the murderers of Dollfuss, and appoint Nazis to key posts. Arthur Seyss-Inquart, the leader of the Pan-German Party, was to be appointed Minister of Interior, with unlimited control of the national police. Taken by surprise and overwhelmed by Hitler's threats, the forty-two-year-old chancellor capitulated. Under the Austrian constitution, only President Wilhelm Miklas had the authority to appoint cabinet members and grant amnesty, but Schuschnigg gave his own assent to the agreement.[507] Badly shaken, Schuschnigg was even expecting to be arrested, when Hitler made a tactical shift:

> I have decided to change my mind—for the first time in my entire life. But I warn you this is your very last chance. I have given you three more days before the agreement goes into effect.[508]

What Schuschnigg did not know was that Hitler was actually bluffing, as he did not think his army was ready to take on Britain and France if they should come to Austria's aid. After Schuschnigg left, Hitler ordered his generals to fake maneuvers near the Austrian border for the next three days to induce President Miklas to ratify the agreement. Under this apparent threat of attack, Miklas granted amnesty to the Austrian Nazis in prison, but he vigorously objected to the appointment of Seyss-Inquart to a position where he would hold power over the police and the army. Finally, Miklas bowed to the pressure, and news of the secret meeting in Germany began to spread to the coffeehouses, the unofficial parliament of Austria. An uneasy spirit soon pervaded the nation.[509]

On February 20, Hitler made an eagerly awaited speech to the Reichstag, and it was broadcast throughout Austria. After announcing that he and Schuschnigg had "made a contribution to the cause of European peace," he accused Austria of mistreating its German minority.[510]

On March 9, 1938, Chancellor Schuschnigg made a speech of his own and struck a match lighting a fire that would engulf humanity in the greatest tragedy it had ever known. Schuschnigg stepped up to the podium in the Tyrolean city of Innsbruck, dressed in the traditional Austrian gray jacket and green waistcoat, and announced that in just four days, on Sunday, March 13, there would be a plebiscite, and the Austrian people would be asked one question: "Are you in favor of a free, German, independent, social, Christian and united Austria? *Ja oder Nein.*"[511] Schuschnigg had challenged Hitler by calling directly on the Austrian people, and he ended his speech with an emotional appeal to their patriotism: "Men, the hour has struck. Red-white-red unto death!"

The people of Vienna responded. On the morning of March 10, the city awoke to a fever of patriotic fervor. Schuschnigg's portrait was painted on walls and streets throughout the city. Lorries draped in the national colors were packed with men and women shouting, "Red-white-red until death!" All day, the radio played Austrian military marches.[512] Though

Schuschnigg was not the dictator Hitler was, William Shirer thought the plebiscite could scarcely be freer than those he had seen in Germany.[513] There had been no free elections in Austria since 1933, and it was naive to think that four days would give opponents time to campaign. Since the voting age in Austria was twenty-four, and most of Hitler's followers were younger than that, the vote was bound to result in an overwhelming victory for an independent Austria.

The next morning, on March 11, Georg and his parents, Ernst and Stella, went about work and school as usual, feeling quite confident that the plebiscite would succeed, and worries about German domination would evaporate. At lunchtime that day, the radio was assuring everyone that rumors of a postponement of the plebiscite were untrue and merely the work of Austria's enemies. Georg arrived home at about six o'clock, leaned his bike against the wall in the hallway, and entered his apartment. He opened the dining room door to see his father standing to greet him, with his mother close behind. "The plebiscite has been called off," his father said. "The radio has just announced that the plebiscite is post-poned." "But it is only postponed," Georg said. "To postpone after the tremendous buildup can only mean it will never take place," his father replied. Even though their family history had been so deeply linked with Austria for so long, the Klaars knew that life as they had known it in their country was over.[514]

Schuschnigg's announcement of the plebiscite on Austrian indepen-dence had brought about the unintended effect of forcing Hitler's hand. A national vote for a free and united Austria, which was the likely outcome, would mean the delay, if not the end of Hitler's dream of the *Anschluss*. And since Germany's union with Austria was a necessary preliminary step toward eastward expansion, the plebiscite had also threatened to wreck Hitler's entire program of "Lebensraum," or additional "living space" for the Germans.[515] He had to do something to stop it.

Finis Austriæ came with an early morning telephone call to Chancellor Schuschnigg from his chief of police, reporting that the German border at Salzburg had been closed, and all railway traffic would stop at ten o'clock that morning. Seyss-Inquart demanded Schuschnigg's immediate resignation and the postponement of the plebiscite for two weeks. Chancellor Schuschnigg and President Miklas were faced with an unpleasant choice between submission and defiance, and they chose submission. After announcing the postponement of the plebiscite, on the same afternoon, Schuschnigg resigned.

President Miklas refused to appoint Seyss-Inquart Chancellor of Austria, but Seyss-Inquart responded by ordering all National Socialists into the streets throughout the country, saying "If Miklas could not understand the situation in four hours, he'll understand it in four minutes."[516] The president's approval was a moot point anyway, as Seyss-Inquart was already taking control in the name of law and order. The Austrian Army offered no resistance, as it had ceased to exist. General Zehner, the last Austrian Defense Minister, had been murdered, the Commander-in-Chief and twenty generals dismissed, and one third of the general staff officers pensioned off. In no other country which Hitler later overran would the grip of the Gestapo ever be so strong, so soon, and so securely organized.[517]

At eight o'clock on the evening of March 11, when Hitler's divisions had already marched into his country, Chancellor Schuschnigg addressed the Austrian people in what William Shirer described as the most moving speech he had ever heard: "President Miklas asked me to tell the people of Austria that we have yielded to force." Shirer thought the chancellor's voice would break as he concluded, "I take leave of the Austrian nation with a farewell which also expresses my heartfelt wish: God save Austria!"[518]

The possibility that Hitler's threat of force was a bluff was not considered in Vienna, London, or Paris; but when the German 2nd Panzer Division entered Austria on the morning of March 11, it was more of a maneuver than an invasion. The soldiers were using tourist maps, and their refueling was done at local gas stations. There was hardly an Austrian leader who can be proud before history and conscience of the role he played on that terrible day. Some fled, but the majority hung around in dejected groups in the chancellor's marble anteroom, waiting for history to overtake them.[519] And, what of the Austrian people? Many of them had been ready to die for independence just days before, but they now greeted the German troops with ecstatic cheers, women and children carrying flowers, and homes decorated with swastika flags.[520]

The manner of Austria's death in March 1938 might have been different under a leader other than President Miklas, but its ceasing to exist as an independent state was beyond the power of any Austrian to prevent.[521] Miklas was thought by many to be a plodding, mediocre man, whose chief accomplishment was to have fathered a large brood of children. But there was in Miklas a certain peasant strength, and after fifty-two years as a state official, he displayed more courage than most Austrians by resigning his presidency rather than agreeing to Germany's annexation of his country.[522]

For Jews, the *Anschluss* brought catastrophe. Schuschnigg's resignation ignited new disturbances in the streets. Austrian storm troopers and their sympathizers crossed the Danube Canal to the Jewish Quarter in Leopoldstadt shouting: "Sieg Heil! Down with the Jews! Heil Hitler! Kill the Jews! Hang Schuschnigg!"[523] The atrocities committed against the Jews during the first few days of the *Anschluss* were acts of pure sadism: Jewish men were herded into schools and forced to do calisthenics, go without food, and sleep while standing up. Jewish women were forced to dance naked, and Jews held in the Prater were made to lie down and eat grass. Austrian members of the Hitler Youth movement, ranging in age from fourteen to thirty, including the League of German girls, were principal perpetrators of these brutal acts. Automobiles owned by Jews were immediately confiscated, and complaints to the police were answered with arrest or physical violence.[524]

The atmosphere in Vienna changed overnight. One example of this was recorded by a visitor who recalled her experience fifty years later: She had entered a cinema at five o'clock on the afternoon of March 11, when many streets were still awash with red-white-red Austrian flags. When she emerged from the theater two hours later, the entire city was bedecked with red-white-black swastika flags. The optimism that most Jews had clung to in the last years and months of Austrian independence had vanished, although wishful thinking never completely disappeared. Many Jews tried to console each other with rumors that Hitler had throat cancer and was expected to die any day.[525]

Jews were not the only targets as the Nazis took over. It is estimated that 90,000 Austrians were arrested by the Gestapo in Vienna and the provinces during the first ten days of the *Anschluss,* including Jews, government officials, and military officers. They were imprisoned for what they represented rather than anything they did. The entire leadership of a nation was wiped out in a few days.[526]

Days after the *Anschluss,* when the phone rang at Georg Klaar's apartment, he answered it to hear the voice of his girlfriend, Lisl. Her emotional tone told him she was upset, as she explained that her family had received visitors and asked Georg to come over right away. During the twenty-minute walk to her apartment, Georg was careful to avoid the roving S.A. bands. When he arrived, Lisl told him that the "visitors" had been Austrian S.A. men, some wearing tin hats and jackboots, and all carrying revolvers or rifles. They had searched the flat, confiscated a few pieces of family silver, taken all the cash they could find, and helped themselves to some alcohol. They had also left an almost unreadable note stating that the S.A. had searched the flat, and the owners were not to be troubled further.[527]

Georg stayed with Lisl and her family until things calmed down, but then he ran back to his own home. There, he found his father, mother, Uncle Alfred, and Cousin Hedi visibly shaken. His mother's hands were trembling, and his father and uncle were pale, with their suits dirty and covered with white paint. Hedi's dress was stained and dirty, and she had a defiant look on her face. Right after Georg had left the house, two men of the Austrian S.A. had entered their home and, without saying anything, had marched Georg's father, uncle, and Hedi down to the street and ordered them to get on their knees and scrub Schuschnigg slogans off the walls and sidewalks.[528]

During the first few days after the *Anschluss,* an orgy of plundering and brutality was directed against the Jews. But only rarely were these anti-Semitic acts committed by German Nazis and even less often by German soldiers. Many German Army officers were openly disgusted by the spectacle of jeering Austrians compelling elderly Jews to scrub streets and public buildings with an acid preparation which made the victims scream with pain.[529] It was the Austrian Nazis, and even the non-Nazis, who were releasing pent-up hatred toward the Jews.[530] William Shirer expressed his dismay in this vivid eyewitness account:

What one saw in Vienna was almost unbelievable. The Viennese usually so soft and sentimental were behaving worse than the Germans, especially toward the Jews. Every time you went out you saw gangs of Jewish men and women, with jeering storm troopers standing over them and taunting crowds shouting insults, on their hands and knees scrubbing Schuschnigg slogans off the sidewalks and curbs. I had never seen this much humiliating scenes in Berlin, or such Nazi sadism.[531]

When the German Nazis marched into Austria, the Viennese population rallied to support them with greater enthusiasm for anti-Semitism than the Germans themselves displayed. It would take Hitler's program of degradation, terror, and expropriation against the Jews five years to build up in Germany, but German anti-Semitic fervor was matched and even surpassed by Austrians over just a few months' time.

Restructuring Austria's government also took little time. Gestapo Chief Reinhard Heydrich was already examining books and records seized from the Austrian police as the German Army entered Vienna on March 11. Nearly two thousand apartments in the 1st District alone were quickly "Aryanised" by the Austrian S.A., and those who tried to defend their homes were sometimes beaten to death.

On the streets, Jewish shops were invaded, robbed, and their owners beaten. Arbitrary arrests deprived families of fathers who were simply never seen again.[532] Hundreds if not thousands of Jews committed suicide to avoid arrest and maltreatment, and the main railway stations of Vienna were thronged with Jews trying to escape the city. They were going anywhere—Switzerland, Prague, or Budapest—it did not matter. Terrible scenes took place when the trains were stopped and boarded by the Gestapo before they reached the Austrian frontier. Many Jews were turned back or left to starve in the no-man's land between frontier towns.[533]

At about six in the evening on March 11, William Shirer took the subway downtown to get a firsthand look at the crowds gathering in the central city. He emerged from the station at Karlsplatz, amazed to see several thousand shouting, hysterical Austrian Nazis and Nazi sympathizers milling around the vast square. In the growing darkness, he found himself swept up by the riotous, yelling throng that reached out past the Ringstrasse and down the narrow street where the fashionable shops were located. He followed the crowd now singing Nazi songs to the office of the German Tourist Bureau, where a flower-draped portrait of Adolf Hitler already hung in the window.

The Austrian Nazi crowds were different from those Shirer had been among in Germany: As he moved among them, he had never seen anything like the degree of hysteria he was witnessing. Many faces were contorted with emotion, with popping eyes and gaping mouths screaming, "Sieg Heil!" A few Austrian police were standing by, but they were already wearing red-black-white swastika armbands, and they did nothing to intervene when things turned ugly.[534] Further along Kärntnerstrasse, young toughs were heaving paving stones into the windows of Jewish shops, surrounded by groups who roared their approval.[535]

Shirer was trying to get a broadcast out to New York, but as he approached the Austrian Broadcasting Company studio, he was greeted by steel-helmeted soldiers in field-grey uniforms, standing guard with fixed bayonets. They were very businesslike, but after some discussion, he was allowed into the building. In the vestibule and further down the corridor were scenes of mass confusion, as young men in all kinds of Nazi uniforms milled about, shouting and brandishing revolvers.

Shirer quickly realized that trying to get news out of Vienna was hopeless, and he decided to fly to London the next day. A phone call to the Aspern Airport revealed that flights to London were full, but he could get a flight through Berlin to Amsterdam. He went back to his apartment, unsure if he would even be allowed to leave the city. When his phone rang, he picked it up to find that Edward R. Murrow was calling from Warsaw, Poland, to ask for news on the situation in Vienna. Shirer told Murrow what he had observed and said he was planning to go to Amsterdam to get away from Nazi censors in Vienna and Berlin.[536]

When Shirer was able to fly out the next day, he left a Vienna that he described as scarcely recognizable. Swastika flags were waving from nearly every house, and the Aspern Airport was crowded with German war planes. His plane lifted from the runway at eight o'clock in the morning, with stops at Prague and Dresden, and it was noon when he arrived in Berlin's Tempelhof Airport. He was greeted there by newspaper headlines that screamed in three-inch type, "GERMAN-AUSTRIA SAVED FROM CHAOS!" The story was about violent disorder on the streets of Vienna, including fighting, shooting, and pillage.

In Amsterdam, Shirer went live on the air to New York with a fifteen-minute news report. It was a groundbreaking event, the first time that CBS had allowed one of its own to go on the air with a firsthand account of a currently volatile situation. The next day, Shirer and Murrow jointly presented the first-ever world live news roundup.[537]

By Wednesday, March 16, things in Vienna had calmed down a bit, and Ernst Klaar returned to work at the Länderbank. When Ernst entered his large office, he looked around the room to take in the heavy oak desk that faced a conference table surrounded by six plush red chairs. His eyes lingered on the blue-patterned oriental carpet that covered the parquet floor and on the bookcase and hat stand that completed the furnishings. This office had been his second home for many years, but Ernst had the distinct feeling that he would not be there much longer.[538]

Ernst had hardly settled behind his desk when Dr. Hilger entered his office. Hilger was a bank employee who had served with Ernst during the Great War, but when he came into the room, he clicked his heels, raised his right arm, and shouted, "Heil Hitler, Ernst!" With an arrogant tone, he said, "I've come to tell you, Ernst, and I trust you will understand my reasons, that as of today I can no longer work for or accept instructions from a Jew." Hilger then turned his back and abruptly left the room.[539] Three weeks later, after almost thirty years of loyal service, Ernst received a letter with the notification he had been expecting: "You are simultaneously suspended from all further active employment and, until further notice, will be on leave of absence."[540]

After Ernst lost his job with the bank, he sank deeper and deeper into a lethargic depression. Georg's mother, by contrast, was becoming stronger. With patience, willpower, and love, she presented a well-reasoned appeal to her husband's highly developed sense of responsibility. This motivated Ernst to become active again on his family's behalf, and together Georg's parents began to explore every possible way to get the family out of Austria. Ernst wrote to a friend who was president of a Paris bank, and he received a reply that the man was trying to help all his former employees. This glimmer of hope revived Ernst's spirits.

The family's big break came from, of all places, an Aryan contact who was the director of Austria's largest hat factory. Ernst Klaar had audited this man's business for years, and he was an ardent anti-Nazi, eager to move his factory to Ireland. He put Ernst in touch with Emil Hirsch, an employee of his who had already begun negotiations with the Irish government about transferring the factory. Ireland was eager to industrialize and increase employment opportunities, so their government was offering incentives to foreign industrialists to relocate. The Klaars needed no such incentives! Ernst was assured that it would take only a few weeks to process the formalities, giving the family time to prepare their documents and ship their belongings to Ireland.[541]

When William Shirer flew back to Vienna from Amsterdam, he was met at the Aspern Airport by his friend and colleague, Edward R. Murrow, who had already returned to Austria. Shirer's wife, Tess, was in a Vienna hospital, about to give birth to their first child, and she was having a difficult time. Murrow assured his colleague that Tess would be fine, but the fearful effects of the Nazi takeover were being felt even in her maternity ward. Tess's Jewish doctor had disappeared without a word, and a Jewish mother across the hall had jumped out of the hospital window, killing herself and her baby.[542]

When the two men arrived at Shirer's apartment in the Plösslgasse, S.S. guards in steel helmets with bayonets refused to let them enter the building. Next door, at the palace of Baron Louis Rothschild, there was a platoon of S.S. men guarding the entrance to that residence as well. Shirer and Murrow were escorted to the palace by an S.S. soldier to meet with the commanding officer in charge. At the entrance, they saw S.S. men carting up silver and other valuables from the basement. Even the unit commander came up the stairs loaded down with a heavy box of silver knives and forks, but, not the least bit embarrassed, he put the box down, listened to their story, and said they could enter Shirer's apartment. Once in the Shirer home, the two friends poured themselves a strong drink, and watched from the window as the S.S. men continued to carry valuables, paintings, and other art objects from the Rothschild home.

Murrow began to tell Shirer about his experiences in Vienna while Shirer had been in Amsterdam, and Shirer could tell that his friend was depressed by all he had seen the week before: A Jewish man getting drunk in a bar and slashing his throat with a straight razor he pulled from his pocket; hysterical crowds chanting hate-filled slogans, and Nazi bully boys committing sadistic acts in the streets. But they both believed they had accomplished something by being radio's first eyewitness reporters, and Murrow said, "We have found a format for rounding up the news. Maybe now, my friend, we can go places."[543]

Hitler returned to his hometown of Linz on April 8 to meet with his old friend, Gustl Kubizek. As they sat in the lobby of a Linz hotel and talked of old times, Hitler asked Gustl what had become of his musical career. Gustl answered that his career was finished, but he had three boys who were also musically gifted. Hitler immediately responded that he would assume responsibility for their training: "I don't want gifted young people to have such a hard time of it as we had. You know best what we had to go through in Vienna!"[544] Hitler then visited his parents' gravesite in the Leonding churchyard, and after taking a wreath from his valet, he told him to retire with the rest of the staff so he could meditate. He then placed the wreath against his parents' grave marker and stood silently for several minutes.[545]

Instead of the *Anschluss*, Hitler had initially considered something more like the loose union such as Austria already had with Hungary. But the enthusiastic reception he received upon entering his homeland on March 11 had convinced him that complete absorption of Austria into the German Reich was the direction to take. Reflecting his decision, he turned to his valet and said, "It is fate, Linge. I am destined to be the führer who will bring all Germans into the Greater German Reich."[546]

Hitler scheduled a new plebiscite in Austria for April 10 on the *Anschluss*, but the result of the vote was a foregone conclusion. Catholics in this very Catholic country were swayed by the statement of Cardinal Innitzer urging a *Ja* vote. Witnesses to the Nazi hysteria in the streets feared that a failure to cast a *Ja* vote might be found out and punished. When Shirer visited one polling station, he noticed a fairly wide slit in the corner of the voting booth that gave Nazi election committee members a good view of how each person voted.[547] By this time, many Austrians believed that their country simply could not survive unless linked to Germany, and the *Ja* vote reflected an immense relief that the issue was finally settled. The exhausted people of Austria felt their country's independent existence was no longer viable, and they saw the annexation as bringing a welcome end to years of instability, insecurity, and uncertainty.[548]

During the summer after the *Anschluss,* Nazi outrages against the Jews abated. But by October, they began again with a vengeance. Jews were hauled out of their beds and taken away by Nazi functionaries. If a gentile streetcar passenger did not like the looks of a Jewish rider, he could have the trolley stopped and the Jew thrown off. Jews could even be ejected from a cinema in the middle of a performance if someone complained about their presence.[549] Jews were sometimes notified by a piece of paper on their front door that they had days, or even hours, to move out of their apartment.[550]

By the end of 1938, 44,000 of an estimated 70,000 Jewish apartments had been "Aryanized." German citizens now flocked to Austria so they could buy homes and businesses formerly owned by Jews at a fraction of their value. They could also pay with marks for extravagant meals not available in Germany and take bargain-priced vacations amid Austria's matchless mountains and lakes. The confiscation of Jewish homes and businesses probably had less to do with Nazi ideology than it did with economic self-enrichment or just pure, old-fashioned greed.[551]

German S.S. Lieutenant Adolf Eichmann's goal was to get Jews out of Austria as quickly as possible, and he was demanding financial tribute from those with the means to pay. But getting out of Austria was not going to be as easy for the Ernst Klaar family, as Ireland was not in a hurry to receive them. The Klaars were not the exception, as no country seemed to want "Eichmann's Jews." Georg Klaar described the family's feelings at this time: "We were like screaming, helpless travelers on a nightmarish big dipper racing upwards towards peaks of hope only to plough down even more rapidly and deeply into ravines of despair."[552]

The Klaars started up the dipper toward hope as they received word that their Irish visas had finally been granted. All they had to do was travel to Berlin to the Irish Legation for Germany and Austria, present their passports, and have their entry permits stamped. The family made the arrangements to pack up and ship all of their personal belongings, furniture, pictures, and other household items to Ireland. The Klaars' housekeeper, Helene, was put in charge of shipping everything after they left Vienna. Helene was planning to marry that year, and, as a token of gratitude, the Klaars gave her their double bed as a wedding present.[553]

To their surprise, on arriving in Berlin, the Klaars were shown great kindness by the railway porter as he loaded their bags on the trolley that took them to the Hotel Excelsior. With 600 rooms, this hotel was the largest and most luxurious in Europe, and again they were treated with the utmost courtesy. Georg was amazed at how Jews were being treated in Berlin in September of 1938. The Klaars felt free to do things they would not have considered doing in Vienna, such as visiting coffee houses and places of entertainment. Some Jews still owned stores and cars, and they could shop wherever they pleased. It was strange to say, but for the Klaars, after living for months in Nazi Vienna, being in Berlin felt almost as though they had already emigrated to a place far from Hitler's rule.[554]

The next morning, however, the Klaars took another plunge down the big dipper toward despair. When they went to the Irish Legation, they found out there were no instructions from Dublin to issue visas for the family. Now they had to wonder how long it would take to receive their visas and how much money they would need until then. Ernst cabled his contact in Ireland and received a reply that he would check into their situation immediately. But one week later, the Irish Legation had still heard nothing from Dublin. The family moved from the Hotel Excelsior to a more affordable boarding house, where their remaining funds would last longer. They were happy to find their rooms were comfortable, and the food was very good.[555]

After three weeks, the Klaars were informed by the Irish Legation that the Irish authorities thought it was too risky to allow a Jewish family to enter the country before they had confirmation that the company's machinery, which is all they really cared about, was on its way. Since the machines were not due to be shipped before the end of October, it would be at least six weeks more before they received their visas. But staying in Berlin that long was risky for the family. The crisis over the Sudetenland in Czechoslovakia was increasing the chances of a German war with Britain and France. Georg's eighteenth birthday was only three weeks away, and he was sure Hitler would use him as cannon-fodder if war did break out.[556]

On October 5, the big dipper took another plunge downward. The Austrian government decreed that all passports issued to Jews had to be stamped with a large red "J." That meant that the family had to make the treacherous trip back to Vienna. They arrived safely and stayed with Ernst's brother and his wife, Georg's Uncle Paul and Aunt Alice. They were planning to be in the city only two days if they had no trouble getting the "J" stamp on their passports. Happily, the man at the passport office was friendly, and things went quickly.

But the dipper took another drastic dip when Ernst and Stella decided to visit their old residence. There was no answer at the door, so Ernst used his key, and they let themselves in. As they had expected, the rooms were empty except for the bedroom, but they soon realized that Helene had kept not only the double bed they had given her but had taken all of Stella's clothes and the rest of the family's furniture. At that moment, Helene returned, and when she saw them, her face turned as red as her hair. But she soon regained her composure and told them that either they leave Vienna immediately, never to return, or she would go to the police and accuse Ernst of forcing himself on her. If she carried out the threat, the Klaars knew they would probably all be arrested, so they left for Berlin that evening.[557]

In Berlin, the news turned good again when Ernst received a letter offering him a job at a bank in Paris. He was ecstatic! A bank wanted to hire him, and once he was in Paris, he could speed up the entry permits for Stella and Georg. In two weeks' time, the family might be together in Paris, economically secure, and safe from the Gestapo.[558]

On November 9, however, before the family could act on the news from Paris, Nazi Germany turned on its Jewish citizens the full force of anti-Semitic fervor. The date is remembered in history as Kristallnacht: The Night of Broken Glass. In reprisal for the shooting of a German diplomat by a Polish Jew, Hitler Youth and S.A. thugs burned down synagogues and smashed plate glass windows throughout the city, as the Gestapo rounded up Jews in their homes and led them away. Some Jews were lynched on the spot, and others never returned. By some miracle, the Nazis did not go through the boarding houses, and the Klaars were spared. The next morning, Stella received a call from the Irish Legation to come quickly. Irish visas had been granted for Stella and Georg.[559] There was not a moment to lose, and Georg and his mother decided to leave for Ireland immediately.

At Tempelhof Airport, after Georg was searched by two Gestapo officers, he was allowed to board the plane, but he had another half-hour of anxious waiting before his mother finally boarded. Stella had been searched by a female customs inspector, even to the point of having to remove all of her clothes, including underwear. Finally, the plane left for England. In 1981, Georg Klaar would write of his arrival in London in 1938:

And that smell of London, when we were out again in the street, that unforgettable smell of prewar London! It remained forever in my nose. That tangy, smoky, foggy air possessed for me the fragrance of freedom.[560]

On Hitler's orders, former Austrian Chancellor Kurt von Schuschnigg was arrested on the morning of March 12, 1938, and kept under house arrest until May 28 of that year. During this time, the Gestapo deprived him of sleep by keeping the lights and radio on for twenty-four hours a day. Schuschnigg was next moved to Gestapo headquarters in Vienna, where he lived in a small room for the next seventeen months, forced to clean washbasins, slop buckets, and latrines of the S.S. guard. He lost fifty-eight pounds before being transferred to Dachau Concentration camp, where he would spend the rest of the war years.

On May 1, 1945, Schuschnigg was moved from Dachau with other important prisoners to prevent their liberation by American troops. The Gestapo officer in charge informed Schuschnigg that, on Himmler's orders, he and the others would be killed before they would be allowed to fall into the hands of the Americans. His spirits fell with the news that he was now to die, at the very end of the war, after he had survived Nazi brutality for so long. But his diary entry on May 4, 1945, triumphantly records, "At two o'clock this afternoon, alarm! The American detachment takes over the hotel. We are free!"[561] Schuschnigg left Europe for the U.S. to become a university professor of political science from 1948 to 1967 at St. Louis University, but he later returned to Austria. He died near the town of Innsbruck in 1977.[562]

Toward the end of November 1938, Ernst Klaar also received his Irish visa. He flew to London to meet his wife and son for a joyful reunion, and the family left the next day for Dublin. But Ernst could stay only for two days as he was needed at the bank in Paris. Ernst loved Paris and his new job to the extent that Paris became home to him, and he often asked himself how he could have believed that he could be happy only in Vienna. With war clouds on the horizon, however, he wondered if he should bring Stella and Georg to join him in France. Further from Germany, Ireland seemed safer than Paris; but France had a strong army, and the Maginot Line France had built after the Great War was designed to be impregnable against a German attack. They needed to make a decision, because Stella missed her husband, and their separation was taking its toll. She had lost weight, her face had become haggard, and her eyes were red from crying most of the time.

In March of 1939, Ernst called Stella to say that her French visa had come through, and she could now come to Paris. After telling her the news, he asked to speak to his son, and it was a conversation that would haunt Georg for the rest of his life. Ernst asked Georg what he thought they should do: Should Stella come to Paris, or should he join her in Ireland? Georg replied, "Daddy, the bank has been your life. You love Paris. Of course, you want to stay."

Georg was speaking to his father as Hitler's troops were marching into Czechoslovakia, and the question to ask about Germany's next invasion was "when" rather than "if." The safety of the family was the first priority, so Ernst asked Georg the unanswerable question, "What if the Germans win? What if Hitler occupies France?" Georg gave another response he would never forget: "That's quite impossible. They didn't get further than the Marne last time, and the French didn't have the Maginot Line ..."[563]

In late March of 1939, a sad-faced fifty-year-old lady entered the French Embassy in London, and a smiling bride came out, holding a French visa in her passport. The next day, Stella was on the boat-train heading to Paris. Many years later, Georg wrote:

> *When I settled her in her compartment and there were only a few moments left, tears came into her eyes, but they were very different from those bitter ones she had shed in Ireland. These were soft ones, tears one could smile through, tears of love and care for me, warm but not burning, and they flowed without sobs gently and tenderly.*[564]

The war between France and Germany began on September 3, 1939, and on September 4, there was a knock on the door at the furnished flat of Ernst and Stella Klaar in Paris. Outside stood two French policemen whose business it was to round up all male German nationals and take them to an internment camp. Stella found out where her husband was being held, and she was able to join him there. The commandant of the camp was a decent, humane man, and when the armistice between France and Germany was signed in May of 1940, the Klaars were released.

To avoid further contact with the Germans, Ernst and Stella made their way to the South of France to the vicinity of Marseilles, where they were able to write their son for the first time since the war had begun the previous year. They stayed in the Marseilles area until January 1941, when they were forced, with other Jews, to move, to the small village of St. Pierreville so the French Vichy government could keep better track of them. The people of St. Pierreville were good to them, and they were free to pass the time as they pleased except when they were required to report to the local gendarmerie.[565]

When Georg Klaar joined the British Army, he changed his name to "George Clare," to prevent his immediate identification as a Jew in case he was captured by the Germans. One day in late August of 1942, while having tea in the regimental canteen and listening to the BBC news on the radio, he heard, "Recent rumors are that foreign-born Jews are to be deported from unoccupied France."[566] Vichy France ordered all of the mayors to immediately erase from national registers the names of the Jews who were arrested and deported to the occupied zone. Once this happened, the deported Jews ceased to have any legal existence, and their whereabouts became untraceable. As George Clare would later write:

My parents, my beloved Mother and Father, had disappeared with the many millions in the gruesome anonymity of impersonal mass-murder. Ernst and Stella's lives had been erased.[567]

Out of power at the time of the *Anschluss,* Winston Churchill's words were a lonely voice in the wilderness of British politics when he said:

The gravity of the event of March 12 cannot be exaggerated. Europe is confronted with aggression and there is only one choice open, either to submit like Austria or else to take effective measures while time remains. How many friends will be alienated, how many potential allies shall we see go, one by one down the grisly gulf? A long stretch of the Danube is now in German hands. The mastery of Vienna gives to Nazi Germany military and economic communications of southeastern Europe, by road, by river, and by rail. What is the effect of this on the structure of Europe?[568]

The annexation of Austria was a great victory for Hitler, giving him momentum that would be hard to stop. At no cost to Germany, he had seized the key to Danubian communications, isolated Czechoslovakia, and shown the world that he could blatantly defy the Versailles Treaty with no fear of reprisal.[569] The military forces of Britain, France, or Russia could have easily overwhelmed him, but without firing a single shot, he had added seven million people to his Third Reich. The clever coup had strengthened his hold on the German Army and established the precedent that he alone would make decisions on foreign policy. Henceforth, the army's role would be to supply the force behind Hitler's will. By their inaction, other European countries had demonstrated that that they would not lift a finger to stop him.[570]

Austria had passed, for the moment, out of history, its very name suppressed by an Austrian who never forgave his country for not recognizing his true worth. Vienna had become just another German city. Once a vagabond in the city of Vienna, this now-mighty German dictator had wiped his native land off the map and deprived the glittering capital that had rejected him of its last shred of significance.[571]

Where were the good people of Germany, Europe, and the world when the Holocaust was taking place over the days, weeks, months, and years of Hitler's Third Reich? The best answer may be that of Martin Niemöller, pastor of a church at Dahlem, a suburb of Berlin, when Hitler came to power. Commander of a submarine in World War I, he was a nationalist hero who initially welcomed the Nazi regime. But when he refused to recognize the right of the Nazi state to supremacy over Christians because he took the position that only God and God's word had that right, he was sent to Dachau. After the war, he recorded his thoughts about the world's response to the Holocaust:

First the Nazis went after the Jews, but I was not a Jew so I didn't react. Then they went after the Socialists but I wasn't a Socialist. Then they went after the trade unions, but I wasn't a worker, so I did not stand up. Then they went after me, and by that time it was too late for anybody to stand up.[572]

The famous words of eighteenth-century philosopher and politician, Edmond Burke, were indeed borne out as millions of Jews and others suffered immeasurable horror under the Nazis: "All that is necessary for the triumph of evil is that good men do nothing."

CHAPTER 9

He Prepared Us to Be Free

Our journey through Austrian history has led us from Roman Vindobona in the second century AD, through the blooming and fading of the mighty Habsburg Empire, to the bleak events surrounding the outbreaks of the First and Second World Wars. The seeds of the Holocaust were sown and the plant nourished, tended, and pruned for centuries before the fruit was finally harvested by Adolf Hitler. Ancestors of the Ernst Klaar family in Vienna could be traced back to the days of Habsburg Emperor Josef II in 1780, but the long and honorable history of a family made no difference when the hyper-inflation and Great Depression had ruined the financial future of most Austrians. By 1938, people were looking for a place to lay the blame, and the Jews were their convenient target.

After reviewing more than 1700 years of social, political, and economic history in Austria, it is timely to examine the life and work of Voltaire, a brilliant eighteenth-century Frenchman who remains one of the most influential philosophers produced by Western Civilization. Almost 250 years after his death, Voltaire's writings continue to have a profound impact on Western culture, politics, religion, and systems of justice, so it is important to understand what he said and why. The fact that our modern civilization still reflects many of the principles Voltaire espoused is enough to give us hope for our complex and volatile times.

Though he was never in Vienna, Voltaire's grand ideas stand in stark contrast to the dark thoughts of Hitler and the entrenched attitudes that kept Europe fragmented, caused two World Wars, and still contribute to international tensions. Voltaire had his own flaws and blind spots, but he used his sharp wit, keen intelligence, and the power of the written word to consistently resist injustice, intolerance, superstition, and hypocrisy wherever he found it. In his best-known book, *Candide,* his hero learned that this is not the best of all possible worlds, but human beings can make things better.

Voltaire's France was the wealthiest and most powerful nation in the world, but the country's wealth was concentrated in the hands of a few. France was inhabited by nineteen million people divided into three classes, or *états:* the nobility, the clergy, and everybody else. The higher clergy could be seen as part of the nobility, as all bishops were appointed by the king. The Church owned a quarter of all of the wealth in France, and its income and possessions were tax exempt. Wielding unquestioned authority, the clergy ruled hand in hand with the king.

Known as the "Third Estate," 90 percent of the population lived in poverty and ignorance, with few rights to protect them from the whims of those in power. Many were peasants who spent their lives in feudal servitude, subject to both governmental taxes and ecclesiastic tithes. They were required to give their local lord several days of labor each year, plowing and planting his fields, reaping his harvest, and stowing his barns. They paid the lord a fee to fish in his lakes and streams and tend their cattle in his pastures. They were also obliged to pay for the use of his mill, bakery, and wine or oil presses.[573]

Writing many years later, another champion of social justice, Victor Hugo, said that France was ruled by intolerant religion and unjust law.[574] The purpose of a trial was not to find truth, but to prove guilt, preferably based on a suspect's confession. A private citizen accused of a crime was often subjected to torture, with the operative principle being that a man will say what you think he should say if you hurt him enough. Trials were deliberately rigged against the suspect in favor of the State. The accused usually did not know much about the charges or evidence against him, the witnesses, or the questions he would be asked. He was allowed a lawyer to represent him, but the lawyer could not be present during questioning of the accused, which took place behind closed doors.[575]

As for religion, French Protestants, or Huguenots, were outlawed. A Protestant wife was legally considered a concubine, and her children were deemed illegitimate and unable to inherit property. For men, the punishment for participating in Protestant worship was a life sentence in the galleys, and for women it was life imprisonment. Once convicted, their personal property was confiscated by the Church. Protestants were required to baptize their children into the Catholic Church within twenty-four hours of their birth and to pledge to bring them up in a Catholic home.[576]

Paris was a turbulent city of magnificent palaces amidst dismal slums, and among its 800,000 people, there were 100,000 servants and 20,000 beggars. Dark alleys and seedy streets were hidden behind fashionable boulevards. Street lamps cast shadows on dirt roads only when the moon was not full enough to light them. Rats competed with people for shelter within the poor housing facilities of the city, and men, women, and children barely rivaled the rats in the ongoing race for food.[577]

As for freedom of thought and speech, it did not exist. Publishing any piece of writing required the author to obtain "privilege" or royal permission. The body responsible for approving publications saw itself as a standards watchdog, but it effectively suppressed freedom of expression. This explains why nearly half the books written in France during the eighteenth century were published outside of the country.[578]

To the degree that we can take for granted the existence of freedom, tolerance, and justice in our modern Western society, we can thank people like Voltaire, who proclaimed the value of such principles even when the expression of such views was neither free nor tolerated. It was, in fact, likely to result in unjust punishment. In spite of the significant risks within eighteenth-century France and the entire known world of his time, no one proclaimed these values louder and longer than Voltaire.[579]

Voltaire was born François-Marie Arouet in Paris on November 21, 1694, to a father who was an affluent attorney and a mother who was of slightly noble lineage. Voltaire remembered little of his mother, as she died when he was a young boy. François was a sickly child who was not expected to live long, and he suffered from real or imagined ill health throughout his life. His father was well connected and fully expected his son to follow him into the law. The two quarreled repeatedly over François' desire to become a writer.

At the age of ten, Voltaire was sent by his father to the oldest and most respected school in Paris, Collége Louis-le-Grand, a Jesuit school favored by the rich and powerful.[580] While there, he was offered a good education in the classics, literature, and especially drama, but like most great men, he was largely self-taught. At Louis-le-Grand, he learned Latin, work habits, ambition, and the Jesuit tradition of performing school plays in Latin.[581] One of his teachers predicted that the young wit would become the standard bearer of French deism—a school of thought that discarded nearly all theology except belief in God, playing down the more supernatural or miraculous aspects of the Christian story. There is no doubt that the Jesuits imbued Voltaire with a love of literature and taught him the secrets of how to write.[582]

In 1711, seventeen-year-old François was fresh out of school, oozing with self-confidence and filled with hormones that urged him to rebel. The future lay before him to be conquered, the present to be ridiculed, and the past to be outdone.[583] He initially planned to comply with his father's wishes and study for the bar, but he soon developed a reputation with poets and men of rank for having distinguished manners, being bright and witty, and having a gift for throwing off graceful and flattering verse. By 1714, François had begun to make a name for himself in the Paris world of letters. He competed for a prize awarded by the French Academy for the best poem on the new choir at Notre Dame, but the prize was awarded to an elderly abbé. He was disappointed enough to write a stinging response that earned him a budding reputation as a satirist—a reputation which would follow him the rest of his life.[584]

Louis XIV died in 1715, when his son was only five years old, and Philippe d'Orléans was selected as regent until Louis XV became old enough to reign. After the gloomy years of Louis XIV, the young king brought in a new order of boldness, experimentation, satire, mockery, and unrestrained pleasure. Plays, gambling, and masked balls at the opera were now all the rage, though some thought things were going too far. One young writer who seemed to go too far was François-Marie Arouet.[585]

At twenty-one, the young upstart described himself as "thin, long, and fleshless, without buttocks." When the king's regent reduced half the horses in the royal stables, François Arouet quipped that Philippe would have done better to dismiss half the asses that crowded his Highness's court. He got into serious trouble when his poem about the regent's daughter, the Duchesse de Berry, contained some lines about her loose morals. The regent could pardon lampoons of himself, but he was deeply offended by the biting criticism of his daughter.[586] François had underestimated the absolutism and repressive nature of the powerful regency. On May 16, 1717, he was sent to the Bastille without trial, and he was imprisoned for almost a year.

The Bastille was no château. Though François was allowed some books and writing paper, conditions were harsh. The walls of the Bastille were ten feet thick, and there were triple locks on the gates. His cell had no window for sunlight, and the food was poor. His arrest on the orders of Philippe d'Orléans meant that the duration of his detention was indefinite, and it could last as long as the regent wished. François was learning firsthand how French law worked: it was arbitrary, despotic, and determined by royal decree.[587]

His time in the Bastille was a turning point in young François' life, and he resolved never again to run the risk of imprisonment. Because he had suffered under the name Arouet, he decided to change it. Celebrated writers before him had changed their names, and he believed he could not become immortal under the name Arouet. He began the process by signing his name as "François-Marie Arouet de Voltaire," gradually dropping Arouet from his signature. In a few months, he became known simply as "Voltaire."[588]

Voltaire spent much of his time writing his first play, *Edipe*, in which he railed against the injustice of the gods. It was based on the greatest tragedy in classical Greek mythology, made famous by Sophocles' play, *Oedipus Tyrannus*, or Oedipus the King. Voltaire was drawn to the subject not only because of its power but also because a controversy was raging within the Catholic Church between the Jesuits and the Jansenists over the nature of sin, grace, and predestination. Voltaire's play depicted the Jesuit vision of a just God in conflict with the Jansenist God of wrath. The story proposed that the world could be a better place through human free will and action, if only the gods and their priests would get out of the way.[589] In the Greek tragedy, Oedipus killed his father and married his mother. Could he have avoided his sin? Was it the fault of the gods? In Voltaire's version, the mother of Oedipus criticizes the role of the priest: "Our priests are not what the foolish people imagine; their wisdom is based solely on our credulity." This little maxim has remained to this day one of Voltaire's most frequently cited quotations.[590]

When it opened at the Comedie Francaise on November 18, 1718, *Edipe* was an immediate sensation. By January 1719, there had been twenty-nine performances, and some 25,000 people had seen the play. Overnight, Voltaire had become what he was to remain for sixty years, the chief ornament of French letters. Audiences applauded his attack on "fraudulent priests," but the play was also a declaration of war against established ideas. The gauntlet had been thrown down.[591] Among the innumerable lines of attack open to satirists of his day, Voltaire had chosen the one that would be characteristic of him throughout his life: he would consistently use his humor, wit, and intelligence to oppose any system or thought that fostered injustice or unreason.[592]

By the middle of 1719, the money Voltaire made from *Edipe* was running out, and his next play was so bad that he closed it almost immediately. The challenge of how to make a living was made even more difficult by the fact that he had to work under the country's oppressive system of censorship and its lack of any copyright law. Anyone could copy his work.[593] On January 1, 1722, Voltaire's father died at the age of seventy-one. His estate was divided among his three children, but the inheritance did not eliminate Voltaire's financial difficulties. He was to receive only the income from his third of the estate until he became thirty-five. And even then, he would be able to claim his full share only if he could persuade a court of his respectability.[594]

Voltaire's next literary offering was an epic poem, *La Henriade*, recounting the heroic achievements of the French king Henri IV in bringing a truce to end the murderous wars between Catholics and Protestants in the sixteenth century. The poem related the story of the Catholic massacre of up to 30,000 Protestants, or Huguenots, on St.

Bartholomew's Day in 1572. It also recounted religious crimes through the ages, including mothers offering their children to be burned, Romans persecuting Christians, and Christians persecuting heretics. They were all "fanatics invoking the Lord while slaughtering their brothers." For a time, Voltaire enjoyed fame and fortune as the greatest living poet in France, and he hoped that *La Henriade* would become his country's national epic. The critics applauded his work, and he was even received at the court of Louis XV.[595]

Though he had received praise for *Edipe* and *La Henriade*, Voltaire was being watched by the police. And in December 1725, an incident took place that would change his life. While at the opera, his talk irritated a young nobleman from the great house of Rohan, and a fight ensued. The police again whisked Voltaire away to the Bastille.[596] This time, he was given a choice: he could leave Paris and endure the obscurity of the provinces or be imprisoned in the Bastille indefinitely, without trial. As always, innocence carried with it no guarantee of justice.[597]

Voltaire had already been thinking of visiting England to see if he could get *La Henriade* published there. Even after his early successes, he realized he could not continue to publish his work in France without the constant threat of imprisonment. As long as he was in a totalitarian society, merit was not enough to allow him to express independent thought.[598] His offer to be exiled to England was readily accepted by the French authorities, who were eager to see the last of him. A new chapter in his life was about to begin.[599]

Voltaire touched the shores of England at Greenwich, near London, in May of 1726. The challenge of living alone in London was great. In French society, which he had known all his life, he was already recognized as a rising poet, and he had made his way through his gift of words. In England, he was reduced to silence, impotence, and obscurity. To make matters worse, he was penniless. Before leaving France, he had put together as much money as he could and sent a letter of credit to a London banker, but when he arrived in the city, he found that his banker had gone bankrupt. The man's father, who had broken the news to Voltaire, may have given him a small amount to tide him over, but exactly how he got through his first few days in England is not clear. A young man from a prominent merchant family who specialized in trading wool and silk with the Middle East asked Voltaire to stay with him, and he gratefully accepted the invitation.[600]

Voltaire resolutely set about to learn the English language, and by the end of 1726, he was writing letters in English. His three-year stay in London may not have left any particular mark on England, but England produced a lasting and profound effect on him. In discussing the differences between the theaters of the two countries, he observed, "The Englishman says whatever he please, the Frenchman only what he can."[601] And about English taxes, Voltaire said:

You do not hear in England of one kind of justice for the higher class, a second for the middle class, and a third for the lowest. Englishmen of the noble class are not exempt from paying certain taxes. The peasant is not afraid to increase the number of his cattle, or to cover his roof with tiles, lest his taxes be raised next year.[602]

Soon Voltaire began to think of writing a book about his observations on England. He wanted to acquaint his countrymen with the contrast between what he admired in free England and what he disdained in despotic France.[603] The book that emerged after seven years of gestation, *Letters on England*, was the first major work of the French Enlightenment. It was an attack on religion and political intolerance and a defense of the experimental methods of science—in short, the blueprint for a bourgeois, liberal society of progressive views and prosperous ways. Voltaire wanted to tell the world how men like Isaac Newton and John Locke contributed to the sum of human knowledge, a loud testament to the benefits of free thinking.[604]

When finally published, *Letters on England* masqueraded as a pseudo-journalistic description of England, but it was also a satirical, backhanded attack on the French establishment. It was a masterpiece and one of his most important works. It served as the manifesto for the New Enlightenment, reverberating through the fifty years until the French Revolution and beyond.[605] Reflecting his intense interest in the beliefs, values, and mores of the English Quakers, Voltaire presented in the opening chapter a fictional conversation between himself and a nameless Quaker, contrasting the Quaker's plain speaking, simplicity, contempt for titles, abhorrence of war, and general non-conformity with his own Parisian urbanity and worldliness. While seeming to belittle the Quaker, it had the effect of underscoring his honesty, sincerity, and good sense:

"'My dear sir,' say I, 'were you ever baptized?' 'I never was,'
replied the Quaker, 'Nor any of my brethren.' 'Zounds!' say I to
him, 'You are not Christian then.' 'Friend,' replies the old man in
a soft tone of voice, 'Swear not; we are Christians, but we are not
of opinion that the sprinkling of water on a child's head makes him

> *a Christian.' 'Heavens,' say I, shocked at his impiety, 'You have*
> *then forgot that Christ was baptized by St. John.' 'Friend,' then*
> *replies the mild Quaker once again, 'Swear not, Christ indeed was*
> *baptized by John, but he himself never baptized anyone. We are*
> *the disciples of Christ, not of John.'"* [606]

Voltaire liked the practicality of the English, with their respect for facts, reality, and utility, and their simplicity of manners, habits, and dress. He especially liked the English middle class. Comparing the English with their beer, he said they were like "froth at the top, dregs at the bottom, but the middle excellent." [607]

Voltaire left England rather suddenly in late 1728, perhaps because he had borrowed money to live on during 1726 and 1727 and found himself unable to repay his debts. By this time, he also had powerful friends in the French Ministry who were able to arrange for his return from exile. At thirty-four, he was determined to become financially independent, and soon after his return to Paris, an unusual opportunity presented itself. When it did, he exhibited a financial dexterity that was to become habitual.

In April of 1729, Voltaire had a chance encounter with an old friend, Charles Marie de La Condamine, a brilliant young mathematician who had recently spotted a loophole in the new state lottery system. In order to liquidate a portion of the public debt, the government had developed the lottery, but the French Finance Minister had not done his math properly. The prize money was much larger than the total value of all possible ticket sales, and if an individual or group of speculators bought all the tickets, the net profit would be one million livers. [608] As a result of learning this from his friend, Voltaire formed a syndicate to act on the information. When the finance minister realized his mistake, he tried to change the rules, but a court decided against him. Voltaire's syndicate made a lot of money, and it was distributed among the associates.[609]

After this windfall in November of 1729, Voltaire turned thirty-five and came into his inheritance, which was considerable. Now a seriously rich man, Voltaire treated his newfound wealth as a serious matter deserving serious attention, because it might not come around again.[610] He invested heavily in a hugely profitable business that provided supplies to the French army, including fodder for the horses, food for the soldiers, and cloth for their uniforms. He also had a large interest in a commercial house in Cadiz, Spain, which owned a number of vessels employed in the American trade. He had become not only a man of letters but also an able businessman, and he had made a colossal fortune.[611] If he had not acquired the independence that came with his fortune, he could not have done the things for which he deserves our attention.

Voltaire had earned a reputation as poet and playwright, and he now set out to write tragedies that centered on the conflicts and emotions of his characters.[612] In May of 1733, he was living in an obscure apartment in Paris, renting from a corn merchant with whom he had made a substantial investment in the cereal trade. Among his visitors was a brilliant young woman who would have a strong influence on his career and with whom he would have a long intimacy. She was Madame du Châtelet, the "divine Émilie" who appeared in much of Voltaire's prose and verse. Émilie's father, the Baron de Breteuil, was a nobleman of an ancient family who had been a client of his own father, and Voltaire had known Émilie since her childhood. He was thirty-nine and unattached, while Émilie was twenty-seven and married with three children; but they were both look-ing for love. Émilie was a woman of striking appearance and impressive intellect who loved going to parties, dances, the theatre, and the opera, or even slumming in city bars. She had already had two rather public affairs, but they were over, and she was free to give her heart to Voltaire.[613]

Voltaire wanted to continue living in Paris, as some of his recently acquired wealth had come from lending to reliable borrowers at 10 percent interest. He also believed that he should have earned the right to publish what he wanted, and his experience in England had made him fond of this practice.[614] But, in the summer of 1733, his relations with French authorities were once again at the breaking point, and he had to be careful. On April 24, 1734, Voltaire's *Letters on England* began to appear in Paris, and on May 13, the State issued a warrant for his arrest. His book was publicly burned on the steps of the Palais de Justice as "scandalous and contrary to religion, to morality, and to the respect due to authority."[615]

Warned by friends of the arrest warrant, Voltaire had to leave Paris quickly, and he was offered the château of Émilie's husband, the Marquis du Châtelet. Situated near the Village of Cirey, in the Champagne region of France, the château was in poor condition, but Voltaire was wealthy enough to transform it into a comfortable residence for himself and Madame, far away from the prying eyes of Parisian gossips and the French police. He was now the paying guest of his mistress and her husband, entering a period of time that would become the happiest of his life.

With the bird flown off to Cirey, the State withdrew the arrest order on the condition that Voltaire would remain a respectful distance from Paris.[616] Though he was eager for Émilie to join him at the château, the previous month of madness and passion with her had taken a toll on forty-year-old Voltaire, and he ended up in bed, alone. He would have to wait another five months for Émilie to arrive.[617]

The village of Cirey consisted of 230 inhabitants and no more than a dozen houses. It was not easily accessible from other areas of France, and this is still somewhat true today. The nearest large town in northeastern France is Nancy, and it is more than fifty miles from Cirey by road. Paris was normally three or four days away, but more in bad weather. Voltaire found that he loved the isolation of being in a quiet spot nestled in a small river valley surrounded by forest. It was certainly better than the Bastille! Living in the country meant fresh eggs, milk, and poultry to soothe his tortured stomach. It was an idyllic setting in which to study science, write history and philosophy, and be forgotten by the French government.[618]

The château itself was a dilapidated relic of the thirteenth century, rarely used by its owners, as the Marquis du Châtelet had neither the interest nor the funds required to repair it. But the Marquis gave Voltaire not only permission to stay at Cirey but also to do whatever was needed to make the château more hospitable. After years of wandering, Voltaire enjoyed being able to create a home of his own, and he began a far-reaching program of improvements. All he needed was "the divine Émilie" to share his new paradise with him.[619] When she finally arrived, with 200 boxes of baggage, she immediately began to revise Voltaire's repairs to her own taste before settling down to a life of study and bigamous devotion. The amiable Marquis sometimes stayed with Émilie and Voltaire, gracefully keeping a separate apartment and separate mealtimes, but he soon began to spend much of his time with his regiment.[620]

Paris society was consumed with curiosity and hunger for news or even gossip about life in the ménage à trios at Cirey. The most controversial writer of the age had set up house with a brilliant and passionate woman in a remote country château, with the approval of her tolerant husband. They were said to be living a life of extravagant luxury and shocking decadence, and Voltaire did nothing to discourage the reports. "Not without some champagne and some excellent food, for we are very voluptuous philosophers," he wrote. The gossips would be disappointed to know that Voltaire and Émilie spent much of their time in serious study and earnest conversation. They often worked late into the night, while the Marquis busied himself with business affairs of the estate.[621]

In addition to her love for Paris nightlife and her interest in redecorating her country home, Émilie was unquestionably an intellectual who was a leading scientist and mathematician of her day. In her youth she had learned several languages, and she knew by heart the finest passages of the Roman writers Horace, Virgil, and Lucretius. She had also read Milton and Locke in the original. But for all of her obvious intelligence, she was an oddity in the eyes of "good society." At the age of nineteen, she had married the Marquis du Châtelet, a career army officer with limited intellectual and cultural interests. After having three children, Émilie believed that she had done her duty by the Marquis, and he was smart enough to recognize that it was not in her nature to be a dutiful wife managing his home. She needed to be free to pursue her own life.[622]

Émilie was genuinely attracted to Voltaire, and he was virtually bowled over by this remarkable and beautiful woman who was the first female intellectual he had encountered. She shared his deistic outlook, and she was in serious pursuit of intellectual study, lively parties, and cultural delights, including the theatre. She had long, dark hair and a fiery personality that beguiled and bewitched Voltaire. During the next sixteen years, he relished Émilie's companionship; in her company, he came into the fullness of being a philosopher, a natural scientist, and a freethinking deist.[623]

To catch a glimpse of Voltaire's life at Cirey, we have the journal and correspondence of Mme de Graffigny, who came to visit on December 3, 1738, and stayed for two months. She wrote a letter only hours after arriving to relate that the roads were good at first but finally became so bad that the coachman refused to go any further. She had to go by public coach from Joinville and was turned out with her maid at the foot of a mountain. They had to tramp through the mud to reach Cirey, where she was received kindly by Mme Du Châtelet and enthusiastically by Voltaire.[624] Two days later, on December 5, Mme de Graffigny described her surroundings at the château:

I went down to coffee at eleven o'clock ... and which lasted an hour and a half. I came upstairs to write to you and to describe my room. It is like a barn, it is so high and so wide. All the winds whistle through the thousand cracks around the window, and which I should like to stuff up, if God gives me life. There is a vast fireplace, but though it burns a great quantity of wood, the room remains very cold. The window gives little light and little view, since an arid mountain shuts it out. Such is my room, which I really hate. In fact, everything in the house is disgusting, apart from the apartments of the lady and Voltaire.[625]

Despite Émilie's efforts to rein him in, Voltaire kept writing things that got him into trouble with the French authorities. His long satirical poem, *Jeane du Pucelle* (Joan the Maid), was a bawdy satire ridiculing the idealization of Joan of Arc, whose virginity was constantly threatened by lustful monks or licentious soldiers but always saved in the nick of time. Any derision of France's national heroine was bound to cause offense.[626] In some ways, Mme Du Châtelet was bad for Voltaire. She wanted to keep him out of trouble, but when trouble came, she made it worse by losing her head. Yet no one in his life provided greater stimulation, kept better pace with him intellectually, or joined him more wholeheartedly in creating at Cirey an exhilarating refuge.[627]

Around 1740, Voltaire wrote what he thought was his best play: *Mahomet.* A tragedy set in an exotic location, the play told a story about mistaken identity, illicit love, and the discovery of a long-lost father and his children, culminating in murder and suicide. What made the play controversial was Voltaire's depiction of Mahomet, the founder of Islam, as an impostor and fanatic. He portrayed him not merely as the prophet of a new religion that he knew to be totally false, but as someone who wanted to use that religion to enslave the Arabs and conquer the world. It was the first time a play had treated the topics of superstition and fanaticism in the theatre.[628]

In the story, Mahomet has a definite plan and a terrifying purpose, and the play's second act conveys a political message that reverberates in our own time. Zopire, the Sheik of Mecca, laments the disturbed state of the country, and asks Mahomet, "Tyrant of your country, is it thus that you bring it peace and announce a god?" And Mahomet replies, "Many great empires have had their day, now it is the turn of the Arabs. A new religion, new chains, a new god are needed for the blind universe. By the right of superiority and determination over vulgar humanity."[629]

In 1741, the play opened triumphantly in the town of Lilly, but the critics saw the play directed not so much against Mahomet as against Jesus Christ. The French ministry concluded that it was directed against all religions, and the Paris censor refused to authorize the performance of the play in Paris until 1742. The outcry was so loud that Voltaire was forced to withdraw *Mahomet* from the stage after only three performances.[630]

Was *Mahomet* anti-Muslim, anti-Christian, or anti-religious? It was clearly against fanaticism and bigotry. Mahomet was portrayed as a conscious deceiver who foisted his new religion upon a credulous people and then used their faith as a spur to war. But Voltaire denied that the play was an attack upon any religion or individual. Instead, he said it was a plea to make Christianity more Christian.[631]

As early as 1740, Voltaire and Émilie were at odds, having become divergent in their interests and starting to pull in different directions. By 1748, fifty-four-year-old Voltaire had realized he could not give Émilie the love and passion that she needed. Émilie was forty-one, a dangerous age for a woman whose lover had become only a devoted friend. Predictably, she fell head over heels with a young captain of the guards, thirty-one-year-old Marquis Jean François de Saint-Lambert. She wrote love letters of almost girlish abandon to the handsome young officer, who may have assumed that a fling with Émilie du Châtelet was without meaning or consequence. If so, he had not reckoned with Émilie's fiery temperament and her desperate craving for love.[632]

On December 24, 1748, Émilie broke the news to Voltaire that she was pregnant by Saint-Lambert. She and Voltaire agreed that they had to legitimize the pregnancy by having everyone believe that her husband was the father of the child. Émilie had not had sexual relations with the

Marquis du Châtelet for some years, so she and Voltaire staged a marital reconciliation. They invited him to Cirey, and he was more than delighted when Émilie went through the motions of seducing him. When she later told the Marquis that she was pregnant, Emile reported to Voltaire, "He hopes I will give him a son."[633]

Émilie was now forty-two, and childbirth at her age was considered dangerous. Toward the end of April 1749, she had a premonition of her death and arranged all her papers in sealed packets, writing on them the names of those to whom they were to be delivered. On the night of September 3, 1749, with her three lovers in attendance, Émilie gave birth to a baby girl. When the delivery proved remarkably easy, Voltaire immediately announced the birth, with great joy, to all his friends. But his happiness would not last long. Within days, Émilie developed a fever, no doubt from an infection, and, though doctors were called, she died during the night of September 9, 1749. Her baby daughter died soon after. Voltaire was devastated. He wrote to his niece, Mme Denis, "My dear child, I have just lost a friend of twenty years."

The death of Émilie was a traumatic loss for Voltaire, and one from which he probably never fully recovered. Using his own poetic talents, he penned a few simple verses and attached to them a portrait of the person who would remain the greatest love of his life:[634]

The world has lost thee, noble Émilie,
Who lovedst art and truth and pleasures free.
The gods who did bestow their soul on thee,
Withheld no gift but immortality.[635]

Voltaire felt that if he stayed at Cirey, he would waste away in isolation. His only choice was to go back to Paris, and on October 12, 1749, he sent his books and his art collection to the city. He established himself in a spacious mansion on the Rue Traversière and asked his niece to join him there to be his hostess. Marie Louise Mignot, born in 1712, was the daughter of Voltaire's sister, and when his sister died, he had assumed protection of her children. In 1738, Marie Louise had married Captain Nicolas Charles Denis, but Captain Denis died in 1744, and she had turned to Voltaire for comfort. Mme Denis was worldly, materialistic, and self-centered, but she was also pretty, sexy, lively, fond of music and theatre, and something of a French literary figure. By the time she joined Voltaire at his mansion in Paris, she was thirty-seven.[636] He was in his fifties and chronically unwell. He needed her more than she needed him.[637]

For several years, Frederick, King of Prussia, had been urging Voltaire to come and join his court, but Voltaire had been so comfortable in Cirey with Émilie that he had not wanted to go. After moving to Paris, he received a new offer from Frederick: the post of chamberlain, free lodgings, and a salary of five thousand thalers. Voltaire asked the permission of Louis XV, who quickly agreed, saying, "This will make one madman the more at the Court of Prussia, and one less at Versailles." Voltaire's duties included dining or at least supping with the king and correcting his verse or prose. Frederick would be the pupil who submitted his homework to Voltaire, the teacher. Voltaire wrote in the early months of his stay, "This is a paradise of philosophers, there is the charm of retirement, there is the freedom of court life, with all the little comforts which the host of a château, who is also a king can procure for his very humble guest."[638]

Voltaire wrote to Mme Denis, asking her to join him in his new paradise, but she preferred Paris and its young men. She did warn him against staying too long in Berlin: "Friendship with a king is always precarious; he changes his mind and his favorites; one must be always on one's guard not to cross the royal mood or will." Mme Denis also said that sooner or later he would find himself a servant or a prisoner rather than a friend.[639]

Paradise was lost in November 1752, when Voltaire published a wickedly satirical pamphlet poking fun at the head of the Berlin Academy, Pierre Louis Maupertuis, called *Diatribe of Dr. Akakia*. The Greek word, *Akakia*, was used to indicate guileless simplicity. Frederick was furious to see his academy, its president, and, by implication, himself publicly ridiculed across Europe, just when his whole purpose was to establish Berlin as an important intellectual center.[640]

Once again, Voltaire had worn out his welcome, this time in Berlin, and he was unsure of where to go next. A chance meeting with Dr Théodore Tronchin of Geneva inspired him to move to Switzerland, as it pleased him to live near the famous doctor. In the early spring of 1755, Voltaire leased a house in Geneva, which he christened *Les Délices*.[641] Soon after the move, he wrote:

The house is pretty and convenient. Its charming aspect surprises and never wearies. On one side is the Lake Geneva, on the other the town. In the distance soars the Alps covered with eternal snow. Pleasant and intellectual society fills up the moments left me by study and by the care of my health.[642]

It was time for Voltaire to finally settle down, and he wanted Mme Denis to be his life companion, but she had to decide whether or not she could give up Paris and attach herself permanently to this extraordinary man. She was still in her early forties, while he was sixty and not in the best of health, so she might soon inherit a fortune. If not, she could still enjoy the wealth, her lovers, and being with Voltaire, as life with him was never dull.[643]

Voltaire kept himself occupied by building, gardening, planting, laying out poultry yards, and forming a dairy. Though he was merely leasing the property, he had a home that he felt was his. He described the gardens at Les Délices as a "comparable to the most beautiful near Paris." By April 1755, he had employed two master gardeners, twenty workers, and twelve servants. Later, the number of gardeners would rise by four. By the following spring, he had also hired four carriages, a coachman, six horses, a postillion, a valet, a French cook, a scullery boy, and a secretary.[644] He was now living the opulent lifestyle of a country gentleman.

At Les Délices, Voltaire received visitors from all over Europe, and anyone traveling to Switzerland made it a point to call on him. Many of his guests were strangers who just invited themselves, but Voltaire was having a wonderful time in his new home. In September of 1755, he wrote:

I haven't a moment to myself. I have to spend time with the procession of the curious who come from Lyon, Geneva, Saxony, Switzerland, and even from Paris. Almost every day, I have seven or eight people come to have dinner with me.[645]

Voltaire gave an indication of how happy was his life at Les Délices in his 1756 response to the invitation of the Empress of Austria, Maria Theresa, when she sent him a "most flattering" message asking him to her court. He might have jumped at the chance earlier, but now he replied:

I shall not go to Vienna. I am too comfortable in my retreat Les Délices. Happy he who lives in his own house with his niece, his books, his garden, his vines, his horses, his cows, his eagle, his fox, and his rabbits that caress their noses with their paws. I have all that and the Alps as well.[646]

Voltaire is often described as sometimes sad, sometimes moved, but never serious; yet he became serious on November 1, 1755, when the civilized world was rocked with the news that a terrible earthquake had struck Lisbon, Portugal. The quake struck at ten o'clock in the morning when the faithful of that very Catholic city were celebrating Mass on All Saints Day. During their worship service, their city was destroyed, and an estimated 30,000 people were killed.

The catastrophe set off a major debate across Europe about the problem of evil: If God is good, how can he permit such a catastrophe? How can man reconcile the goodness of God with the mindless cruelty of the disaster in Lisbon? An idea popular at the time was that "whatever is is right," and therefore, "all is well." This concept was unsatisfactory to Voltaire, and he would write after the earthquake that only the laws of physics could bring about such frightful disasters in this "best of all possible worlds."

From 1756 to 1760, Voltaire spent his time writing novels, including his most enduring work, *Candide,* the timeless tale of an innocent boy who is convinced that everything happens for the best. He discovers from bitter experience that evil in the world is real and that it can be remedied only by works and not through faith.[647] In *Candide*, Voltaire takes pointed issue with the idea that "all is well," by repeatedly ridiculing the persistent optimism of Dr. Pangloss.[648] In the short space of one hundred pages, *Candide* is a mix of autobiography, pacifism, anti-clerical satire, skepticism, good humor, and good sense.[649]

The best of all possible satire, *Candide* is Voltaire's attempt to confer freedom on his readers: freedom to think, feel, and speak by the light of human reason. All is not for the best in this world. And what is good does not make up for what is bad. It is up to us to lift ourselves from the slough of despondency through our actions. Metaphorically speaking, we are the ones who must cultivate our gardens to eliminate the brambles of old customs and prejudices, give them new soil, sun, air, and light, and rid their fruit trees from caterpillars and parasitic insects of all kinds.[650]

The world was astonished that the sixty-five year old writer could have produced this youthful voice. The authorities immediately tried to suppress *Candide*, but their efforts were overwhelmed by its instantaneously popular success throughout Europe. By March 1759, 6,000 copies had been sold in Paris alone, and by year's end, perhaps as many as 30,000.

Les Délices had been just the right setting in which to compose *Candide*, Voltaire's iconic story about the human condition, but the years following the earthquake increased Voltaire's pessimism. He was happy at Les Délices, but he continued to fear that the authorities might conspire against him, and he was conscious that he was always walking the fine line between acceptable celebrity and dangerous notoriety. Calvinist Geneva was intellectually enlightened, but serious about its religion, so not the ideal location for his satirical wit. For an adventurous philosopher such as Voltaire, it might actually be best to return to France when Swiss Calvinistic intolerance threatened and to quickly retreat to Switzerland when the winds of French Catholic intolerance blew with fury.[651] But he was not sure that he wanted to end his days on Swiss soil.[652]

Fortune was in Voltaire's favor when the new French minister of foreign affairs turned out to be a fan who would turn a blind eye if the famous heretic returned to France. So in the autumn of 1758, he did just that, buying the château de Ferney, the home with which he is now most associated. He could live primarily on French soil, on the north shore of the lake, but still only three and a half miles from Geneva. Ferney also had considerable acreage that was well suited to planting, gardening, and farming.

The busy country gentleman did not neglect his writing at Ferney. He resolved to carry on his persistent systematic warfare to *ecrasez l infâme*, or crush superstition. To Voltaire, religion was the primary source of the superstition that led to injustice and fanaticism.[653] Religion enforced its doctrines with sword, fire, and threats of imprisonment or eternal damnation. In the name of religion, the massacre on the night of St. Bartholomew had been carried out, and religion had been used to gloss over royal sins. It benefitted the rich, who could pay for the remission of their sins, and it served as a shield for tyranny and oppression that ground down the poor and kept wretchedness wretched forever.[654]

Ecrasez l infâme cannot easily be translated into English, and historians have used differing literal translations. Tallentyre translates it as *intolerance*, and Gastineau translates it as *Let us crush the wretch, for if you do not crush him, he will crush you.* Espinasse translates it as *Crush the infamous one,* where "infamous one" is superstition, with its threat of everlasting torture in the next world and its demand for unquestioning obedience from all men, whether they be in Paris, Vienna, or Geneva.

In Voltaire's time, the official Christian view was that the purpose of religion was to ensure eternal happiness in the afterlife for a few select human beings. The Enlightenment had a single outstanding characteristic which distinguished it from all preceding philosophies: a belief in progress through human reason. This belief leads to humanism, for humanism is the religion of progress, not of science. During the Enlightenment, people began to look around them rather than upward; in doing so, they saw that the world was not good, but evil could be resisted.[655]

Voltaire constantly calls on his readers to put two and two together, to "dare to know." For him, the Enlightenment meant getting people to think for themselves and to see through the nonsense that had held them in thrall.[656] Voltaire also had a fixation on justice as the most fundamental principle, and this explains much of his life. If the malice of a critic or the inefficiency of an official exasperated him, it was because he experienced malice and inefficiency as unjust behavior.[657] At Ferney, Voltaire was the universal advocate of humanity, the judge of the public conscience, and the champion of justice. From all parts of France came the unfortunate, the oppressed, and all who were molested in their freedom of conscience. They came for support, advice, and money, and Voltaire refused no one. Ferney became the Mecca of free thought.[658]

Voltaire had spent many of his sixty years in a quasi-nomadic existence, in constant search of fame, fortune, security, and freedom. Now the world came to his doorstep: the great, the small, and the good, to be given shelter against persecution and injustice against the *Infâme.*

His secretary took dictation and sent letters daily to all corners of the European world. A remote corner of France had become the intellectual and cultural nerve center of Europe, all because of the personality and magnitude of François Marie Arouet de Voltaire. He was rich, old, and free, so he could do exactly what he wanted. And what he wanted was to write plays and fight the good fight for reason over superstition.

In Catholic Europe, human beings were free neither to worship a God of their own choosing nor to trust in their own innocence as a guarantee against criminal conviction. For Voltaire, such a state of affairs was intolerable. At sixty-five, he was still blessed with indefatigable zeal. His critics said that he had forgotten to die. His remaining hair might be white and all his teeth gone, but he appeared to have taken out a new lease on life, and he was ready to have the Church for breakfast.[659]

The breakfast Voltaire hungered for was being prepared in 1761 in the southern French city of Toulouse. In order to understand what followed, we must understand that the region surrounding Toulouse was an area of intense hatreds between the Catholics and the Huguenots. Each side had committed atrocities over the years, and 200 years after the St. Bartholomew's Day Massacre of 3,200 Protestants, Catholics still celebrated the horrific event with enthusiastic zeal, including widely held ceremonies and religious processions.[660]

At sixty-four, Jean Calas was one of a small group of Huguenots still residing in Toulouse. He had lived there for forty years with his wife, their four sons, and their two daughters, above a small shop the family owned on the main street of town. His oldest son, Marc Antoine, had studied law, but knowing that Protestants were forbidden to enter the profession, he had tried to conceal his Protestantism. The deceit was discovered, and Marc Antoine had become moody, taking to gambling and drinking.[661]

On October 13, 1761, the Calas family gathered for dinner in their rooms above the store, including their Catholic governess and a friend of Marc's. After the meal, Marc went down to the shop but did not return. Wondering why, his brother Pierre and Marc's friend went down the stairs to find Marc's lifeless body hanging from a beam. Pierre alerted his family and rushed to get a doctor. After the police arrived on the scene, curious onlookers gathered, and a voice suddenly exclaimed that the young man had been hanged by his family for wanting to turn Catholic. The crowd immediately took up the cry, and soon the entire Calas family was imprisoned.

A trial was held on March 9, 1762, by the Parliament of Toulouse, consisting of lawyers who were not elected by the people. One witness, a painter named Mattei, testified that his wife had told him that a person named Mandrille had told her that he had heard Marc Antione's cries at the other end of the town. On this and similarly doubtful testimony, Jean Calas was condemned to be tortured, in order to extract a confession of guilt, and then broken on the wheel; after this, his body was to be burned and his ashes scattered to the winds. The rest of the Calas family was released from prison, but all of their assets were confiscated by the authorities.[662]

The authorities had pre-judged Jean Calas and then looked for hard evidence to support their assumptions. Even though no such evidence was ever produced, a narrow majority of the court ruled that Calas was guilty and subject to be tortured and broken on the wheel.[663] The proceedings were so secret that even Jean's wife and family neither read nor heard the sentence before it was carried out on the day following the trial. Jean Calas unflinchingly bore the excruciating torture to which he was subjected. His arms and legs were stretched on the rack before he was forced to drink two jugs of water that ballooned his body to almost twice its size. Still he made no confession. At the foot of the scaffold, a priest asked again for a confession, only to receive the reply, "Do you also believe it is possible for a father to murder his son?" Calas was judicially murdered on March 10, 1762.[664]

On March 22, a news item about the Calas incident caught Voltaire's attention. Initially taking the report of Jean's guilt at face value, he wrote to a friend, giving an indication of his feelings about all organized religion: "We may not be worth much, but the Huguenots are worse, and in addition they preach against play acting."[665] This was Voltaire's first reference to what would become famous as the Calas Affair, and his involvement with it would cause a dramatic turning point in his life. Three days later, a visit from one of the surviving Calas sons caused his attitude to completely change.

Convinced of Jean Calas' innocence, Voltaire went to work to clear his name, with all the energy the sixty-eight-year-old could muster. He had the money, the influence, and the determination, but most of all, he had the power of his pen. He published a pamphlet that told the story as if it were a letter from Mme Calas to her sons, giving her version of what had happened. The pamphlet itself was an indictment of the French judicial system, especially of its secrecy, brutality, and haste, in contrast to the relative openness of the English system.[666]

In fighting for justice for the Calas family, the greatest obstacle Voltaire faced was the dogged refusal of the Toulouse Parliament to release the records of the legal proceedings. Final victory did not come until March 9, 1765, when the French court in Paris recommended the posthumous exoneration of Jean Calas, almost exactly three years after the Parliament of Toulouse sentenced him to death in 1762. On April 11, a generous Louis XV decreed that the family be compensated from the royal purse in the amount of 36,000 livres, the French currency at that time. Voltaire wrote, "I forgot all my ills when I learned of the king's generosity; I felt young and vigorous again."[667] His efforts to expose the injustice done to the Calas family had led Voltaire to his most important victory in the campaign against the *Infâme,* and it defined him for all time as the champion of human rights.[668]

Like the Lisbon earthquake, the Calas affair had a lasting and profound effect on Voltaire. He realized even more than he had before that his writings could evoke a vast response throughout the civilized world. He knew, beyond a doubt, that his words could help to form and harness public opinion against superstitious explanations, not only for natural disasters, but for legal assassinations provoked by religious hysteria.[669] Especially through his actions in the Calas case, Voltaire was perhaps the first to demonstrate that public opinion could be a powerful force in the life of a civilized community.

Voltaire had wielded his powerful pen, and it had been a successful strategy, even in the face of authoritative, fanatical, and unscrupulous opposition. While this was a tremendous step forward in the evolution of human freedom, superstition, intolerance, and injustice die hard. In the twentieth century, especially during World War II, they would rise to heights not seen before.[670]

Following the Calas Affair, seventy-one-year-old Voltaire became heavily involved with the Sirven case, where a father was accused of murdering his daughter to prevent her conversion to Catholicism. But of all the cases that Voltaire championed, the one that most moved him, because of the youth of the accused and the barbarity of the authorities, occurred in Abbeville, in what was supposed to be a more tolerant region of northern France: In August 1765, young Jean François Lefèvre, chevalier de La Barre, was alleged to have committed the illegal acts of singing anti-religious songs, maliciously damaging a crucifix, and showing disrespect to a religious procession. He was charged with blasphemy and sacrilege, and the verdict was *guilty*. The sentence for the twenty-year-old was to have his tongue torn out, his head severed from his body, and his body burned on a pyre.[671] The primary evidence against young La Barre was that a search of his apartment revealed that he had in his possession books by Voltaire. La Barre was spared no torture, and the manner of his death was out of all proportion to his supposed offense. His fate affected Voltaire deeply, and it would haunt him for the rest of his life.[672]

Two ideals fired Voltaire's passion: Justice and Reason. They were an intimate part of his make-up and the basis for all that he thought, felt, wrote, and did. In a civilized State, Voltaire maintained, the law must not only be just, but it must have supreme authority. Any theology not based on reason was, for him, no more than superstition, and he saw organized religion as useless.[673]

Through the years, Voltaire has been thought of as an atheist, but he was never that. His enduring opposition to religion did not negate his belief in God. In May of 1775 or 1776, he had been reading Jean Jacque Rousseau's description of the splendors of God's creation, and he wanted to see for himself if Rousseau was right. At three in the morning, he put on his best clothes and awakened a house guest. The two men walked for two hours with only the light of a lantern, reaching a valley just as dawn was breaking. There, they beheld a glorious sight: Before them stood the magnificent grandeur of the Jura Mountains, with the dark green tips of the trees etched against the pale blue light of morning. On the far horizon they saw the sun, rising in a semicircle of purple fire. Voltaire removed his hat and prostrated himself on the ground, improvising a poetic chant of worship: "Almighty God, I believe." Rising to his feet, and resuming his now-stooped posture, he replaced his hat, dusted the dirt from his elegant breeches, eyed the heavens, and added, "As for Monsieur, the son, and Madame, the mother, that is quite another matter."[674]

The truth of this account is debatable. After all, a steep climb following a two-hour walk on the part of an eighty-two-year-old suggests a good story and nothing more. But elements of the dramatic account ring true: Voltaire had an abiding desire to see things for himself. He was prone to theatrical performances, including spontaneous verse, and there was the parting shot, with his typical witty irreverence to reassert his independence. Characteristically, he would believe what he felt was rational, but he would never let himself be duped.[675]

During the winter of 1777-1778, Mme Denis and Voltaire wearied of the cold, dark solitude of Ferney. They longed for Paris, and the recent death of Louis XV had removed the main obstacle to their return. Voltaire was also concerned about receiving adequate medical care for his failing health, and Dr. Tronchin now lived in Paris. Voltaire suffered from gout and from urine retention, an early symptom of the prostate cancer that would kill him. Both conditions were extremely painful.[676]

On February 5, 1778, Voltaire set off for Paris accompanied by his secretary and his cook, all traveling in his specially adapted sleeping carriage, kept warm by a portable stove. They arrived at the gates of the city on February 10, 1778, where the customs officers asked if he had anything liable to duty. Voltaire responded, "Gentlemen, I am the only contraband here."[677] The party went straight to the Hotel de Villette, located on the left bank of the Seine on the street now named Rue Voltaire.[678]

The news of Voltaire's arrival in Paris spread like wildfire throughout the city. A crowd filled the salon where he and Mme Denis were staying, and Voltaire received them in his dressing gown and night-cap.[679] The hotel was besieged with more than 300 would-be visitors from every walk of life. On the streets of Paris, Voltaire was a comical-looking figure, wearing his long, sable fur coat and his large, old-fashioned wig topped off with a red bonnet, and carrying a walking stick with a handle carved in the shape of a crow.

On March 30, 1778, Voltaire felt strong enough to attend a performance of one of his plays at the Comédie Francaise. The crowd surrounding him was so thick that his carriage could barely move.[680] At the theatre, the audience gave him a standing ovation lasting more than twenty minutes. Upon leaving, he was again thronged by so many that the horses could proceed only at a walk. People on the street hailed him as "the man of the Calas." They had come to honor this frail, elderly man who had triumphed over injustice against all odds. There was no revolutionary anger in their cheering. By his very presence, Voltaire had united people from all walks of life and given them hope. He was their hero, saint, and god, occupying a position usually reserved for the monarch. But King Louis XVI and his queen, Marie Antoinette, were conspicuous by their absence—an absence by which the royal couple foolishly displayed their growing irrelevance to the life of the French nation.[681]

Voltaire's health continued to deteriorate, and he became concerned about how he would be buried if he died in Paris. His antagonist, the Church, would not allow him to be buried in consecrated ground, which meant his body would be dumped into a pit and covered with lime. He was advised to make whatever peace he could with the Church. In hopes of satisfying the bishop, he made a brief "confession," but given his nature, this was not an easy task. He said, "I die, adoring God, loving my friends, not hating my enemies, and detesting superstition."[682]

On May 30, 1778, the abbé of St. Sulpice made another effort to receive a declaration of faith from the dying man. But when the abbé asked if he believed in Jesus Christ, Voltaire replied, "In the name of God, Sir, do not speak to me anymore about that man, and let me die in peace." He died at eleven o'clock that night.[683]

The story of Voltaire's death and burial is no less interesting than many stories of his life. His family decided to dress his body as if he were still alive and travel by carriage back to Ferney. On the day after he died, an autopsy was performed and the body embalmed. That evening, after dark, his body was fully dressed and propped up in his carriage between two relatives, as if he were still alive, and the funeral party set off in the direction of Ferney. Two problems remained: first, it was not assured that the bishop of Ferney would allow the burial of Voltaire; and second, the government might guess that the funeral party would head to his home abbey and interfere with the proceedings. So after leaving the city, the carriage turned due east, toward the Champagne region and the abbey of Scelliéres. The abbé there, a nephew of Voltaire, had agreed to bury him in sanctified ground.

The funeral party arrived at Scelliéres on June 1, and everything was prepared for a formal funeral Mass to be held the next day. They were just in time. On June 2, the local bishop was alerted and wrote to the prior at Scelliéres, forbidding him to bury Voltaire. But he was too late. By then, Voltaire had been buried, and his body was to remain at the abbey for the next thirteen years. After the French Revolution, his remains were removed from Scelliéres and reburied in the Panthéon in Paris on July 11, 1791.[684]

Most people are not familiar with Voltaire's books, poems, or plays, with the possible exception of *Candide.* And why should anyone care about a man who died almost 250 years ago? Many of us live in a world where we are free to worship, or not, as we wish, and to say, within reason, dumb things. We can read favorite publications that support our own views of world affairs, even if those views are different from our neighbors, our employer, or our government.

Voltaire understood that freedom of speech is the basis for all freedom—the means by which we enlighten each other.[685] To be happy, people must be free, and freedom depends on the rule of just law. Hence, the best government is one which guarantees to everyone, without exception, the greatest liberty he can enjoy without harm to his fellows. Voltaire saw the law, born of justice and reason, as the source and basis for civilization. As he said, "Liberty consists of dependence on nothing but law."[686]

Voltaire was not a revolutionary. He actually preferred the rule of one individual head of State, such as a benevolent absolute monarchy, to the rule of a body of men. He wanted the monarch to have sole power, but only on the condition that this power would be exercised with wisdom and toleration. He also said that the monarch should be subject to the law, along with everyone else. Still, the French Revolution paid homage to Voltaire's achievements. On the catafalque bearing his coffin back to

Paris, the inscription read, "Poet, philosopher, historian. He gave a great impetus to the human spirit and prepared us to be free."[687]

After a lifetime of dogged determination, Voltaire had cleared the ground and made it ready for the planting of the Tree of Liberty. Whoever sits under that tree in any country, free to worship God as he will, and to think, learn, and do all that does not impede the freedom of others, is one who can progress to unrestricted heights of light and knowledge. Those who live in such freedom should, in gratitude, remember Voltaire.[688]

CHAPTER 10

A United States of Europe: Is It Possible?

Voltaire's life and work inspire hope that human longing for freedom and justice may prevail against intolerance, but the preceding chapters tell the darker tale of a history that reflects much about human desire for wealth and dominance. Anti-Semitism is only one example of hatred too often exhibited by the powerful toward those perceived as "different" or "less than" in some way. Europe's story is one of nations consumed with suspicion, fear, and hatred of the *other* person, religion, culture, or country.

In 1740, Voltaire wrote what he considered to be his best play, *Mahomet*. The story illustrated how religion based on false miracles and ruthless fanaticism can greatly influence or even control docile or credulous people. In a letter to King Frederick II of Prussia, much to the king's delight, Voltaire described his play as being about "the love of mankind and the hatred of fanaticism, two virtues that adorn your throne, guided my pen."[689] He sent the king a condensed version of the story, about a young man born virtuous but seduced by fanaticism, who murders an old man who loves him. The youth thinks he is serving Mahomet, who has ordered the murder and promised a reward, but he discovers that the old man is his long-lost father and the reward, his long-lost sister.

Voltaire shared with Frederick his opinion that young men are more vulnerable to seduction and madness than others in society because their reason may fail them in the face of fanaticism: "It is remarkable how easily nature is sometimes sacrificed to superstition. Every day, superstition does all the mischief it possibly can: disunites friends, separates the kindred and relations, destroys the wise and worthy by the hands of fools and enthusiasts."[690] Years later, Voltaire again expressed his attitude toward blind belief when he wrote, "Those who can make you believe absurdities can make you commit atrocities."[691]

Voltaire's words were written more than two hundred years ago, but are they still relevant today? They apply all too well in our time, where people everywhere face the growing threat of terrorism motivated by religious extremism. More than ever, we need ideas like Voltaire's to restore sanity and balance within our international community.

Early in 2015, two young brothers entered the Paris offices of the French magazine, *Charlie Hebdo,* and carried out the planned massacre of eleven employees in retaliation for the magazine's publication of satirical cartoons of Muhammad. On the same day, a co-conspirator of the brothers killed a policewoman and occupied a Jewish delicatessen, taking its occupants hostage and killing four of them. Unlike the Nazis, who committed most of their atrocities behind behind the barbed-wire of their death camps, terrorists like those in the Paris attacks have been proud of their actions, seeking publicity by "claiming responsibility" for killing innocents and filming their horrific crimes for display on YouTube. Their intent is to strike fear in the hearts of those they consider to be political or religious opponents.

Citizens of the United States, Europe, and many nations throughout the world see themselves as belonging to a civilization based largely on the writings of early Greek and Roman philosophers and continuing through Voltaire's Age of Reason to today. To civilized people everywhere, the violent actions of fanatic extremists are unfathomable, unjustifiable, and unacceptable. After the attacks in Paris, people of many nations and religions united to raise their voices for freedom of speech and in opposition to terrorism. But as acts of terror persist, will the solidarity of those who deplore and resist such acts persist as well?

Too often, reasonable people have been relatively quiet when insanity hijacks their national, religious, or cultural group. Many ordinary Austrians and citizens of other countries were silent as Jews among them were persecuted, deprived of their homes and possessions, and deported to death camps. As a college student during the American Civil Rights Era, I wanted to ask people of the American South where they were when police, with impunity, used fire hoses on peaceful black youths who wanted only to eat at a Woolworth lunch counter or attend an integrated school. I recall no large demonstration in the streets to express opposition to such brutality. When contemporary terrorism is carried out in the name of Islam, Muslims have not publicly opposed such acts on a consistent basis. In all such instances, silence can look like acquiescence.

The French Revolution was, in part, inspired by Voltaire, and the French are among those who most highly value his writings in defense of free speech. Muslims who have lived in France for generations are well integrated into French society, and while they probably do not approve of satire published about the founder of their religion, they understand freedom of speech. After the attacks in Paris, many of them spoke out to decry the violence perpetrated by extremists in the name of Islam.

But what about Muslims who have more recently immigrated to Western nations to flee from poverty and political unrest? Most immigrants everywhere are seeking only security and peace for their families, but their compliance with the values, norms, and even laws of their new places of residence cannot be taken for granted. Many of them are ill-informed about societies different from their own, and some have little to no understanding or experience of Western values, including freedom of speech. Some may even believe that such freedom leads to evil. They have emigrated from countries where public criticism of religion or government can lead to lashings, years of imprisonment, or even death.

Today's terrorism has a decidedly international face. It may be sponsored by a state or an organization, but it is often the product of the determined zeal of religious fanatics who act independently or in relatively small numbers within multiple countries, especially where there is political unrest or a weak government. Perpetrators have included recent immigrants who have failed either to understand or to embrace the cultures and laws of the countries to which they have moved.

What is the solution? If a nation values equal rights for its citizens under its laws, it must require its new immigrants to become educated about those laws and compliant with them. Without freedom of speech, no other freedoms can be sustained. And while people may fear voicing opposition to extremism, the desire to remain silent in the face of very real threats to security and freedom must be resisted. If those who value freedom do not continue to speak out, only the terrorists acting in the name of religion will have the floor.

In addition to facing terrorist threats, Europe continues to face the serious threat of economic decline. Not only must European Union strengthen collaborative security efforts among its member nations, it must pro-actively and collectively confront its economic problems. To support its fragile common currency, Europe must overcome the financial crises that followed profligate spending during the era of low interest rates and an initially successful euro.

Years after Greece first experienced economic disaster, large European economies remain on the brink of deflation. Only a few structural changes engineered by Germany stand between them and another major financial crisis. A divided European leadership lost the chance to place France and Italy in a mode of serious structural reform, and with one-fifth of the world's output coming from Europe, pervasive stagflation and falling prices make the collapse of the euro increasingly likely. Only a truly unified fiscal policy can save it.

The debt of many nations due to entitlement promises made during good times are the elephant in the room nobody wants to talk about. Debt is already causing investors to avoid Europe, especially Italy and Greece, turning up the volume on separatist talk throughout the continent. Impending deflation is always a serious problem because people and businesses postpone spending, thinking that prices will fall still lower. Loan defaults rise as demand sinks.

Many believe that the world economy can grow sufficiently to bring national debts down to a reasonable level. But what if that doesn't happen? Japan's economy has been deflated for twenty years and counting. Germany is the manufacturing power that has been the engine of the European economy, but what if their customers are too broke to buy their products? The United States is doing reasonably well, but it will face the same problem Germany faces if Europe, its largest trading partner, falls into deflation and Europeans can't buy U.S. goods.

Several recent books have discussed how Europe "sleepwalked" into the First World War during the early twentieth century due to a lack of leadership, and there are many striking parallels between then and now. While Europe did act to develop a unified currency, the euro, the lack of strong leadership allowed this to happen without the necessary foundation of a unified fiscal policy.

A lack of leadership in both the U.S. and Europe has also left the West with no unified strategy to defeat current security threats from Russia and militant religious extremists. The reluctance of U.S. and European governments and peoples to go to war encourages our enemies to be more aggressive in advancing their agendas. In reflecting on critical decisions being made by today's Western leaders, we may someday be asking the question that Margaret MacMillan asked in her book on World War I, *The War That Ended Peace*: "What were they thinking?"

Greater European unity is the key to strengthening its military security and to solving its economic problems. Is it possible? Earlier chapters related how, in 1900, prior to World War I, European nations worked hand in hand to collaborate on the successful international relief expedition to aid people affected by the Boxer Rebellion in China. During the same era, important artists and musicians from many nationalities were celebrated throughout Europe. Affordable and convenient travel made it possible for Europeans to move freely on the continent to enjoy the sights of London, Paris, Vienna, and Rome. For a brief time, Europe was the very model of community and interdependence. But in the post-war era, all that has changed.

From the days of mud huts in Germany across the Danube to the Roman fortress city of Vindobona, moving through time to the Baroque buildings of eighteenth-century Vienna, European towns and rural areas have developed around common languages, religions, and cultures. This has ultimately led to narrow nationalistic views that helped to trigger two World Wars. Nationalistic fervor has reared its head again in the Middle East and in Eastern Europe, reminding us of similar passions in the Balkans before 1914. Europeans have been down this road before, and they know it does not end well. On December 21, 2013, this statement appeared in an article in *The Economist*: "Politicians are playing with nationalism just as they did a hundred years ago. The European Union is looking more fractious and riven by more incipient nationalism than at any point in its formation."

When we look back at events a hundred years ago, we see unnerving similarities to economic and political trends in our own times. During the last decades of the nineteenth century and the early years of the twentieth century prior to the World Wars, anarchists were committing barbaric terrorist acts with the aim of destroying Western Civilization. They were willing to commit violence against all forms of social or political organization, which they deemed to be tools of oppression. A bomb thrown by an anarchist into an audience at a performance in Barcelona, Spain, killed twenty-nine theatre-goers. When anarchists were sentenced in Paris for participating in a violent demonstration, their supporters blew up the homes of the judge and the prosecutor. People were reluctant to go into public places in Paris for fear of where the terrorists would strike next.

When they were caught, terrorists of that era often had no clear vision for why they had committed such brutal acts. Empress Elizabeth of Austria was stabbed simply because she was the accessible monarch. America was not immune: President William McKinley was shot and killed by an assassin who only said, "I have done my duty." While campaigning in an attempt to reclaim the office of president, Theodore Roosevelt was wounded in an assassination attempt by a man who simply thought he should not be seeking a third term.[692]

International leaders bungled things in ways that helped to cause World War I, but that wasn't the only problem. According to Stefan Zweig in his book, *The World of Yesterday*, leaders in place after the war also bungled the peace:

It was only after the smoke of war had lifted that the terrible destruction that had resulted became visible ... How could the people rely on the promises of a State which had annulled all those obligations to the citizens which it could not conveniently fulfill? It was the same old clique, the so-called men of experience who now surpassed the folly of war with their bungling of the peace ... The peace offered one of the greatest, if not the greatest, moral potentialities of history. Wilson knew it. In his comprehensive vision he sketched the plan for a veritable and enduring world agreement. But the old generals, the old statesmen, the old captains of industry

had snipped that great concept to bits and reduced it to worthless
paper.[693]

Is it any wonder that political ineptness leading first to war and then to a botched peace ultimately led to the hyper-inflation that resulted in the Great Depression? Everyone felt cheated, including mothers who had lost their children in the war and people who had patriotically bought now-worthless war bonds. In France, Austria, and Germany, a whole generation of young men were lost—killed or crippled by the war. Survivors who had dreamed of a better world after the war were disillusioned. Youth who were too lucky or too young to have participated in the war had festering suspicions of authority, including the State, their parents, and their teachers. Their protests took various forms, including "boyish bobs" for young women and feminine-looking apparel for young men. Open homosexuality became trendy, partly as a statement against the established order.

Are things different today? On October 16, 2014, in *The Wall Street Journal,* Daniel Hemminger wrote:

In Italy and Spain youth unemployment is above 40%. These young people have become bitter at their parents' generation for wallowing in a system whose labor protections suppress the creation of new jobs. Economic anxiety has fueled the rise of extremist political movements in France, Germany, England and elsewhere. Weak economic growth is a grave danger to European stability especially since they are missing the key element to recovery. That element is political courage. A political leader willing to stand up against

finance ministers and a financial press that will ride previously failed
models off another cliff. Germany was the key here but they don't
know what to do and nobody is helping them.

The monetary policy which created the euro was a step forward, but it failed to include a true Federal Reserve, a real fiscal union, or commonly elected leaders, so no definition exists of the common economic good for all of Europe. Logic demands that these things be in place, but history shows how difficult it would be to create them. Every war described in the preceding pages has started as a European civil war, with the exception of the small unified effort to repel the Turks from the gates of Vienna in 1683. In fact, some would say that the major reason for creating the unified currency, the euro, was to prevent another civil war among the European nations.[694]

Recent crises have not resulted in a structural unification of Europe, though some have wanted to achieve this. In the past, the megalomaniac Napoleon tried to create a common legal system for all the countries he defeated through relentless warfare; Hitler tried to form an international political union through the systematic use of sheer terror and brute force, and Stalin successfully consolidated East European nations and East Germany by taking them as spoils of war, until the Soviet Union's brand of international communism crumbled. At no time have European leaders been able to convince all of their governmental peers or their people that a voluntary United States of Europe is the best way to protect their freedom and achieve economic stability.

If a true fiscal and political union is needed to ensure the survival of the euro and the security of Europe, let's go back and ask again, what will it take for European nations to be willing to form such a union? We can turn to the history of our own United States for perspective.

While it is not fully known to what degree the philosophy of Voltaire influenced America's Founding Fathers, a number of them embraced views that were consistent with those of the European Enlightenment. Even so, there was sincere and passionate disagreement among them as to how the United States of America should take shape. Soon after the war with England, the fragile American union was facing a crisis that almost destroyed its ability to survive.

The Treaty of Paris ending the Revolutionary War in 1783 required the British to evacuate their forts in the Great Lakes region, but knowing the weakness of the newly liberated American states, they were in no hurry to abide by these terms. Refusing to recognize American control of the vast area west of the Appalachians, Spain soon closed the Mississippi River to American commerce. In so doing, they were hoping to induce populations in the West to shift their shaky allegiance to Spain in exchange for access to this vital waterway.[695] After a trip to check on his land holdings in the West, George Washington recognized the danger and reported that the inhabitants of the area he visited were only "sketchily loyal to their new nation and a touch of a feather would turn them any way."[696] Both England and Spain would have been quite happy to regain their former colonies. The thirteen states of the new confederation were broke, and there was no adequate army either to enforce the Treaty of Paris with the British or to force Spain to open the Mississippi River.

There were problems within the new country as well. In January 1782, there was a plan for a federal customs duty of 5 percent to provide funds to pay an already impatient army whose soldiers had refused to disband without at least part of their back pay. But consent of all thirteen states was required, and the plan was blocked by Rhode Island. Instead, Rhode Island proposed to abolish all of its federal debt and divide any remaining wealth equally among its own residents.

In 1783, pamphlets were beginning to appear encouraging soldiers to retain their arms, replace General Washington and all other commanders who counseled moderation, march on the new Congress, and hold its members captive until they received their promised pay. Most of the soldiers had already served eight years without income from any source.[697] In order to feed, equip, and pay the Continental Army during the war, Congress had turned to the easiest financial expediency—the printing press. Some soldiers were so indebted because of the devalued currency that they expected to be jailed upon being discharged from the army.

The federal government of 1783 had the power to raise an army and navy and to coin and borrow money, but it did not have the power of taxation in order to fund these activities. Congress could only apportion federal costs among the thirteen states according to the value of each state's surveyed land and wait for each state to send its share of the money. Some states paid promptly, but most were seriously in arrears, and some, notably New Jersey in 1785, just said no. Under the Articles of Confederation, the federal government was much like the United Nations today—more or less powerless.[698]

Many creditors and property owners in youthful America were disturbed by the mounting power of state governments and dismayed by the impotence of a federal government that had sold off its last warship and let the army shrink to an insignificant force of 700 soldiers. The federal treasury was empty, so debt could not be serviced in order to establish

American credit abroad. Fearing that foreign creditors would not show the patience of domestic creditors, Alexander Hamilton warned, "They have the power to enforce their demands and sooner or later they may be expected to do it."[699]

In June 1783, rebellious troops in Philadelphia sent a petition to Congress demanding their money in threatening terms. Two days later, eighty armed men seized control of several arsenals and prepared to raid the local bank. A portion of the revolutionary army had turned into a mob that was intimidating the enfeebled federal government, and Hamilton was seeing his worst fears coming true. He warned Congress that the British were still "an enemy vigilant, intriguing, and well acquainted with our defects and embarrassments." Hamilton chose this time to unveil his plan to pay the national debt through customs duties and the sale of federal government bonds.[700]

Today, a visit to our nation's capital will expose one to monuments that rightly reflect the greatness of George Washington, Thomas Jefferson, Abraham Lincoln, and more recently, Franklin Roosevelt. While there is a modest statue of Alexander Hamilton in front of the U.S. Treasury Building, the writer George Will said, "If you seek a monument to Hamilton you need only look around. You are living in his memorial. We honor Jefferson but we live in Hamilton's country."[701]

Jefferson's vision of America was a nation of self-sufficient farmers, with each of its states holding the dominant power. In contrast, Hamilton saw a national, integrated urban economy that could compete with European manufacturers. He also envisioned a federal judiciary with powers sufficient to protect property and liberties against democratic excess. Finally, he proposed a professional army and navy, with a chief executive who had commander-in-chief powers, to enable the young country to repel foreign attacks and suppress domestic insurrection. Hamilton was at home in the city, and he knew the theory and practice of finance. He saw more clearly than Jefferson how the winds of economic change were blowing in the late eighteenth century. With a vision of American greatness, he was ultimately the most potent influence in calling for a Constitutional Convention.[702]

In June of 1787, Hamilton had one purpose: to push forward a plan for a federal financial system that would both cement the union and enable the government to pay its debts. His success is demonstrated by the transformation of the country's financial condition. In the 1780s, the United States was a financial basket case, but by 1794, the country had the highest credit rating in Europe, and some of its bonds were selling at a 10 percent premium.[703]

It would take another extraordinary crisis to completely solidify the union Alexander Hamilton helped to develop. The American Civil War made the United States a country where its people were Americans first, and Virginians or New Yorkers second. During two thousand years, Europeans have never considered themselves to be Europeans first and Austrians, French, or Germans second. This attitude not only hinders structural unification today, it has contributed to intra-European conflict, competition, and war for centuries. It also paved the way for racial anti-Semitism in Austria that intensified prior to World War II.

After 200 years of working in professional occupations in Vienna, members of Georg Klaar's family were considered Jews, never Austrians. In 1938, madness took over, and rational thought disappeared, leading first to inhumane attitudes and then to brutal acts. Anti-Semitism has evolved over time: During the Middle Ages, Jews were hated for their religion, a religion held responsible for the killing of Christ. In the twentieth century, religious hatred became racial hatred that made the Holocaust possible. Today, we see an entirely new twist: The world is witnessing a resurgence of anti-Semitism as both Israel and the Jews are held disproportionately responsible for the perpetual conflict in the Middle East.

As I've said, Hitler did not cause the Holocaust. Many have tried to place responsibility on a few fanatics, saying that the rest of the German military and the general population were only "following orders." But Hitler would have ridden any horse to obtain the power he craved, and he recognized in his early days in Vienna that anti-Semitism was an easy horse to ride. Individual acts of cruelty and mass slaughter of the Jews were not carried out by those who were reluctantly following orders. There are too many accounts of concentration camp guards, with no reason to stay at their posts, who were still murdering Jews after the last shot of the war was fired.

When I was researching material for this book, the information I read about Catholic efforts to portray Jesus as Aryan surprised me. But then I thought of several visits I had made to Florence, Italy, each time viewing Michelangelo's awesome masterpiece, the statue of David. The last time I visited, I remember thinking to myself as I walked away, "David doesn't look Jewish." Both Jews and Christians often seem to ignore the reality that Jesus was Jewish, even though that very fact has the potential to bring members of the two religions closer together.

America is not a perfect country, and its history of slavery, racism, and prejudice against Catholics, Jews, and other ethnic groups is sad evidence of this. But one thing that makes this country great is its persistent, if sometimes halting attempt to live up to its original ideals of equality and justice. Compared to many nations, America has displayed an extraordinary ability to embrace people from widely varied backgrounds and to take pride in the diversity within its borders. Even when some states have faltered in their determination to be inclusive, America's strong federal union and national identity have helped the country to move toward compliance with its founding principles.

My ancestry in Britain and America goes back for many generations, while my barber is a young Hispanic woman born outside of the U.S.A. After nearly nine years of cutting my hair, she happily announced that she was going to become a naturalized citizen of the U.S. I was very pleased for her and said that when she raised her right hand and assented to be a citizen, she would be as American as I am. In another example, I have seen and enjoyed many shows and movies directed by the brilliant Mike Nichols, who died in November 2014. The announcement of his death included biographical information along with a listing of his outstanding achievements and awards. Before his death, I had not even known that Nichols was a naturalized U.S. citizen of German-Russian-Jewish heritage. The "myth" that America is *uniquely* a melting pot is not really a myth.

On reflection, I cannot think of another country whose citizens from all ethnic, cultural, and social backgrounds are as well integrated as they are in the U.S. If I moved to any country in Europe, learned its language and history, and became a citizen, I could never become truly French, Austrian, or even British. It will not be easy, but Europe must gain a greater ability to embrace the diversity among its member nations and peoples. This is a vitally necessary step if their military, political, and economic union is to survive. It is the only way to achieve a true United States of Europe.

All bigotry, in Europe, America, or anywhere, is the inability of people and governments to make space for human differences, yet the capacity and willingness to do this is the essential foundation of a free society. Wherever these attributes are absent, we will continue to see horrors such as those demonstrated by groups of extremists who feel completely justified in violently assaulting anyone who comes from a different culture, religion, or even a different tradition within their own faith. But if enough countries and people develop these attributes, we have reason for hope. The challenge, always, is to move beyond lip service to the ideal and actually learn to accommodate differences for the sake of the common good.

What is the answer? We can look to Voltaire and his lifelong fight for social justice and freedom of expression. We can look to early American leaders who sought, debated, and won a way toward freedom, equality, and economic security for all. Americans have persevered in this direction in spite of blatant and tragic steps in the opposite direction. We can see from our own experience in the U.S. that freedom, tolerance, justice, and unity are not easy to achieve and maintain. But we can also see that they are worth any price.

There is an urgent need for greater unity in Europe than we have seen. Hopefully, an international awakening to this fact will not require an economic or military crisis greater than those the world has recently experienced. I may be deemed idealistic or naïve to a fault, but I am suggesting that it is past time for people of all religions, as well as those with no faith but reason, and people of all countries who espouse freedom to stand together. In Europe, in the West, and in the world, no less than our future is at stake.[704]

NOTES

[1] Connelly, Bernard. *The Rotten Heart of Europe, The Dirty War for Europe's Money,* 223. London: Faber and Faber, 1995.

[2] George Clare, *Last Waltz in Vienna: The Rise and Destruction of a Family 1842-1942* (New York: Holt Rinehart Winston, 1980), 29.

[3] Clare, *Last Waltz,* 184.

[4] Ibid.

[5] Ibid., 178.

[6] Ibid., 171.

[7] Ibid., 16.

[8] Ibid., 187.

[9] Ibid., 177.

[10] Ibid., 189.

[11] Ibid., 185.

[12] Ibid., 186.

[13] Ibid., 159.

[14] Ibid.

[15] Ibid., 191.

[16] Ibid., 205.

[17] Ibid., 18.

[18] Yehudu Bauer, *A History of the Holocaust* (Danbury, CT: Franklin Watts, 1982), 116.

[19] Ibid., 132.

[20] Clare, *Last Waltz*, 176.

[21] Ibid., 191.

[22] Ibid., 192.

[23] Bruce F. Pauley, *From Prejudice to Persecution: A History of Austrian Anti-Semitism* (Chapel Hill, NC and London, 1992), 275.

[24] David Jonah Goldhagen, *Hitler's Willing Executioners: Ordinary Germans and the Holocaust* (New York: Alfred A. Knopf, 1996), 286.

[25] Clare, *Last Waltz*, 190.

[26] Frank McLynn, *Marcus Aurelius, a Life* (Cambridge, MA: Da Capo Press, 2009), 150.

[27] Will Durant, *The Story of Civilization, Part III: Caesar and Christ: A History of Roman Civilization and of Christianity from Their Beginnings to AD 325* (New York: Simon & Schuster, 1944), 72.

[28] Nicholas Parsons, *Vienna: A Cultural History* (Oxford: Oxford University Press, 2009), 93.

[29] Michaela Kronberger, editor, "Vindobona: Roman Vienna" (Vienna, Austria: Museum of Rome, Hoher Market, 2013), 24.

[30] Ibid., 26.

[31] Durant, *Story of Civilization, Part III*, 375.

[32] Kronberger, "Vindobona: Roman Vienna," 46.

[33] Ibid.

[34] Ibid.

[35] Ibid., 75.

[36] Durant, *Story of Civilization, Part III*, 376.

[37] Ibid., 324.

[38] Ibid.

[39] Ibid., 226.

[40] Ibid., 61.

[41] Ibid., 67.

[42] Ibid., 68.

[43] Edward Gibbon, *The Decline and Fall of the Roman Empire: A One-Volume Abridgement*, ed. D.M.Low (New York: Harcourt, Brace & Co, 1960), 637.

[44] Ibid., 643.

[45] McLynn, *Marcus Aurelius, a Life*, 352.

[46] Gibbon, ed. Low, *Decline and Fall of the Roman Empire*, 629.

[47] Ibid.,1.

[48] Durant, *Story of Civilization, Part III*, 426.

[49] Ibid., 431.

[50] Ibid.

[51] McLynn, *Marcus Aurelius, a Life*, 246.

[52] Parsons, *Vienna*, 96.

[53] McLynn, *Marcus Aurelius, a Life*, 248.

[54] Ibid., 254.

[55] Durant, *Story of Civilization, Part III*, 480.

[56] Will Durant, *The Story of Civilization, Part VI: The Reformation: A History of European Civilization from Wyclif to Calvin, 1300-1564* (New York: Simon & Schuster, 1957), 143.

[57] Ibid., 145.

[58] Gordon Shepherd, *The Austrian Odyssey* (London: MacMillan; New York: St. Martin's Press, 1957), 25.

[59] Ibid., 33.

[60] Ibid., 35

[61] Parsons, *Vienna*, 126.

[62] Will Durant, *The Story of Civilization, Part IV: The Age of Faith: A History of Medieval Civilization-Christian, Islamic, Judaic-from Constantine to Dante: AD 325-1300* (New York: Simon & Schuster, 1950), 514.

[63] Ibid.

[64] Ibid., 621.

[65] Ibid., 835.

[66] Ibid.

[67] Ibid., 837.

[68] Ibid., 839.

[69] Ibid., 826.

[70] Ibid.

[71] Joseph R. Strayer and Dana C. Munro, *The Middle Ages, 395-1500* (New York: Appleton-Century-Crofts, 1959), 498.

[72] Ibid., 504.

[73] Paul Kennedy, *The Rise and Fall of the Great Powers: Economic Change and Military Conflict from 1500 to 2000* (New York: Random House, 1987), 35.

[74] Parsons, *Vienna*, 126.

[75] Ibid., 139.

[76] Ibid., 142.

[77] Ibid., 152.

[78] Will Durant and Ariel Durant, *The Story of Civilization, Part VII: The Age of Reason Begins: A History of European Civilization in the Period of Shakespeare, Bacon, Montaigne, Rembrandt, Galileo, and Descartes: 1558-1648* (New York: Simon & Schuster, 1961), 567.

[79] Kennedy, *Rise and Fall*, 44.

[80] Durant and Durant, *Story of Civilization, Part VII*, 568.

[81] Ibid., 569.

[82] Ibid., 568.

[83] Kennedy, *Rise and Fall*, 46.

[84] Will Durant and Ariel Durant, *The Story of Civilization, Part VIII: The Age of Louis XIV: A History of European Civilization in the Period of Pascal, Moliere, Cromwell, Milton, Peter the Great, Newton, and Spinoza: 1648-1715* (New York: Simon & Schuster, 1963), 420.

[85] Durant and Durant, *Story of Civilization, Part VII*, 571.

[86] Parsons, *Vienna*, 158.

[87] Ibid., 156.

[88] Durant and Durant, *Story of Civilization, Part VIII*, 423.

[89] Parsons, *Vienna*, 161.

[90] Durant and Durant, *Story of Civilization, Part VIII*, 424.

[91] Ibid., 426.

[92] Edward Crankshaw, *The Fall of the House of Habsburg* (New York: The Viking Press), 1963), 9.

[93] Lady Mary Wortley Montague, *Letters of Lady Mary Wortley Montague: Written During Her Travels In Europe, Asia, And Africa, To Which Are Added Poems* (Paris: P. Didot the elder, and F Didot, 1800), 17.

[94] Will Durant and Ariel Durant, *The Story of Civilization, Part IX: The Age of Voltaire: A History of Civilization in Western Europe from 1715 to 1756 with Special Emphasis on the Conflict between Religion and Philosophy* (New York: Simon & Schuster, 1965), 205.

[95] Montague, *Letters of Lady Mary*, 18.

[96] Parsons, *Vienna*, 173.

[97] Will Durant and Ariel Durant, *The Story of Civilization, Part X: Rousseau and Revolution: A History of Civilization in France, England, and Germany from 1756, and the Remainder of Europe from 1715 to 1789* (New York: Simon & Schuster, 1967), 345.

[98] Montague, *Letters of Lady Mary*, 55.

[99] Durant and Durant, *Story of Civilization, Part X*, 345.

[100] Montague, *Letters of Lady Mary*, 23.

[101] Durant and Durant, *Story of Civilization, Part IX*, 432.

[102] Montague, *Letters of Lady Mary*, 30.

[103] Durant and Durant, *Story of Civilization, Part IX*, 431.

[104] J. Alexander Mahan, *Maria Theresa of Austria* (New York: Thomas Y. Crowell Co, 1932), 14.

[105] Durant and Durant, *Story of Civilization, Part IX*, 435.

[106] Ibid., 434.

[107] Mahan, *Maria Theresa of Austria*, 36.

[108] Ibid., 56.

[109] Durant and Durant, *Story of Civilization, Part IX*, 435.

[110] Ibid., 436.

[111] Brendan Simms, *Europe: The Struggle for Supremacy from 1453 to the Present* (New York: Basic Books, 2013), 96.

[112] Durant and Durant, *Story of Civilization, Part IX*, 431.

[113] Simms, *Europe*, 97.

[114] Mahan, *Maria Theresa of Austria*, 174.

[115] Durant and Durant, *Story of Civilization, Part IX*, 453.

[116] Mahan, *Maria Theresa of Austria*, 98.

[117] Simms, *Europe*, 98.

[118] Durant and Durant, *Story of Civilization, Part IX*, 457.

[119] Ibid., 436.

[120] Mahan, *Maria Theresa of Austria*, 228.

[121] Parsons, *Vienna*, 176.

[122] Ibid., 312.

[123] Ibid., 244.

[124] Ibid., 176.

[125] Durant and Durant, *Story of Civilization, Part X,* 348.

[126] Ibid., 349.

[127] Ibid., 354.

[128] Parsons, *Vienna,* 178.

[129] Mahan, *Maria Theresa of Austria,* 137.

[130] Durant and Durant, *Story of Civilization, Part X,* 355.

[131] Derek Beales, *Joseph II, Volume II, Against the World, 1780-1790* (Cambridge, MA, Cambridge University Press, 2009), 69.

[132] Ibid., 272.

[133] Parsons, *Vienna,* 186.

[134] Durant and Durant, *Story of Civilization, Part X,* 357.

[135] Ibid., 359.

[136] Ibid.

[137] Ibid., 356.

[138] Ibid., 358.

[139] Ibid., 360.

[140] Ibid.

[141] Ibid., 359.

[142] Ibid., 355.

[143] Ibid., 364.

[144] James D. Hardy, Jr., "Joseph II (Holy Roman Empire) 1741-1790," *Europe, 1450-1789: Encyclopedia of the Early Modern World* (Farmington Hills, MI: Gale Group, Inc., 2004).

[145] Parsons, *Vienna,* 186.

[146] Durant and Durant, *Story of Civilization, Part X,* 366.

[147] Ibid., 941.

[148] Tim Fitzpatrick, "Napoleon's Final Triumph," *Military History Magazine* (March 2010), 49.

[149] J. Christopher Herold, *The Age of Napoleon* (New York: American Heritage, 1963), 276.

[150] Fitzpatrick, "Napoleon's Final Triumph," 49.

[151] Herold, *Age of Napoleon,* 276.

[152] Ibid., 12.

[153] David King, *Vienna, 1814: How the Conquerors of Napoleon Made Love, War, and Peace at the Congress of Vienna* (New York: Harmony Books, 2008), 2.

[154] Ibid., 9.

[155] Ibid., 12.

[156] Ibid., 13.

[157] Ibid., 228.

[158] Ibid., 323.

[159] Ibid.

[160] Will Durant and Ariel Durant, *The Story of Civilization, Part XI: The Age of Napoleon: A History of European Civilization from 1789 to 1815* (New York: Simon & Schuster, 1975), 777.

[161] Beales, *Joseph II*, 244.

[162] Shepherd, *Austrian Odyssey*, 47.

[163] A.J.P. Taylor, *The Habsburg Monarchy 1809-1918: A History of the Austrian Empire and Austria-Hungary* (Chicago and London: University of Chicago Press, 1948), 10.

[164] Beales, *Joseph II*, 246.

[165] Ibid., 243.

[166] Durant and Durant, *Story of Civilization, Part XI*, 776.

[167] Crankshaw, *Fall of the House of Habsburg*, 11.

[168] Simms, *Europe*, 183.

[169] Crankshaw, *Fall of the House of Habsburg*, 12.

[170] Taylor, *Habsburg Monarchy*, 23.

[171] Crankshaw, *Fall of the House of Habsburg*, 21.

[172] Taylor, *Habsburg Monarchy*, 12.

[173] Crankshaw, *Fall of the House of Habsburg*, 24.

[174] Ibid., 23.

[175] Parsons, *Vienna*, 2392.

[176] Crankshaw, *Fall of the House of Habsburg*, 24.

[177] Taylor, *Habsburg Monarchy*, 31.

[178] Simms, *Europe*, 194.

[179] Crankshaw, *Fall of the House of Habsburg*, 56.

[180] Ibid., 14.

[181] Simms, *Europe,* 211.

[182] Taylor, *Habsburg Monarchy,* 38.

[183] Simms, *Europe,* 215.

[184] Crankshaw, *Fall of the House of Habsburg,* 26.

[185] Ibid.

[186] Ibid., 27.

[187] Ibid., 30.

[188] Ibid., 29.

[189] Taylor, *Habsburg Monarchy,* 30.

[190] Crankshaw, *Fall of the House of Habsburg,* 26.

[191] Ibid., 38.

[192] Ibid., 50.

[193] Ibid.

[194] Shepherd, *Austrian Odyssey,* 52.

[195] C.E. Black and E.C. Helmreich, *Twentieth Century: A History* (New York: Alfred A. Knopf, 1961), 18.

[196] Shepherd, *Austrian Odyssey,* 38.

[197] Simms, *Europe,* 220.

[198] Crankshaw, *Fall of the House of Habsburg,* 100.

[199] Ibid., 103.

[200] Ibid., 108.

[201] Ibid., 207.

[202] Black and Helmreich, *Twentieth Century,* 36.

[203] Charles Emmerson, *1913: In Search of the World Before the Great War* (New York: Public Affairs, 2013), 90.

[204] Parsons, *Vienna,* 2481.

[205] Ibid., 2481.

[206] Ibid., 2487.

[207] Crankshaw, *Fall of the House of Habsburg,* 260.

[208] Parsons, *Vienna,* 2545.

[209] Emmerson, *In Search of the World,* 96.

[210] Barbara W. Tuchman, *The Proud Tower: A Portrait of the World Before the War, 1890-1914* (New York: MacMillan, 1966), 71.

[211] Crankshaw, *Fall of the House of Habsburg*, 261.

[212] Ibid., 265.

[213] Black and Helmreich, *Twentieth Century*, 24.

[214] Crankshaw, *Fall of the House of Habsburg*, 279.

[215] Emmerson, *In Search of the World*, 98.

[216] King, *Vienna, 1814*, 320.

[217] Black and Helmreich, *Twentieth Century*, 21.

[218] Ibid., 11.

[219] Ibid., 10.

[220] Ibid., 13.

[221] Simms, *Europe*, 289.

[222] Crankshaw, *Fall of the House of Habsburg*, 280.

[223] Ibid., 282.

[224] Emmerson, *In Search of the World*, Introduction.

[225] Ibid., 98.

[226] Andy Walker, "1913: When Hitler, Trotsky, Tito, Freud and Stalin All Lived in the Same Place," *BBC News Magazine*, April 18, 2013.

[227] Ibid.

[228] Emmerson, *In Search of the World*, 101.

[229] Walker.

[230] Taylor, *Habsburg Monarchy*, 9.

[231] Black and Helmreich, *Twentieth Century*, 19.

[232] Walker.

[233] Emmerson, *In Search of the World*, 93.

[234] Black and Helmreich, *Twentieth Century*, 42.

[235] Simms, *Europe*, 290.

[236] Black and Helmreich, *Twentieth Century*, 47.

[237] Martin Gilbert and Richard Gott, *The Appeasers* (Boston: Houghton Mifflin, 1963), 4.

[238] Black and Helmreich, *Twentieth Century*, 52.

[239] Simms, *Europe*, 292.

[240] Taylor, *Habsburg Monarchy*, 231.

[241] Anna Eisenmenger, *Blockade: The Diary of an Austrian Middle Class Woman, 1914-1924* (London: Constable, 1932), 12.

[242] Black and Helmreich, *Twentieth Century*, 54.

[243] Barbara W. Tuchman, *The Guns of August* (New York: MacMillan, 1962), 462.

[244] John Keegan, *The First World War* (New York: Alfred A. Knopf, 1999), 15.

[245] Ibid., 426.

[246] Crankshaw, *Fall of the House of Habsburg*, 388.

[247] Black and Helmreich, *Twentieth Century*, 345.

[248] Adam Fergusson, *When Money Dies. The Nightmare of Deficit Spending, Devaluation and Hyperinflation in Weimar Germany* (New York: Public Affairs, 2010), 6.

[249] Black and Helmreich, *Twentieth Century*, 109.

[250] Fergusson, *When Money Dies*, 6.

[251] Black and Helmreich, *Twentieth Century*, 116.

[252] Ibid., 103.

[253] Simms, *Europe*, 313.

[254] Shepherd, *Austrian Odyssey*, 47.

[255] Black and Helmreich, *Twentieth Century*, 116.

[256] Parsons, *Vienna*, 2767.

[257] Ibid.

[258] Black and Helmreich, *Twentieth Century*, 117.

[259] Fergusson, *When Money Dies*, 18.

[260] Frederick Taylor, *The Downfall of Money: Germany's Hyperinflation and the Destruction of the Middle Class* (New York: Bloomsbury Press, 2013), 154.

[261] Black and Helmreich, *Twentieth Century*, 301.

[262] Fergusson, *When Money Dies*, 255.

[263] Ibid., 4.

[264] Ibid., 19.

[265] Eisenmenger, *Blockade*, 13.

[266] Ibid., 4.

[267] Ibid., 63.

[268] Ibid., 21.

[269] Ibid., 62.

[270] Ibid., 115.

[271] Taylor, *Downfall of Money*, 212.

[272] Eisenmenger, *Blockade*, 33.

[273] Ibid., 45.

[274] Fergusson, *When Money Dies*, 24.

[275] Eisenmenger, *Blockade*, 120.

[276] Ibid., 91.

[277] Fergusson, *When Money Dies*, 24.

[278] Eisenmenger, *Blockade*, 149.

[279] Taylor, *Downfall of Money*, 268.

[280] Ibid., 271.

[281] Fergusson, *When Money Dies*, 84.

[282] Taylor, *Downfall of Money*, 268.

[283] Eisenmenger, *Blockade*, 151.

[284] Fergusson, *When Money Dies*, 59.

[285] Ibid.

[286] Eisenmenger, *Blockade*, 222.

[287] Taylor, *Downfall of Money*, 206.

[288] Fergusson, *When Money Dies*, 85.

[289] Eisenmenger, *Blockade*, 78.

[290] Ibid., 79.

[291] Ibid., 80.

[292] Taylor, *Downfall of Money*, 265.

[293] Ibid., 281.

[294] Eisenmenger, *Blockade*, 133.

[295] Taylor, *Downfall of Money*, 182.

[296] Ibid., 92.

[297] Ibid., 96.

[298] Ibid.

[299] Ibid., 97.

[300] Ibid., 99.

[301] Ibid., 100.

[302] Ibid., 223.

[303] Eisenmenger, *Blockade*, 267.

[304] Ibid., 272.

[305] Taylor, *Downfall of Money*, 336.

[306] Ibid.

[307] Fergusson, *When Money Dies*, 23.

[308] Black and Helmreich, *Twentieth Century*, 350.

[309] Eisenmenger, *Blockade*, 209.

[310] Black and Helmreich, *Twentieth Century*, 308.

[311] Ibid., 301.

[312] Simms, *Europe*, 341.

[313] Black and Helmreich, *Twentieth Century*, 308.

[314] Ibid.

[315] Ibid.

[316] Ibid., 306.

[317] Ibid.

[318] Ibid., 304.

[319] Ibid.

[320] Ibid.

[321] John Toland, *Adolf Hitler, Vol 1* (Garden City, New York: Doubleday & Co., 1976), 4.

[322] Ibid., 5.

[323] Ian Kershaw, *Hitler 1889-1936: Hubris* (New York; London: W.W. Norton & Co., 1998), 11.

[324] Toland, *Adolf Hitler, Vol 1*, 7.

[325] Kershaw, *Hitler 1889-1936*, 11.

[326] William L. Shirer, *20ᵗʰ Century Journey: A Memoir of a Life and the Times, Vol. 2, The Nightmare Years, 1930-1940* (Boston and Toronto: Little, Brown, and Co., 1984), 6.

[327] Kershaw, *Hitler 1889-1936*, 12.

[328] Ibid.

[329] Shirer, *20th Century Journey*, 10.

[330] Kershaw, *Hitler 1889-1936*, 15.

[331] Ibid., 16.

[332] Shirer, *20th Century Journey*, 11.

[333] Kershaw, *Hitler 1889-1936*, 21.

[334] Ibid., 14.

[335] Toland, *Adolf Hitler, Vol 1*, 20.

[336] Shirer, *20th Century Journey*, 16.

[337] Toland, *Adolf Hitler, Vol 1*, 22.

[338] Ibid., 25.

[339] Kershaw, *Hitler 1889-1936*, 23.

[340] Toland, *Adolf Hitler, Vol 1*, 27.

[341] Kershaw, *Hitler 1889-1936*, 23.

[342] Ibid., 25.

[343] Shirer, *20th Century Journey*, 17.

[344] Ibid.

[345] Toland, *Adolf Hitler, Vol 1*, 30.

[346] Ibid., 31.

[347] Kershaw, *Hitler 1889-1936*, 30.

[348] Shirer, *20th Century Journey*, 17.

[349] Toland, *Adolf Hitler, Vol 1*, 33.

[350] Ibid., 38.

[351] Kershaw, *Hitler 1889-1936*, 38.

[352] Ibid., 47.

[353] Toland, *Adolf Hitler, Vol 1*, 32.

[354] Kershaw, *Hitler 1889-1936*, 44.

[355] Ibid., 39.

[356] Toland, *Adolf Hitler, Vol 1*, 39.

[357] Kershaw, *Hitler 1889-1936*, 31.

[358] Shirer, *20th Century Journey*, 18.

[359] Kershaw, *Hitler 1889-1936*, 29.

[360] Toland, *Adolf Hitler, Vol 1*, 39.

[361] Shirer, *20th Century Journey*, 18.

[362] Kershaw, *Hitler 1889-1936*, 52.

[363] Toland, *Adolf Hitler, Vol 1*, 42.

[364] Kershaw, *Hitler 1889-1936*, 54.

[365] Ibid., 53.

[366] Ibid., 54.

[367] Shirer, *20th Century Journey*, 19.

[368] Kershaw, *Hitler 1889-1936*, 55.

[369] Shirer, *20th Century Journey*, 25.

[370] Kershaw, *Hitler 1889-1936*, 56.

[371] Ibid., 31.

[372] Ibid.

[373] Ibid.

[374] Shirer, *20th Century Journey*, 23.

[375] Kershaw, *Hitler 1889-1936*, 33.

[376] Ibid., 18.

[377] Ibid., 34.

[378] Shirer, *20th Century Journey*, 21.

[379] Kershaw, *Hitler 1889-1936*, 36.

[380] Shirer, *20th Century Journey*, 22.

[381] Kershaw, 36.

[382] Shirer, *20th Century Journey*, 23.

[383] Ibid., 24.

[384] Kershaw, *Hitler 1889-1936*, 35.

[385] Shirer, *20th Century Journey*, 24.

[386] Ibid.

[387] Kershaw, *Hitler 1889-1936*, 34.

[388] Ibid.

[389] Toland, *Adolf Hitler, Vol 1*, 45.

[390] Kershaw, *Hitler 1889-1936*, 61.

[391] Ibid., 50.

[392] Toland, *Adolf Hitler, Vol 1*, 46.

[393] Kershaw, *Hitler 1889-1936*, 50.

[394] Ibid., 66.

[395] Toland, *Adolf Hitler, Vol 1*, 50.

[396] Shirer, *20ᵗʰ Century Journey*, 21.

[397] Kershaw, *Hitler 1889-1936*, 63.

[398] Toland, *Adolf Hitler, Vol 1*, 45.

[399] Shirer, *20ᵗʰ Century Journey*, 27.

[400] Kershaw, *Hitler 1889-1936*, Intro.

[401] Clare, *Last Waltz*, 29.

[402] Jacob Katz, *From Prejudice to Destruction: Anti-Semitism, 1700-1933* (Cambridge, MA: Harard University Press, 1980), 316.

[403] Pauley, *From Prejudice to Persecution*, 14.

[404] Ibid., 15.

[405] Katz, *From Prejudice to Destruction*, 36.

[406] Ibid., 23.

[407] Ibid., 20.

[408] Ibid., 24.

[409] Ibid., 28.

[410] Ibid., 29.

[411] Ibid., 34.

[412] Ibid., 43.

[413] Ibid., 40.

[414] Ibid., 44.

[415] Ibid., 24.

[416] Pauley, *From Prejudice to Persecution*, 16.

[417] Ibid., 18.

[418] Katz, *From Prejudice to Destruction*, 53.

[419] Ibid., 94.

[420] Ibid., 225.

[421] Pauley, *From Prejudice to Persecution*, 20.

[422] Katz, *From Prejudice to Destruction*, 223.

[423] Pauley, *From Prejudice to Persecution*, 21.

[424] Clare, *Last Waltz*, 10.

[425] Ibid., 15.

[426] Julius Braunthal, *The Tragedy of Austria* (London: Victor Gollancz LTD, 1948), 59.

[427] Ibid., 58.

[428] Frederick A. Hayek, *The Collected Work of Frederick A. Hayek, Volume II, The Road to Serfdom*, edited by Bruce Caldwell (Chicago: University of Chicago Press, 1944, Kindle edition), 198.

[429] Pauley, *From Prejudice to Persecution*, 10.

[430] Clare, *Last Waltz*, 256.

[431] Katz, *From Prejudice to Destruction*, 304.

[432] Ibid., 306.

[433] Ibid., 307.

[434] Ibid., 308.

[435] Pauley, *From Prejudice to Persecution*, 5.

[436] Katz, *From Prejudice to Destruction*, 309.

[437] Frank Field, *The Last Days of Mankind: Karl Kraus and His Vienna* (London: MacMillan; New York: St. Martin's Press, 1967), 35.

[438] Pauley, *From Prejudice to Persecution*, 35.

[439] Ibid., 36.

[440] Ibid., 37.

[441] Braunthal, *Tragedy of Austria*, 60.

[442] Ibid., 63.

[443] Ibid.

[444] Braunthal, *Tragedy of Austria*, 66.

[445] Clare, *Last Waltz*, 188.

[446] Pauley, *From Prejudice to Persecution*, 59.

[447] Katz, *From Prejudice to Destruction*, 325.

[448] Pauley, *From Prejudice to Persecution*, 45.

[449] Ibid., 66.

[450] Ibid., 69.

[451] Ibid., 70.

[452] Ibid., 60.

[453] Katz, *From Prejudice to Destruction*, 87.

[454] Bauer, *History of the Holocaust*, 66.

[455] Clare, *Last Waltz*, 32.

[456] Field, *Last Days of Mankind*, 124.

[457] Katz, *From Prejudice to Destruction*, 311.

[458] Ibid., 229.

[459] Pauley, *From Prejudice to Persecution*, 192.

[460] Ibid., 193.

[461] Ibid., 82.

[462] Ibid., 80.

[463] Bauer, *History of the Holocaust*, 361.

[464] Pauley, *From Prejudice to Persecution*, 97.

[465] Ibid., 116.

[466] Ibid., 197.

[467] Bauer, *History of the Holocaust*, 362.

[468] Pauley, *From Prejudice to Persecution*, 130.

[469] Ibid., 201.

[470] Ibid., 268.

[471] Ibid., 191.

[472] Ibid., 260.

[473] Field, *Last Days of Mankind*, 192.

[474] Ibid., 72.

[475] Braunthal, *Tragedy of Austria*, 65.

[476] Pauley, *From Prejudice to Persecution*, 263.

[477] Bauer, *History of the Holocaust*, 142.

[478] Clare, *Last Waltz*, 42.

[479] Pauley, *From Prejudice to Persecution*, 270.

[480] Bauer, *History of the Holocaust*, 134.

[481] Ibid., 114.

[482] Stefan Zweig, *The World of Yesterday*, trans. B.W. Huebsch and Helmet Ripperger (Plunkett Lake Press, 2011, Kindle edition), 381.

[483] Clare, *Last Waltz*, 160.

[484] Ibid., 164.

[485] Ibid., 165.

[486] Ibid.

[487] Ibid., 27.

[488] Ibid.

[489] Ibid., 28.

[490] Ibid., 29.

[491] Ibid., 163.

[492] William L. Shirer, *20th Century Journey: A Memoir of a Life and the Times, Vol 2, The Nightmare Years, 1930-1940* (Boston and Toronto: Little, Brown and Company, 1984), 288.

[493] Clare, *Last Waltz*, 161.

[494] Shirer, *Nightmare Years*, 291.

[495] Simms, *Europe*, 355.

[496] Shirer, *Nightmare Years*, 287.

[497] Shepherd, *Austrian Odyssey*, 129.

[498] Toland, *Adolf Hitler, Vol 1*, 431.

[499] Field, *Last Days of Mankind*, 230.

[500] Toland, *Adolf Hitler, Vol 1*, 433.

[501] Black and Helmreich, *Twentieth Century Europe*, 522.

[502] William L. Shirer, *The Rise and Fall of the Third Reich: A History of Nazi Germany* (New York: Simon & Schuster, 1960), 324.

[503] Toland, *Adolf Hitler, Vol 1*, 433.

[504] Shirer, *Rise and Fall of the Third Reich*, 326.

[505] Ibid.

[506] Toland, *Adolf Hitler, Vol 1*, 433.

[507] Shirer, *Nightmare Years*, 291.

[508] Toland, *Adolf Hitler, Vol 1*, 435.

[509] Ibid., 436.

[510] Ibid., 437.

[511] Shirer, *Nightmare Years*, 295.

[512] Clare, *Last Waltz*, 174.

[513] Shirer, *Nightmare Years*, 295.

[514] Clare, *Last Waltz*, 176.

[515] Toland, *Adolf Hitler, Vol 1*, 442.

[516] Ibid., 447.

[517] Shepherd, *Austrian Odyssey*, 144.

[518] Toland, *Adolf Hitler, Vol 1*, 447.

[519] Shepherd, *Austrian Odyssey*, 137.

[520] Toland, *Adolf Hitler, Vol 1*, 451.

[521] Shepherd, *Austrian Odyssey*, 109.

[522] Shirer, *Rise and Fall of the Third Reich*, 331.

[523] Toland, *Adolf Hitler, Vol 1*, 448.

[524] Pauley, *From Prejudice to Persecution*, 287.

[525] Ibid., 279.

[526] Shepherd, *Austrian Odyssey,* 143.

[527] Clare, *Last Waltz*, 193.

[528] Ibid., 194.

[529] Field, *Last Days of Mankind*, 236.

[530] Pauley, *From Prejudice to Persecution*, 280.

[531] Shirer, *Nightmare Years*, 314.

[532] Bauer, *History of the Holocaust*, 114.

[533] Field, *Last Days of Mankind*, 236.

[534] Shirer, *Nightmare Years*, 295.

[535] Ibid., 100.

[536] Ibid.

[537] Ibid., 303.

[538] Clare, *Last Waltz*, 197.

[539] Ibid., 198.

[540] Ibid.

[541] Ibid., 204.

[542] Shirer, *Nightmare Years*, 312.

[543] Ibid., 313.

[544] Toland, *Adolf Hitler, Vol 1*, 457.

[545] Ibid., 453.

[546] Ibid., 452.

[547] Shirer, *Nightmare Years*, 317.

[548] Parsons 2904.

[549] Pauley, *From Prejudice to Persecution*, 286.

[550] Ibid., 283.

[551] Ibid., 288.

[552] Clare, *Last Waltz*, 206.

[553] Ibid., 208.

[554] Ibid., 209.

[555] Ibid., 211.

[556] Ibid., 212.

[557] Ibid., 224.

[558] Ibid., 225.

[559] Ibid., 229.

[560] Ibid., 233.

[561] Shirer, *Nightmare Years*, 318.

[562] Field, *Last Days of Mankind*, 239.

[563] Clare, *Last Waltz*, 238.

[564] Ibid., 239.

[565] Ibid., 241.

[566] Ibid., 242.

[567] Ibid., 244.

[568] Shirer, *Nightmare Years*, 310.

[569] Black and Helmreich, *Twentieth Century Europe*, 521.

[570] Shirer, *Nightmare Years*, 356.

[571] Ibid., 317.

[572] Bauer, *History of the Holocaust*, 146.

[573] Durant and Durant, *Story of Civilization, Part IX*, 259.

[574] Theodore Besterman, *Voltaire* (New York: Harcourt, Brace & World, 1969), 532.

[575] Ian Davidson, *Voltaire: A Life* (New York: Pegasus Books, 2010), 318.

[576] Roger Pearson, *Voltaire Almighty: A Life in Pursuit of Freedom* (New York: Bloomsbury Publishing, Inc., 2005), 289.

[577] Durant and Durant, *Story of Civilization, Part IX*, 263.

[578] Pearson, *Voltaire Almighty*, 33.

[579] Ibid., 407.

[580] Davidson, *Voltaire: A Life*, 2.

[581] Besterman, *Voltaire*, 36.

[582] Pearson, *Voltaire Almighty*, 30.

[583] Ibid., 33.

[584] Francis Espinasse, *The Life of Voltaire* (Whitefish, MT: Kessinger Publishing, LLC, 2004), 22.

[585] Davidson, *Voltaire: A Life*, 17.

[586] Durant and Durant, *Story of Civilization, Part IX*, 34.

[587] Davidson, *Voltaire: A Life*, 21.

[588] Espinasse, *Life of Voltaire*, 30.

[589] Pearson, *Voltaire Almighty*, 50.

[590] Davidson, *Voltaire: A Life*, 14.

[591] Pearson, *Voltaire Almighty*, 49.

[592] Besterman, *Voltaire*, 90.

[593] Davidson, *Voltaire: A Life*, 27.

[594] Ibid., 30.

[595] Durant and Durant, *Story of Civilization, Part IX*, 40.

[596] Espinasse, *Life of Voltaire*, 46.

[597] Pearson, *Voltaire Almighty*, 34.

[598] Besterman, *Voltaire*, 104.

[599] Davidson, *Voltaire: A Life*, 56.

[600] Ibid., 59.

[601] Besterman, *Voltaire*, 150.

[602] Espinasse, *Life of Voltaire*, 60.

[603] Ibid., 56.

[604] Pearson, *Voltaire Almighty*, 99.

[605] Davidson, *Voltaire: A Life*, 63.

[606] Ibid., 70.

[607] Durant and Durant, *Story of Civilization, Part IX*, 247.

[608] Espinasse, *Life of Voltaire*, 66.

[609] Besterman, *Voltaire*, 161.

[610] Davidson, *Voltaire: A Life*, 77.

[611] Espinasse, *Life of Voltaire*, 69.

[612] Davidson, *Voltaire: A Life*, 78.

[613] Ibid., 100.

[614] Pearson, *Voltaire Almighty*, 96.

[615] Espinasse, *Life of Voltaire*, 22.

[616] Pearson, *Voltaire Almighty*, 118.

[617] Davidson, *Voltaire: A Life*, 109.

[618] Besterman, *Voltaire*, 224.

[619] Davidson, *Voltaire: A Life*, 113.

[620] Durant and Durant, *Story of Civilization, Part IX*, 372.

[621] Davidson, *Voltaire: A Life*, 127.

[622] Ibid., 104.

[623] Pearson, *Voltaire Almighty*, 109.

[624] Besterman, *Voltaire*, 242.

[625] Davidson, *Voltaire: A Life*, 147.

[626] Ibid., 129.

[627] Besterman, *Voltaire*, 186.

[628] Davidson, *Voltaire: A Life*, 176.

[629] Besterman, *Voltaire*, 254.

[630] Ibid., 250.

[631] Durant and Durant, *Story of Civilization, Part IX*, 380.

[632] Davidson, *Voltaire: A Life*, 223.

[633] Ibid., 228.

[634] Ibid.

[635] Benjamin Gastineau, *Voltaire in Exile: His Life and Work in France and Abroad with Unpublished Letters of Voltaire and Mme. du Chatelet*, Trans. F. Vogeli (New York: D.M. Bennett, 1883), 84.

636 Durant and Durant, *Story of Civilization, Part IX*, 392.

637 Davidson, *Voltaire: A Life*, 209.

638 Espinasse, *Life of Voltaire*, 106.

639 Durant and Durant, *Story of Civilization, Part IX*, 461.

640 Pearson, *Voltaire Almighty*, 228.

641 Ibid., 271.

642 Espinasse, *Life of Voltaire*, 130.

643 Pearson, *Voltaire Almighty*, 240.

644 Davidson, *Voltaire: A Life*, 275.

645 Ibid., 279.

646 Besterman, *Voltaire*, 349.

647 Ibid., 418.

648 Davidson, *Voltaire: A Life*, 282.

649 Pearson, *Voltaire Almighty*, 261.

650 Gastineau, *Voltaire in Exile*, 11.

651 Ibid., 105.

652 Pearson, *Voltaire Almighty*, 262.

653 Besterman, *Voltaire*, 397.

654 S.G. Tallentyre, *The Life of Voltaire, Vol. II* (New York: G.P. Putnam's Sons, 1903), 381.

655 Besterman, *Voltaire*, 362.

656 Pearson, *Voltaire Almighty*, 299.

657 Besterman, *Voltaire*, 299.

658 Gastineau, Voltaire in Exile, 134.

659 Pearson, *Voltaire Almighty*, 268.

660 Durant and Durant, *Story of Civilization, Part IX*, 727.

661 Espinasse, *Life of Voltaire*, 147.

662 Tallentyre, *Life of Voltaire*, 419.

663 Davidson, *Voltaire: A Life*, 319.

664 Pearson, *Voltaire Almighty*, 288.

665 Davidson, *Voltaire: A Life*, 316.

666 Ibid., 324.

[667] Davidson, *Voltaire: A Life*, 330.

[668] Pearson, *Voltaire Almighty*, 281.

[669] Besterman, *Voltaire*, 427.

[670] Ibid., 539.

[671] Davidson, *Voltaire: A Life*, 361.

[672] Besterman, *Voltaire*, 450.

[673] Ibid., 529.

[674] Pearson, *Voltaire Almighty*, 360.

[675] Ibid.

[676] Davidson, *Voltaire: A Life*, 445.

[677] Gastineau, *Voltaire in Exile*, 145.

[678] Davidson, *Voltaire: A Life*, 449.

[679] Ibid., 44.

[680] Ibid., 456.

[681] Pearson, *Voltaire Almighty*, 380.

[682] Espinasse, *Life of Voltaire*, 191.

[683] Davidson, *Voltaire: A Life*, 460.

[684] Ibid., 461.

[685] Pearson, *Voltaire Almighty*, 406.

[686] Besterman, *Voltaire*, 300.

[687] Davidson, *Voltaire: A Life*, 461.

[688] Tallentyre, *Life of Voltaire*, 571.

[689] Voltaire, Letter to Frederick II of Prussia, January 20, 1742.

[690] Ibid.

[691] Gordon Crovitz, "Defending Satire to the Death," *The Wall Street Journal*, January 12, 2015. (Quoting Voltaire's *Questions sur les miracles*, 1765).

[692] Margaret MacMillan, *The War That Ended Peace: The Road to 1914* (New York: Random House, 2013), 260.

[693] Zweig, *World of Yesterday*, 302.

[694] Bernard Connolly, *The Rotten Heart of Europe* (Faber & Faber, 2013, Kindle edition), 156.

[695] John Steele Gordon, *Hamilton's Blessing: The Extraordinary Life and Times of Our National Debt* (New York: Walker & Co., 1997), 14.

[696] Ibid.

[697] Nolmie Emery, *Alexander Hamilton: An Intimate Portrait* (New York: G.P. Putnam's Sons, 1982), 79.

[698] Gordon, *Hamilton's Blessing*, 13.

[699] Ron Chernow, *Alexander Hamilton* (New York: The Penguin Press, 2004), 225.

[700] Willard Sterne Randall, *Alexander Hamilton: A Life* (New York: HarperCollins, 2003), 267.

[701] Stephen F. Knott, *Alexander Hamilton and the Persistence of Myth* (Lawrence, KS: University Press of Kansas, 2002), 6.

[702] Ibid., 7.

[703] Gordon, *Hamilton's Blessing*, 38.

[704] Jonathan Sacks, "Europe's Alarming New Anti-Semitism," *The Wall Street Journal*, October 2, 2014.

BIBLIOGRAPHY

Ahamed, Liaquat. "Economics: The Road to Depression." *The Wall Street Journal*, June 20, 2014.

Aurelius, Marcus. *Meditations*. Translated by George Long. Edited by Charles Driver. Digireads.com, 2004. Kindle edition.

Bauer, Yehudu. *A History of the Holocaust*. Danbury, CT: Franklin Watts, 1982.

Beales, Derek. *Joseph II, Volume II, Against the World, 1780-1790*. Cambridge, MA: Cambridge University Press, 2009.

Besterman, Theodore. *Voltaire*. New York: Harcourt, Brace & World, 1969.

Beer, Edith Hahn, with Susan Dworkin. *The Nazi Officer's Wife: How One Jewish Woman Survived the Holocaust*. New York: HarperCollins, 2012. Kindle edition.

Birley, Anthony. *Marcus Aurelius: A Biography*. New York: Barnes & Noble Books, 1966.

Black, C.E., and E.C. Helmreich. *Twentieth Century Europe: A History*. New York: Alfred A. Knopf, 1961.

Bowen, Catherine Drinker. *Miracle at Philadelphia: The Story of the Constitutional Convention May - September 1787*. Boston: Little, Brown and Company, 1966.

Braunthal, Julius. *The Tragedy of Austria*. London: Victor Gollancz LTD, 1948.

Brozgat, Martin. *Hitler and the Collapse of Weimar Germany*. Hamburg: Leamington Spa, 1984.

Buttsworth, Matt. *Democracy and Debt: The European Debt Crisis*. Buttsworth Books, 2011. Kindle edition.

Callahan, North. *Henry Knox: General Washington's General*. New York: A.S. Barnes & Co., 1958.

Chernow, Ron: *Alexander Hamilton*. New York: The Penguin Press, 2004.

Clare, George. *Last Waltz in Vienna: The Rise and Destruction of a Family 1842-1942*. New York: Holt Rinehart Winston, 1980.

Clark, Christopher. *The Sleepwalkers: How Europe Went to War in 1914*. New York: HarperCollins, 2013.

Connolly, Bernard. *The Rotten Heart of Europe*. London: Faber & Faber, 2013. Kindle edition.

Crankshaw, Edward. *The Fall of the House of Habsburg*. New York: The Viking Press, 1963.

Crovitz, Gordon. "Defending Satire to the Death." *The Wall Street Journal*, January 12, 2015.

Davidson, Ian. *Voltaire: A Life*. New York: Pegasus Books, 2010.

Durant, Will. *The Story of Civilization, Part III: Caesar and Christ: A History of Roman Civilization and of Christianity from Their Beginnings to AD 325*. New York: Simon & Schuster, 1944.

Durant, Will. *The Story of Civilization, Part IV: The Age of Faith: A History of Medieval Civilization-Christian, Islamic, Judaic-from Constantine to Dante: AD 325-1300.* New York: Simon & Schuster, 1950.

Durant, Will. *The Story of Civilization, Part V: The Renaissance: A History of Civilization in Italy from 1304–1576.* New York: Simon & Schuster, 1953.

Durant, Will. *The Story of Civilization, Part VI: The Reformation: A History of European Civilization from Wyclif to Calvin, 1300-1564.* New York: Simon & Schuster, 1957.

Durant, Will, and Ariel Durant. *The Story of Civilization, Part VII: The Age of Reason Begins: A History of European Civilization in the Period of Shakespeare, Bacon, Montaigne, Rembrandt, Galileo, and Descartes: 1558-1648.* New York: Simon & Schuster, 1961.

Durant, Will, and Ariel Durant. *The Story of Civilization, Part VIII: The Age of Louis XIV: A History of European Civilization in the Period of Pascal, Moliere, Cromwell, Milton, Peter the Great, Newton, and Spinoza: 1648-1715.* New York: Simon & Schuster, 1963.

Durant, Will, and Ariel Durant. *The Story of Civilization, Part IX: The Age of Voltaire: A History of Civilization in Western Europe from 1715 to 1756 with Special Emphasis on the Conflict between Religion and Philosophy.* New York: Simon & Schuster, 1965.

Durant, Will, and Ariel Durant. *The Story of Civilization, Part X: Rousseau and Revolution: A History of Civilization in France, England, and Germany from 1756, and the Remainder of Europe from 1715 to 1789.* New York: Simon & Schuster, 1967.

Durant, Will, and Ariel Durant. *The Story of Civilization, Part XI: The Age of Napoleon: A History of European Civilization from 1789 to 1815.* New York: Simon & Schuster, 1975.

Eisenmenger, Anna. *Blockade: The Diary of an Austrian Middle Class Woman, 1914-1924.* London: Constable,1932.

Emery, Nolmie. *Alexander Hamilton: An Intimate Portrait.* New York: G.P. Putnam's Sons, 1982.

Emmerson, Charles. *1913: In Search of the World Before the Great War.* New York: Public Affairs, 2013.

Espinasse, Francis. *The Life of Voltaire.* London: Walter Scott Ltd, 1892.

Esposito, Vincent J., John Robert Elting, and U.S. Military Academy, Department of Military Art and Engineering. *A Military History and Atlas of the Napoleonic Wars.* New York: Praeger, 1964.

Fergusson, Adam. *When Money Dies. The Nightmare of Deficit Spending, Devaluation, and Hyperinflation in Weimar Germany.* New York: Public Affairs, 2010.

Field, Frank. *The Last Days of Mankind: Karl Kraus and His Vienna.* London: MacMillan; New York: St. Martin's Press, 1967.

Fitzpatrick, Tim. "Napoleon's Final Triumph." *Military History Magazine,* March 2010.

Gastineau, Benjamin. *Voltaire in Exile: His Life and Work in France and Abroad with Unpublished Letters of Voltaire and Mme. du Chatelet.* Translated by F. Vogeli. New York: D.M. Bennett, 1883.

Gibbon, Edward. *The Decline and Fall of the Roman Empire: A One-Volume Abridgement.* Edited by D.M. Low. New York: Harcourt, Brace & Co, 1960.

Gilbert, Martin, and Richard Gott. *The Appeasers.* Boston: Houghton Mifflin, 1963.

Goldhagen, David Jonah. *Hitler's Willing Executioners: Ordinary Germans and the Holocaust.* New York: Alfred A. Knopf, 1996.

Gordon, John Steele. *Hamilton's Blessing: The Extraordinary Life and Times of Our National Debt.* New York: Walker & Co., 1997.

Hardy, James D. Jr. "Joseph II (Holy Roman Empire) 1741-1790," *Europe, 1450-1789: Encylopedia of the Early Modern World.* Farmington Hills, MI: Gale Group, Inc., 2004.

Hayek, Frederick A. *The Collected Work of Frederick A. Hayek, Volume II, The Road to Serfdom.* Edited by Bruce Caldwell. Chicago: University of Chicago Press, 1944. Kindle edition.

Henninger, Daniel. "A Year of Living on the Brink." *The Wall Street Journal,* October 4, 2014.

Herold, J. Christopher. *The Age of Napoleon.* New York: American Heritage, 1963.

Josephson, Matthew. *Jean-Jacques Rousseau.* New York: Harcourt, Brace, & Co., 1931.

Katz, Jacob. *From Prejudice to Destruction: Anti-Semitism, 1700-1933.* Cambridge, MA: Harvard University Press, 1980.

Keegan, John. *The First World War.* New York: Alfred A. Knopf, 1999.

Kennedy, Paul. *The Rise and Fall of the Great Powers: Economic Change and Military Conflict from 1500 to 2000.* New York: Random House, 1987.

Kennan, George F. *The Fateful Alliance: France, Russia, and the Coming of the First World War.* New York: Pantheon, 1984.

Kershaw, Ian. *Hitler 1889-1936: Hubris.* New York, London: W.W. Norton & Co., 1998.

Knott, Stephen F. *Alexander Hamilton and the Persistence of Myth.* Lawrence, KS: University Press of Kansas, 2002.

Kronberger, Michaela, editor. "Vindobona: Roman Vienna." Vienna, Austria: Museum of Rome, Hoher Market, 2013.

King, David. *Vienna, 1814: How the Conquerors of Napoleon Made Love, War, and Peace at the Congress of Vienna*. New York: Harmony Books, 2008.

MacMillan, Margaret. *The War That Ended Peace: The Road to 1914*. New York: Random House, 2013.

Mahan, J. Alexander. *Maria Theresa of Austria*. New York: Thomas Y. Crowell Co, 1932.

Massie, Robert K. *Dreadnought: Britain, Germany, and the Coming of the Great War*. New York: Random House, 1991.

McLynn, Frank. *Marcus Aurelius, a Life*. Cambridge, MA: Da Capo Press, 2009.

Montague, Lady Mary Wortley. *Letters of Lady Mary Wortley Montague: Written During Her Travels in Europe, Asia, and Africa, to Which Are Added Poems*. Paris: P. Didot the elder, and F. Didot, 1800.

Morton, Frederic. *Thunder at Twilight: Vienna 1913-1914*. New York: Charles Scribner's Sons, 1989.

Parsons, Nicholas. *Vienna: A Cultural History*. Oxford: Oxford University Press, 2009.

Pauley, Bruce F. *From Prejudice to Persecution: A History of Austrian Anti-Semitism*. Chapel Hill, NC and London, 1992.

Pearson, Roger. *Voltaire Almighty: A Life in Pursuit of Freedom*. New York & London: Bloomsbury Publishing, 2005.

Peet, John, and Anton LaGuardia. *Unhappy Union: How the Euro Crisis-and Europe-Can Be Fixed*. London: The Economist Books, 2014.

Randall, Willard Sterne. *Alexander Hamilton, A Life*. New York: HarperCollins, 2003.

Sacks, Jonathan. "Europe's Alarming New Anti-Semitism." *The Wall Street Journal*, October 2, 2014.

Shepherd, Gordon. *The Austrian Odyssey*. London: MacMillan; New York: St. Martin's Press, 1957.

Shirer, William L. *The Rise and Fall of the Third Reich: A History of Nazi Germany*. New York: Simon & Schuster, 1960.

Shirer, William L. *20th Century Journey: A Memoir of a Life and the Times, Vol. 2, the Nightmare Years, 1930-1940*. Boston and Toronto: Little, Brown and Company, 1984.

Simms, Brendan. *Europe: The Struggle for Supremacy from 1453 to the Present*. New York: Basic Books, 2013.

Strayer, Joseph R. & Dana C. Munro. *The Middle Ages, 395-1500*. New York: Appleton-Century-Crofts, 1959.

Tallentyre, S.G. *The Life of Voltaire, Vol. II*. New York: G.P. Putnam's Sons, 1903.

Taylor, A.J.P. *The Habsburg Monarchy 1809-1918: A History of the Austrian Empire and Austria-Hungary*. Chicago and London: University of Chicago Press, 1948.

Taylor, Frederick. *The Downfall of Money: Germany's Hyperinflation and the Destruction of the Middle Class*. New York: Bloomsbury Press, 2013.

Toland, John. *Adolf Hitler, Vol 1*. Garden City, New York: Doubleday & Co., 1976.

Tuchman, Barbara W. *The Guns of August*. New York: MacMillan, 1962.

Tuchman, Barbara W. *The Proud Tower: A Portrait of the World Before the War, 1890-1914.* New York: MacMillan, 1966.

de Voltaire, Jean Francois-Marie Arouet. *Candide.* New York: The Modern Library, 2002.

Voltaire. *Letters on England.* Translated by Leonard Tancock. Penguin Classics, 1980. Kindle edition.

Voltaire. *Philosophical Dictionary.* Translated by Theodore Besterman. Penguin Classics, 1984. Kindle edition.

Voltaire. *Mahomet.* Translated by William F. Fleming. Start Publishing, 2012. Kindle edition.

Walker, Andy. "1913: When Hitler, Trotsky, Tito, Freud and Stalin All Lived in the Same Place." *BBC News Magazine*, April 17, 2013.

Zweig, Stefan. *The World of Yesterday.* Translated by B.W. Huebsch and Helmet Ripperger. Plunkett Lake Press, 2011. Kindle edition.

INDEX

ABOUT THE AUTHOR

Larry Hilton is an avid student of history who has studied and traveled in Europe for more than four decades. With a B.A. degree in history from Arizona State University and a graduate degree from the Southwestern School of Banking at Southern Methodist University, Larry has an extensive background in the financial services industry as a banker, stock broker, and portfolio manager. In *Europe: Chained by History,* he brings history to life by sharing deeply personal stories of those who lived and died in Vienna at critical turning points in time. His lively writing style leads us to a ready understanding of how events in the history of Vienna led to the geo-political dynamics that threaten Europe's survival today. Larry lives, works, and writes in Phoenix, Arizona.

Made in the USA
Charleston, SC
23 December 2015